PRAISE FOR IAN MORTIMER

Medieval Horizons
'A sparkling, eye-opening book' *Mail on Sunday*

The Time Traveller's Guide to Medieval England
'After *The Canterbury Tales* this has to be the most entertaining book ever written about the middle ages' *Guardian*

'The endlessly inventive Ian Mortimer is the most remarkable medieval historian of our time' *The Times*

The Time Traveller's Guide to Elizabethan England
'... as if Mortimer has restored an old painting, stripping it of its cloaking layers of brown varnish to reveal its vitality and life afresh' *Daily Telegraph*

'As Mortimer puts it, "sometimes the past will inspire you, sometimes it will make you weep". What it won't do, thanks to this enthralling book, is leave you unmoved' *Mail on Sunday*

The Time Traveller's Guide to Restoration Britain
'If only they'd taught history like this when I was at school... Irreverent, witty and beautifully democratic, this is a delight' *i*

The Time Traveller's Guide to Regency Britain
'This is ideal history; tales of people like us, who tell you that the past is closer than you think' *Daily Telegraph*

'Mortimer's erudition is formidable.... The learning is lightly worn' *The Times*

ALSO BY IAN MORTIMER

The Time Traveller's Guide to Medieval England
The Time Traveller's Guide to Elizabethan England
The Time Traveller's Guide to Restoration Britain
The Time Traveller's Guide to Regency Britain
The Greatest Traitor: The Life of Sir Roger Mortimer, Ruler of England 1327–1330
The Perfect King: The Life of Edward III, Father of the English Nation
The Fears of Henry IV: The Life of England's Self-Made King
1415: Henry V's Year of Glory
Medieval Intrigue
Centuries of Change (aka *Human Race*)
Medieval Horizons: Why the Middle Ages Matter

MORTIMER'S A TO Zs OF ENGLISH HISTORY

IAN MORTIMER

Published in Great Britain in 2025 by
Old Street Publishing Ltd
Notaries House, Exeter EX1 1AJ

www.oldstreetpublishing.co.uk

ISBN 978-1-91308-367-0
Ebook ISBN 978-1-91308-368-7

The right of Ian Mortimer to be identified as the author of this work has been asserted by him in accordance with the Copyright, Designs and Patents Act 1988.

Copyright © 2025 by Ian Mortimer

Illustrations © 2025 by James Nunn

Every effort has been made to secure permissions for all images reproduced in this volume. Please contact the publisher directly for further information.

All rights reserved. No part of this publication may be reproduced, stored in or introduced into a retrieval system, or transmitted, in any form, or by any means (electronic, mechanical, photocopying, recording or otherwise) without the prior written permission of the publisher.

10 9 8 7 6 5 4 3 2 1

A CIP catalogue record for this title is available from
the British Library.

Printed and bound in Great Britain.

Typesetting by User Design, Illustration and Typesetting, UK

This book is dedicated to my much-loved friends, the 'Hittites' – Ric Horner, Dom Lawson, Elise Mori (née Alergant) and Rich Cooper – who were my companions in creativity and co-conspirators in taking everything to excess at Hitts Farm, Whimple, in 1988–90.

CONTENTS

Introduction	1
PART ONE *A to Z of Medieval England*	7
PART TWO *A to Z of Elizabethan England*	69
PART THREE *A to Z of Restoration England*	125
PART FOUR *A to Z of Regency England*	185
ENVOI *A to Z of Historical Reflections*	247
Further Reading	303
Acknowledgements	311

INTRODUCTION

Many years ago, when working in an archive, I picked up an old copy of *Haydn's Dictionary of Dates* and came across an entry for 'boiling to death'. Apparently Henry VIII made this the statutory punishment for poisoning after the bishop of Rochester's cook, Richard Rose, poisoned seventeen people, two of whom died. The entry went on to say that 'Margaret Davy, a young woman, suffered in the same manner for a similar crime, 26 March 1542.' I was appalled. I already knew that Henry VIII was a nasty piece of work – one of the most unfeeling, selfish individuals ever to wield power in England – but that detail was more revealing of his cruelty than all the hangings and beheadings on trumped-up charges that I had ever associated with him. It spoke of his utter contempt for ordinary people and his vindictiveness, which extended to wanting to cause the maximum amount of suffering when having his subjects killed. It was no surprise to me that this law was repealed soon after his death in 1547.

That one fact taught me an important lesson about writing history. You don't need to use lots of evidence to make a point. One single, vivid detail can be enough. Novelists sometimes employ a similar trick. If you shock people at the outset of a novel by showing your principal character coldly murdering his wife (as Henry VIII did, twice), you can create a sense that that individual is cruel beyond bounds. In the same way that 'an image is worth a thousand words,' a single startling event can reveal more about an individual than pages and pages of nuanced description.

Skip forward to 2012, when my new book, *The Time Traveller's Guide to Elizabethan England*, had just been published. This was based on a very simple idea. How would England appear if you could actually visit it during the reign of Elizabethan I (1558–1603)? For example, what should you wear? Where might you stay? What might you eat? Which diseases might kill you? Which *doctors* might kill you? It seemed to me that if the past really is 'another country', as the writer L. P. Hartley memorably wrote in *The Go-Between*, historians should be able to describe the various epochs in guidebooks in the same way travel writers do foreign countries.

The challenge I faced in promoting my *Time Traveller's Guide* was that there was just too much information to convey to an audience. What should I include? Describing a different world – not just a single person or place but *everything* in that time – takes more than an hour-long talk. Then I remembered Henry VIII boiling Richard Rose and Margaret Davy to death. If a single detail like that could be so evocative – and so shocking that it was still in my mind, twenty years later – perhaps a few well-chosen headings could illustrate the entire reign. After all, anecdotal history is one of the most memorable forms of historical writing. Just think of Alfred burning the cakes; Harold II with an arrow in his eye; Edward II's red-hot poker; Charles II imploring 'Let not poor Nelly starve'; and Queen Victoria being 'not amused'. But which details should I choose to illustrate Elizabethan England? The horrors of the plague? The plays of William Shakespeare? The queen herself? What to use as loo paper? How to cut your toenails?

Those last two points might sound absurdly trivial but they too are revealing of life in different ages. It is not just the answers to these questions that are interesting: the questions themselves alert you to the fact that there are aspects to the past that you have probably never even considered. Drawing attention to such things makes you realise there are things you *don't know* you don't know and *that* opens your mind up to all sorts of new ways of historical thinking. I therefore planned an A–Z to Elizabethan England that was arranged like the pieces on a chess board: small pawns of detail – which would advance steadily and show people that there are things they don't know they don't know – and larger themes – like castles, bishops, knights and queens – to sweep in and demonstrate the harsh and beautiful realities.

My Elizabethan A–Z talks were a success. People sometimes told me after a performance that they had been trying to guess which theme I would choose for a specific letter of the alphabet. Occasionally someone said that they had been meaning to leave by a certain time – to relieve the babysitter or catch a train – but they had simply had to hang on to find out what I would come up with when I reached X, Y and Z. There seemed to be a real enjoyment in this way of hearing about the past. I therefore developed a similar A–Z for my other Time Traveller's Guides – to medieval England, Restoration Britain and Regency Britain.

These four talks constitute the first four-fifths of this book. Well, they do in a manner of speaking. The truth is that all four have developed hugely over the years. For a start, no two performances were ever the same, even if I tried to make them so. New ideas would occur to me each time and so the themes evolved. Moreover, in writing them down for publication, I have found myself expressing things differently – in ways that I hope are both richer and clearer than the original versions. On top of this, I have carried on learning. For example, just after I had written the Elizabethan A–Z, I was contacted by an archaeologist from Austria who prompted me to rethink everything I thought I knew about women's underwear in the fifteenth and sixteenth centuries. Yes, there were such things as medieval bras. This is the marvellous thing about writing a book: you send out an ambassador into the world on your behalf to make friends and contacts, and gradually, if you have done a good job, those friends and contacts get in touch with you and enrich your understanding. In some cases they have resulted in invitations to get further involved. In 2010 I was invited to join the Fabric Advisory Committee of Exeter Cathedral and so learned a great deal about that magnificent building and Decorated architecture in general. A few years later I was invited to give a keynote address on the development of the sense of self to an international conference of psychologists at the University of Southampton. Such events force you to re-examine what you think you know for presentation to new audiences. Hence these A–Zs have grown with me over the years.

Perhaps the most significant of these post-publication revelations was the matter of working-class life expectancy at birth compared to the life expectancy of the wealthy. It was only after finishing my Regency book, when I was thinking about how a labourer's family could only expect to live *half* as long as a prosperous middle-class family in the Regency period, that the question popped into my head: what was the equivalent proportion in earlier and later centuries? How long could a medieval peasant expect to live in comparison to a lord? And a Restoration labourer compared to the emerging bourgeoisie? Was there a progression? I did a little research and, although the results were not directly comparable, it looked very much as if the labouring classes in every other period could expect to live 85–90 per cent as long as their wealthy contemporaries. In fact, so strong was the correlation, it seemed almost a social constant. In this light, the Regency figure of 50 per cent was utterly shocking. And as you will soon discover, some parts of Regency England had a relative life expectancy that was even less than that.

Each of my Time Traveller's Guides ends with an 'envoi': a short farewell from me to the reader. I have also given this book an envoi – in the form of a fifth and final A–Z. In this I attempt to sum up the experience of considering the last 700 years of English history as a series of living environments. I include things like working-class life expectancy at birth. I look back over such things as how the class system survives, why literacy is important, what it means to be English, and the concept of progress. The envoi of this book is thus, in some respects, a review of the entire *Time Traveller's Guide* project to date. But it is not just looking back. These are also themes to carry forward. In fact, re-reading them now, it strikes me how each one is potentially the subject of a whole book. I recall Bob Dylan saying that every line of his song 'A Hard Rain's a-Gonna Fall' was the title of a song he wanted to write but, being in the middle of the Cuban missile crisis, he did not know if he'd live long enough to complete. The themes of this envoi are similar for me. They aren't just what I've learnt from 'living' in the past; they are the themes that I shall continue talking about for the rest of my life, each one a book I'd write if I had world enough and time.

Here, then, are what began as my four A–Z talks, now in their richer, more developed forms, plus a shiny new, previously unheard A–Z in the envoi. I hope that the flashes from the past that follow give you some idea of your place in the great sweep of human existence. That is the main point of writing these books: they should cause us to reflect on what life is like in all ages, and thereby teach us something about ourselves. At the very least, I am sure that you will be as grateful as I am not to be a cook in Henry VIII's kitchens.

PART ONE

A TO Z

OF MEDIEVAL ENGLAND

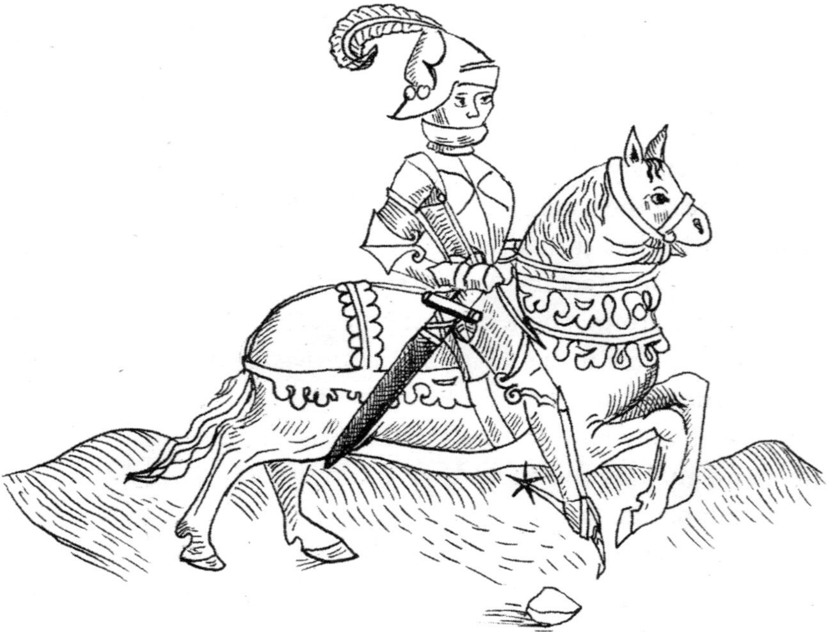

MEDIEVAL ENGLAND

The fourteenth century

What does the word 'medieval' mean to you? For many people, it will immediately trigger thoughts of the 1994 film *Pulp Fiction*, in which one of the leading characters, Marcellus Wallace, declares to a man who has just assaulted him in a most ungentlemanly manner, 'I'm gonna get medieval on your ass.' If this is what comes to mind, you are in good company because that term – 'to get medieval' – is now in the *Oxford English Dictionary*. The truth is that we generally see the Middle Ages as a time of violence and brutality. We only have to think of the crusades and the countless wars between kings, princes and warlords – of castles, walled towns, knights in armour and siege engines – to confirm our impressions. But medieval England was many other things besides violent. It was also innovative, inventive, resilient, responsible and even compassionate. I hope what follows helps you see the bigger picture. Or, rather, the deeper, richer and more interesting one.

Before we start out, however, we have to get one thing clear. What are we talking about when we refer to medieval England? When, exactly, were – or, as we will say here, when *are* the Middle Ages?

The Middle Ages are generally the centuries between the fall of Ancient Rome, around AD 500, and the rise of modern times, in the sixteenth century. The term first appears in English right at the end of that period, in the reign of Elizabeth I (1558–1603). These days historians normally place the end of the Middle Ages in the late fifteenth century or early sixteenth because of the many important social changes between 1450 and 1550. Printing, for example, starts in Western Europe in the 1450s, with the result that about 13 million books have been printed across the Continent by 1500. Guns become instrumental in winning battles in the early sixteenth century. There are important political watersheds at this time too: the final destruction of the Eastern Roman Empire (Byzantium) takes place in 1453. You can also see the expansion of Europe into far-distant lands as marking the end of the Middle Ages. Bartholomew Dias rounding the Cape of Good Hope and sailing into the Indian Ocean in 1487 is a significant event. So too is Columbus's first voyage across the Atlantic five years later. But most of all, it is the Reformation – the break-up of the Catholic Church in the 1520s and 1530s – that makes the old medieval world order seem a thing of the past. As a result, the point at which historians date the end of the Middle Ages varies, depending on the context. Some put it as early as the 1450s, others as late as 1540. In some instances, there are reasons to put it even later, around 1600, when magnifying glasses and telescopes are invented and our horizons are extended towards the very small and very distant, and people generally start to learn there are things they don't know about the world around them. Whichever date you prefer, we are talking about approximately a thousand years of history.

A thousand years is a long time by anybody's reckoning. Life at the end of the Middle Ages has very little in common with life at the start. Therefore, if you are trying to understand everyday life in any great depth, it is wise to stick to just one century. I tend to focus on the fourteenth because it encapsulates all the things that people normally associate with the Middle Ages – castles, knights, monks and friars and, of course, the Black Death. It also allows me to define *England* in relatively simple terms. The fourteenth century is after Edward I has conquered Wales in 1272 but before Henry VIII has made Wales administratively part of the kingdom of England, in 1535. It is also long before the union with Scotland, which is a totally separate kingdom until 1603. Although it is true that the kings of England are also lords of large regions of France – over which they will continue to rule until 1453 – these form parts of the kingdom of France, not England, so the Channel marks a clear line of distinction.

In order to counter the impression that the fourteenth century is all bloodshed and suffering, the first handful of items I've chosen for my medieval A–Z offer a fairly gentle introduction to the period. And what could be more peaceful than a woolly sheep or a cow chewing its cud?

A IS FOR ANIMALS

Why animals? After all, a sheep is a sheep, a pig is a pig and so on. The reason is that we take some things so much for granted that we don't imagine they have altered much over the last 700 years. Yet they have. Hugely.

Take cows, for example. Looking online to check the reports from my local livestock market in Exeter, cows these days weigh between 1,280lbs and 1,896lbs (581kg and 860kg). If you visit the same livestock market in the middle of Exeter in the year 1300, you'll see the animals for sale are about one-third of the size of the *smallest* modern cow, and less than a quarter of the size of the largest.

After you've taken off the horns and the hide and gutted the animal, it weighs roughly five-eighths of its alive, running-around weight. Dressing it to produce meat reduces its weight by a similar proportion. Thus a 1,280lb cow will produce 500lbs of beef. But the average yield from a cow in the early fourteenth century is less than 170lbs. And given the desperate need for food, there isn't a scrap of wastage. A mature live cow in 1300 weighs about 435lbs.

It is not hard to find the reason for the change. Centuries of breeding programmes transform the medieval animals of 1300 into larger, more meat-producing beasts. This process begins in the fourteenth century. Cows are selectively bred to grow bigger so that already by 1400 they are approaching 200lbs of dressed meat, or 512lbs when running around. If you look at medieval byres, you'll see the spaces for cows could not possibly accommodate a modern animal. The twenty-first-century record for a South Devon cow – the local breed to where I live – is over 4,400lbs. That's ten times the size of its average medieval ancestor. That great beast couldn't even get through the door of a fourteenth-century byre.

Much the same can be said for sheep and pigs. They too are about a third of the size of modern animals. Medieval sheep only weigh around 28lbs. Modern *lambs* are twice that when they go to market. Occasionally a ram in the modern world will exceed 350lbs – again, more than ten times as much as its medieval ancestors. Bear this in mind when you look at nature and think it is unchanging. The fields, animals and plants are likely to seem every bit as strange as the people.

B IS FOR BUTTONS

Have you ever stopped to marvel at a button? Do you realise what a wonderful invention it is? Perhaps you don't really think of it as an invention, it is so simple. Given this, you might be surprised to hear that although buttons were used in the ancient world, they are unknown in England in 1300. It is only in the late 1320s that a garment called a *cotehardie* starts to appear at court. As a result, fashion changes forever – and much for the better.

To appreciate this revolution, look how ordinary people dress in 1300. A basic tunic is normally cut from two pieces of cloth, one forming the front of the chest and the front of the sleeves, and the other the back and the back of the sleeves. These are stitched together and the finished article goes on over the head.

But having to get it over your shoulders and wriggle your arms into the sleeves means that it can't be cut that close to the body. It hangs from your shoulders, looking like a repurposed curtain. If wealthy ladies want to have figure-hugging garments – and many do, for obvious reasons – they either have to be sewn into them or they have to have a servant lace them up at the back. And when taking off such garments, they need to be helped out of them. Unsurprisingly, most ordinary men and women normally go for something baggy, so they can squeeze their arms into the sleeves and get dressed without assistance.

Into this world come buttons. And with buttons come front-opening 'coats' and tunics. In the history of fashion, this is a pivotal and exciting moment. As you walk along a row of tailors' shops on a summer's day in London in the 1330s and see the workers sitting cross-legged on their workbenches, all the best ones are sewing a garment that will closely fit their client's body. And these new clothes don't just look good: the wearer can put them on quickly without the assistance of a servant. It's a win-win. A figure-hugging look that used to take a great deal of work is suddenly effortlessly achievable. Up and down the country, provincial tailors and seamstresses see someone in the street wearing a button-fastening close-fitting tunic for the first time – when a fashionable man or woman visits town – and aim to replicate the design. By the mid-1330s, the old hanging-from-the-shoulders look is out. Now, everyone who is remotely fashion-conscious wants a tunic that will cling to his or her body as tightly as possible – because that way they can show off their muscles, hips, waists and breasts. The new look is elegant, refined and sexy. Everyone loves it – everyone, that is, except grumpy old churchmen, who remain steadfastly in their gowns and cassocks, determined to look as unsexy as possible.

C IS FOR CLOCKS

When you think of the fourteenth century in terms of knights in their castles and monks in their monasteries, it is easy to forget that some of the most important social and technological developments affecting our lives originate in this period. One of the most important is the clock.

Just try for a moment to imagine what the world would be like if we had no clocks. You might be thinking, 'I would not know when to turn on the TV'. But that is not the half of it. The broadcaster would not know when to put your favourite programme out. The programme itself could not have been made. In addition, the TV would not exist, nor would the means to broadcast the evening's schedule. This is because most scientific experiments – and therefore most scientific discoveries – depend on a reliable means of measuring time. We'd have no film, no computers, no cars and no trains. Then think, when are you going to turn up for work? When might your employer expect you to turn up? When might anyone work – the government, the health service, the shops? Society as we know it would not exist without a reliable and universally accepted means of telling the time.

This is why it amuses me greatly to think of Edward III visiting Richard of Wallingford at St Albans Abbey in about 1332. On finding the good abbot building a mechanical clock – probably the first in the British Isles – the king tells him he should be doing something more useful.

Most people in the early fourteenth century still tell the time by dividing the day into twelve equal hours and the night likewise. Thus an hour of daylight is twice as long in summer as it is in winter. That's not particularly helpful if you have a loaf in the oven. Some affluent people do have an hourglass for measuring short periods of time. But most do not.

In large towns, a specific church will take the lead in ringing the hour on its bell but the length of the hour is always down to the judgement of the person in charge. Churches and manor houses often have sundials. In addition, those who can use astrolabes can calculate the angle of the shadow cast by the sun from, say, a nearby tree; from this they can work out what time it is at that time of year. Some people put a stick in the ground and estimate the hour from the way the sun casts a shadow – a technique Chaucer mentions in *The Canterbury Tales*. But all these sundials and astrolabes require the sun to be shining. And in England, that is not always the case.

Richard of Wallingford does build his clock. And Edward III eventually sees the error of his ways. In the early 1350s the king pays for several Italian clockmakers to come to England and install mechanical clocks at Windsor Castle in Berkshire, Queenborough Castle in Kent, Westminster Palace and the royal palace at King's Langley in Hertfordshire. Soon, cathedrals and abbeys are following his example. Salisbury Cathedral installs a mechanical clock in 1386. Wells Cathedral does the same in 1397. In 1400 countrymen can still get by with putting a stick in the ground but by then most large towns have recognised the advantages of measured time. Even Barnstaple, a relatively small town on the north Devon coast, has a clock by the end of the century. People listen out for the hour ringing out on the clock of the cathedral or nearest abbey. They talk about meeting each other at five or six 'of the bell' or 'of the clock' – just as we do.

D IS FOR THE DEAD

You can't escape the dead in the Middle Ages. They're all around you – and not just in this country but right across Christendom. Fourteenth-century people's vision of life extends beyond death, so that everyone who has ever lived is in one great big queue and, at death, they pass out of sight of the living in the way that people do when they cross over the brow of a hill or go round a corner. But really they are still in that queue, on their way to their final destination, which is Heaven. And the length of time it will take them to get there depends in part on the living.

The concept of Purgatory is fully developed by the fourteenth century. This holds that, although the saints go straight to Heaven and some terrible sinners are despatched off immediately to Hell, the majority of people's souls are sent to Purgatory when they die. This is a sort of spiritual holding bay. They linger there in considerable discomfort until enough prayers have been said to ease their path onwards into Paradise. As a result, most wealthy families have special relationships with favoured churches where they maintain priests to pray and sing for the benefit of their souls and the souls of their ancestors. In those churches, the names of the dead are repeated every day.

It is also widely believed that close proximity to the bones of the saints – the holy dead – will bring you into direct contact with them. The saints in turn, whose souls are already in Heaven, can intercede with God to turn things to your benefit. In some people's thinking, your dead ancestors can do something similar. If you pray for them in an appropriate fashion they can have a word with the saints, who will intercede with the Almighty. In fact, if your ancestor makes his way through Purgatory and reaches Heaven, he can put in a good word for you himself. Thus there is a whole cycle of goodwill and intercession. You pray for the dead, the dead speak to the saints, and the saints intercede with God on your behalf.

The remains of the holy dead help the living in other ways too. When swearing oaths, relics are produced, so the person taking the oath recognises the seriousness of his promises. Business dealings are often conducted in churches, close to a saint's shrine, for a similar reason. Kings have holy bones carried into battle. Edward III's relic collection includes bones that purportedly come from the bodies of St George, St Leonard, St John the Baptist, St James the Less, St Agnes, St Margaret, St Mary Magdalene, St Agatha, St Stephen, St Adrian, St Jerome and St Edward the Confessor. But the power of relics of saints to perform miracles is perhaps their most important function. People go on long pilgrimages – sometimes all the way to Jerusalem – to be in the presence of the remains of saints in the hope of being cured. Churches go to great lengths to obtain the bones of the most popular miracle-working figures in order to attract the penny-carrying crowds of sufferers desperate for a cure.

It hardly needs saying that Jesus Christ's bones – were they to exist – would be the most treasured relics of all. Unfortunately for medieval people throughout Christendom, they are nowhere to be found. Christians believe he took them with him when he ascended to Heaven. But that does not stop them from venerating the relics that he left behind on Earth, including the shroud, the cross and the thorns from his crown. They also revere the body parts that, logically, he must have deposited here, such as his milk teeth, his sweat and his blood. And his foreskin. About a dozen churches across Europe claim to have Christ's foreskin in their possession. Call me a sceptic but I suspect some of those claims are not genuine. One church in Rome even claims to have his umbilical cord.

E IS FOR THE ENVIRONMENT

What is the most earth-shattering event of the last thousand years? I always come back to two. One is the Black Death, the great plague of the fourteenth century, to which we will return in due course. The other is environmental change.

These days we all understand how environmental change can drastically affect life on Earth. Global warming would be our principal concern worldwide if it weren't for international conflicts taking a higher priority right now (as they have done for centuries). But global warming is not simply a modern phenomenon. A slower, smaller, less-threatening form occurred naturally in the Middle Ages. Historians call it the Medieval Warm Period. It amounts to an increase in the average year-round temperature of about 1 degree centigrade worldwide between the tenth century and the thirteenth. That does not sound particularly significant. If called upon to guess the temperature right now, I would probably be out by at least 1 degree. But a year-round average increase, even on that modest scale, is hugely significant. A rise of just half a degree can bring forward the last frost of spring by ten days. Likewise, it pushes back the first frost of autumn by another ten days. And those extra twenty days of growth, when they are accompanied by warmer weather throughout, can see a considerable difference in harvest yields, especially at altitude. A 1-degree rise in temperature makes it far less likely you will have consecutive harvest failures above 500ft, so you can clear much more rough, uncultivated land and put it to productive uses.

As a result of the Medieval Warm Period, the population in 1290 is far higher than it has been in previous centuries. With more food to go around, more mothers can produce enough milk for a greater number of babies to live beyond infancy. That means more people reach maturity. They in turn can clear more land and create more food surpluses – and yet more babies. Almost all the potential farmland in England is being used by 1290. Not all the extra people are now needed to work on the land of the rural manors, so they start swelling the populations of the towns. More monasteries exist than ever before. More markets do too. Whereas people before the year 1000 are largely subsistence farmers working on their lords' great estates, never handling money, by 1290 they have silver in their purses and might put it to any number of uses. It is largely due to global warming that the commercial revolution of the early Middle Ages takes place, along with most of the cultural developments we think of as medieval.

So far so good. The trouble is that 1290 is when the weather takes a turn for the worse. The Medieval Warm Period comes to a sudden stop. The Earth goes into a phase of global cooling. Frosts last longer and, in autumn, come sooner. Rainfalls are so heavy and persistent that whole summers are wiped out. In 1315 and 1316 the weather is abysmal. Animals are seen drowned in their fields. And it does not get much better over the next few years. As a result, between 1290 and 1325, approximately 600,000 people perish in England. That is 13 per cent of the population. Many families find themselves impoverished. Children with inadequate diets do not grow up properly but are lame or stunted. For the poor, environmental change in the early fourteenth century results in utter misery.

That is worth pausing over. It is somewhat ironic that the biggest threat the fourteenth-century world faces is global cooling – the very opposite of the environmental threat we face today.

F IS FOR FOOD

Carrying on from this point about the environment, you will be shocked to see how expensive food is in the fourteenth century. To give you an idea just how much it costs, consider the standard unit of measurement known as the chicken.

In the late fourteenth century, a skilled worker such as a carpenter or a thatcher earns 4d or 4½d for every day he works. That is approximately what a chicken costs in the market. In the modern world, a free-range chicken costs about £11. No skilled worker in England today would give you a day's work for £11. At the time of writing, the average daily wage in the UK for a carpenter or a thatcher is more than £110. Ten chickens. To appreciate how precious food is to medieval workers and their families, we need to consider our food bills being more than ten times what we pay today but our incomes being the same.

According to the Office for National Statistics, in 2023 the average UK household (with 2.4 people) spent £4,296 on groceries and £1,628 on food outside the home (restaurants and takeaways). That's a total of £5,924 per year, or £494 per month. Imagine the average family of 2.4 people having to spend £4,940 on food every month – almost £60,000 per year. The 'average family' could not afford to do so. But if you're in a family of *four* (as opposed to 2.4), your food shop today is likely to be considerably more than this, perhaps half as much again. To appreciate how precious food is in the Middle Ages, consider the food bill for a family of four being £90,000 per year, or £7,500 every month. Just on food. No alcohol. No rent, no heating, no clothes, no luxuries – just food.

But that is not the end of it. Those figures relate to the *late* fourteenth century, after the Black Death has wiped out a large proportion of the population and wages have risen. In 1300 a thatcher earns only 2½d and a labourer only 1½d, which is less than a chicken costs at the time. Unsurprisingly, very few labourers' families eat meat in the early fourteenth century. Most only have the chance to do so when the lord of the manor provides his tenants with a feast at Christmas or Easter. Cheese is the great saviour of the people, as it is practically the only form of protein that is both cheap and lasts through winter. Indeed, you could say that whoever discovered how to make cheese about 8,000 years ago did more for the wellbeing of humankind than any other individual in history. If you call on your early fourteenth-century English ancestors in a peasant cottage, be prepared to have a limited diet of rye or barley bread, 'pottage' (vegetable stews) normally made with beans, onions and peas flavoured with salt and garlic, and cheese.

G IS FOR GUNS

We don't normally associate guns with the Middle Ages. We prefer to think of knights doing the chivalric thing and looking their enemy in the eye as they charge at them with level lances or raised battle axes. As it happens, the knights in question prefer that too. Guns aren't very chivalric. They're just not cricket. When Henry IV attacks the great fortress of Berwick in the summer of 1405, he first destroys the outer walls with small cannon and then takes out the Constable Tower with a single shot from one of his big guns. End of siege. Or, as we might say today, game over. Where's the fun in that for a self-respecting knight in armour? There's no honour in blasting people and fortifications to pieces from a safe distance.

Gunpowder was first developed in China in the ninth century. Traders bring it to Europe in the thirteenth. Guns, however, are a fourteenth-century invention. The writer Walter de Milemete includes an illustration of a small cannon in a book of princely advice, dedicated to Edward III, in 1326. The first recorded instance of guns actually being used in England is during the Stanhope Park campaign the following year, when the English army fires bombards against the Scots. After that, Edward III pioneers the mass production of gunpowder. By 1347 he has two tons of it stored at the Tower of London.

The irony is that Edward III is also a great champion of traditional chivalric values. He holds events in which his knights take on Arthurian roles. In the 1330s he holds tournaments almost every month in which he and his men joust with each other for glory and honour. The reason why Edward is pushing the manufacture of guns is for them to be a backup for his mass-produced bows and arrows.

At Crécy in 1346 Edward does what few medieval kings dare to do when he confronts the French army in open battle. France has a population of 20 million people – four times that of England – and is a much wealthier kingdom. But Edward has his strategy worked out. He lets the French knights attack him. He has his archers positioned on the flanks. He has his guns at the rear. As the flower of French nobility charges towards the much smaller English army, their front ranks are cut down by the English archers. The ranks behind the French front line lose momentum. Then they too are shot with arrows. As the subsequent waves of French knights try to reach the English army, clambering over their dead comrades, Edward opens fire with his cannon. The French knights can't compete. The age of projectile warfare has arrived.

Guns don't take over immediately. They are slow to load and, being very heavy, difficult to transport. They are expensive to maintain. By themselves, they do not win battles in the Middle Ages. Hence longbow archery remains the mainstay of English military superiority until the mid-fifteenth century. But guns do win sieges, as we have seen with Edward III's grandson, Henry IV, at Berwick. Henry designs and builds his own big guns with the specific intent of demolishing castle walls. The days of besieging castles for months on end are rapidly drawing to a close, courtesy of these two English kings.

H IS FOR HALL HOUSES

If you are looking for somewhere to stay in the late fourteenth century, what sort of accommodation might you expect? Of course, we all think immediately of castles and manor houses, with stone walls, lofty halls and chambers with fireplaces. You might also picture four-poster beds in those chambers, chests around the room, glazed windows and a perch for your favourite hawk. But what if you are not going to stay with one of your wealthy ancestors but a more modest family who make their living from farming a few acres in the countryside?

Much depends on the region, of course. Building materials are cumbersome and heavy so it is difficult to transport them very far. Farmhouses are almost always made of local materials. On Dartmoor, in the southwest, they are normally built with stone walls. Somerset houses are often made with cob – a compound of subsoil, clay and straw. In the Midlands, you are more likely to come across cruck houses. These are made from trees with curved bows that are split to form a pair of cruck blades, which are then placed together to form an arch. Three or four such arches with a ridge piece joining them provide the basic structure. In the southeast, the Wealden type of timber frame becomes common at the end of the fourteenth century. This consists of an open hall with one two-storey block at one end and another similar block at the other. But wherever you go, ordinary people's houses are always built around a main living space, called the hall.

A medieval hall has no ceiling – it is open to the roof beams. Despite this high space, it is quite dark. Windows are made secure by having vertical wooden bars to stop intruders. They do not contain glass. At night they are closed by shutters but during the day, the shutters are kept open to let in the light. People often leave the doors open during the day too, for the same reason.

A hall floor is made of packed earth and covered with straw or rushes. In the centre is the hearth, where cooking takes place on hearth stones. Smoke rises into the roof and either emanates through the thatch or a vent. Only the rich have fireplaces. The result is that the halls of ordinary houses are suffused with smoke – which swirls everywhere on account of the draughts coming in through the windows and the door, even when these are shuttered and closed. If you look up, you'll see the beams and the underside of the thatch roof are black from years of smoke.

Near the fire you'll see cooking apparatus, such as a tripod for suspending a cauldron over the fire, and basins and wooden vessels for holding water. People eat at a trestle table that can be dismantled when not needed. You might also see a coffer or two against the walls for storage, and benches for use at the table. But in many cases that will be all the furniture there is. Working people do not cram their houses with possessions. They do not buy things they don't urgently need because they can't afford to. Most of their money goes on cooking apparatus and the foodstuffs they can't grow for themselves, especially salt. They live in an aromatic world of smoke, cooking smells and the rotting fragments of food that have fallen into the rushes in the dim light.

I IS FOR ILLNESSES

If there is one good reason *not* to visit the fourteenth century, it is the health risk. We are the descendants of people who survive despite all the odds. In the pre-industrial past, injuries are common – there is no health or safety at work – and illnesses are ubiquitous. When you add the dangers of childbirth, it is amazing we are here at all. Giving birth for every woman in the Middle Ages is like playing Russian Roulette with a forty-barrel gun. It doesn't matter how wealthy you are: there is a 2.5 per cent chance of death every time you become pregnant. If you go through childbirth a dozen times, which many medieval women do, the chances of dying in the process are more than one in four. Sadly, the baby's chances of dying are even higher.

Perhaps the thing you'll find most shocking is how helpless people are in the face of physical suffering. They have no idea about germ theory or the circulation of the blood. We live in an age in which we are confident we understand how our bodies work and, if there is something wrong, we know whom to ask for advice. They don't. For most of them, their best hope is prayer or the wisdom of old women who have no formal medical training but who have nursed many sick people through their worst times.

Consider the plight of those who catch leprosy (otherwise known as Hansen's Disease). It is caused by slow-growing bacteria that progress very slowly through the body, removing first the sensations in your hands and feet, and later paralysing your extremities, leaving them badly ulcerated. People who catch it in the Middle Ages have to ring a bell whenever anyone else comes near them. Over the years their fingers and toes melt off. That makes ringing the bell a little more difficult. But that's not the end of their troubles. Their body hair and eyelashes fall out. Normally the bridge of the nose collapses and they are left with a smelly liquid constantly running from the gaping wound. Their teeth fall out, their penises atrophy, their eyeballs become ulcerated, their voices become a croak and their skin marked with large nodules. Ultimately they are left wholly deformed, stinking, repulsive and blind. Hence it is called the 'living death'. The only good thing you can say about it is that it is becoming less common in the fourteenth century. People are dying of tuberculosis instead.

You know what's coming next. In 1348 the Black Death reaches England – and nothing else since the last Ice Age has had such a dire effect on our population.

The Black Death is the name given to the bubonic plague outbreak of 1346–51, which affects almost all of Europe. It is spread by the bacterium, *yersinia pestis*, which lives in the fleas of the black rat. After a flea bites the rat and the rat has died, that flea and its friends seek another host, and given the proximity of rats and people in the fourteenth century, they may well latch on to one of us. If you are unlucky and an infected flea bites straight into a vein, you will die within a matter of hours. If you are bitten on the legs, you will find very sensitive black swellings or buboes developing in the lymph nodes in your groin. They might grow up to the size of an egg. If you are bitten on the upper body, you will feel the buboes in your armpits. Once infected, you can spread the disease to other people through your breath. After the development of the buboes, you will develop an acute fever and experience extreme headaches. If you live long enough, you will start to emit a terrible stench, vomit blood and behave as if in a drunken stupor. According to Gabriel de Mussis, a notary from Piacenza, some victims die on the day they catch the disease, some on day two, but most between the third and fifth days. You might survive – perhaps 40 per cent do – but not if you start vomiting blood.

The scale of the mortality is so great that it is difficult to comprehend. Consider it in relation to the two World Wars. World War I results in the deaths of 1.55 per cent of the UK population over a four-year period. That amounts to an annual mortality rate of just under 0.4 per cent. The Black Death kills at least 45 per cent of the English population in seven months. That is a mortality rate of 77 per cent per year. The mortality impact of the Black Death is thus roughly 200 times as intense as that of World War I. Very broadly speaking, 200 times as many children lose a parent. Two hundred times as many parents lose a child. As for World War II, the population of Japan in 1945 is roughly about 70 million. To have the same impact on that country in 1945 as the Black Death has on England in 1348–49, you'd have to drop two atomic bombs like those dropped on Hiroshima and Nagasaki on two similarly large cities every day for seven months.

The Black Death is just the first wave of a pandemic that continues to kill English people for the next 300 years. It returns in 1361, 1368, 1375, 1390 and then roughly every ten to twenty years after that. Normally, the bigger the city, the greater the percentage of citizens it kills. It results in higher wages and the greater availability of luxuries, such as meat and spices, for the survivors. But it leaves their lives blighted by personal loss and family tragedy on an unimaginable scale.

As for why it is one of the two most earth-shattering events of the last thousand years (along with environment change, already mentioned in E is for Environment), it is probably 'too soon to say'. It boosts capitalism and economic competition. It provides some families with unprecedented opportunities and thereby shakes up the entire social order. It smashes feudalism to pieces. Peasants who were effectively chained to their manors are suddenly made free. The shortage of labour means they can go where they want when they want and demand higher wages. They can marry whomsoever they want. And it changes people's attitudes to illnesses forever. No one can continue to argue that diseases are sent by God as a blessing, so that people can atone for their sins through suffering on Earth. Babies who die in their cradles from plague have nothing to atone for. Ultimately it provokes a lot of serious questioning and soul-searching. What causes it? And what can be done to limit the damage it causes? In many ways, public health starts here.

J IS FOR JOHN MANDEVILLE

Who is John Mandeville, you might ask? The simple answer is that he is an English traveller from St Albans in Hertfordshire. In 1322 he sets out to travel the world and, having seen all he wants to see by 1356, returns to northern France to write a book about his adventures, like Marco Polo seventy years earlier.

John Mandeville's concept of the world is formed around its centre, Jerusalem. So his book begins with directions for prospective pilgrims thinking of setting out for the Middle East. He adds that the Holy Land is in Muslim hands because of the sins of Christians and that his readers, if they are true men of God, will reconquer the land for Christ.

With that preamble set out, John tells English people that to get to the Holy Land they must set off through Germany and travel through the kingdoms of Poland and Hungary down to Bulgaria. They must then pass into Greece or Turkey to reach the city of Constantinople. He suggests various routes through Turkey to the Holy Land. Some of these include detours that you won't find in any modern travel book. For example, on 'the Isle of Lango' – wherever that is – you'll encounter a 100ft-long dragon who was once a beautiful woman. Unfortunately, she has been changed into her current form by the goddess Diana, and she must remain like that until some brave knight kisses her on the lips.

Do dragons have lips? I don't think so. But I love the image.

After a detailed description of Jerusalem and nearby holy places, such as Bethlehem, John tells us about Egypt, Armenia, 'the land of Job', 'the country of the Amazons' (the fighting women of ancient legends) and Ethiopia. Here, he tells you, live the *Sciopods*, the people with only one leg and one large foot, who can nevertheless run very fast on their one limb. When not running they shelter from the heat of the midday sun underneath their foot. Later he describes the *Cynocephales* (the dog-headed men and women of the Near East); the Brahmins of India; the court of the Mongol ruler, the Great Khan, in China; the gold-digging ants of Ceylon; and the Tibetan people who offer their dead ancestors' bodies as feasts for the birds while eating the contents of their ancestors' heads themselves.

That's the simple explanation of who John Mandeville is. But who is he really?

The book is probably the work of a French monk who has never left France but who has custody of a wonderful library of travellers' tales in his monastery. He uses bits of them to form his own travel book, pretending it's an account of the real-life experiences of an Englishman. Whoever he was and whether he really travelled or not, all the stories in *The Travels of John Mandeville* are taken from other travellers' tales. It is thus both a work of fiction and a compendium of medieval knowledge.

What is not in doubt is that the work becomes very popular after it starts to be copied in about 1357. In no time at all, it has been translated into twenty languages. And that demonstrates the important point. Just like the author, everyone in Europe is fascinated by the outside world, even if they can't go there. What's more, the whole idea of travel as a holy enterprise is like an electric charge to the medieval mind. Columbus is just one of the many thousands of people who will be inspired by John Mandeville. Long before his voyage across the Atlantic, people dream of making journeys into the unknown. And in the fifteenth century, the idea of converting the newly discovered parts of the world to Christianity proves an attractive alternative to the crusades.

K IS FOR KINGS

I suspect the images most frequently associated with the Middle Ages are kings, castles and battles. And it is true that the fourteenth-century kings of England fight battles and besiege castles with the same sort of regularity we hold general elections. One of the most common reasons for fighting is, in fact, a bit like a general election, in that its purpose is to determine who will run the country –

who should be king. On 14 October 1066 Harold II loses out in the hustings of Hastings when the Norman Party under Duke William wins a clear majority. Four centuries later, on 22 August 1485, Richard III and the Yorkist Party come second in the ballot of Bosworth when Henry VII and the Tudor Party sweep the field and Richard himself loses not only his seat but also his horse and his life. Battles for the throne thus top and tail our traditional vision of medieval England.

This fact might lead you to think that nothing much changes across the Middle Ages. Despite the passing of 418 years and 312 days between Hastings and Bosworth, it is the same old story of one king bashing another over the head and taking the throne. But almost everything changes. For a start, kingship itself is turned upside down.

Before the early thirteenth century, nothing holds the king in check except a full-blown civil war; he can do whatever he wants. This explains such details as Henry I's twenty or more illegitimate children by as many different mothers and Richard I's reckless exploits on the Third Crusade. But in 1209 the pope puts King John on the medieval naughty step by excommunicating him. Soon afterwards, in 1215, the English barons get together and make John's rule subject to approval by a committee when they force him to agree to Magna Carta (literally 'the Great Charter'). John would rather die than accept such restrictions on his power – and die is exactly what he does the following year. But the principle has been established. Magna Carta gives us the theory and practice of holding kings to account.

In 1265 the first parliament to include elected representatives of the shires and boroughs is held. In 1297 Edward I acknowledges Parliament's right to grant or withhold extraordinary taxation. Kings need taxes to be able to raise armies, so this means Parliament effectively decides whether or not England goes to war, not the king. By 1300 kings can no longer simply do what they want. If they plan to fight battles as often as Edward III, for example, they need the support of Parliament, which means the support of the leading men in the country.

The power of English kings shifts dramatically in the fourteenth century. Never before has an anointed king of England been deposed. After all, without Parliament, how do you depose a king? The answer is that you remove him by force – as in the case of Harold II, William II and Richard I – all of whom found themselves on the wrong end of a high-velocity pointed piece of metal. But then Edward II comes to the throne in 1307. For almost his entire reign he surrounds himself with close friends of relatively low rank who have mocked the most

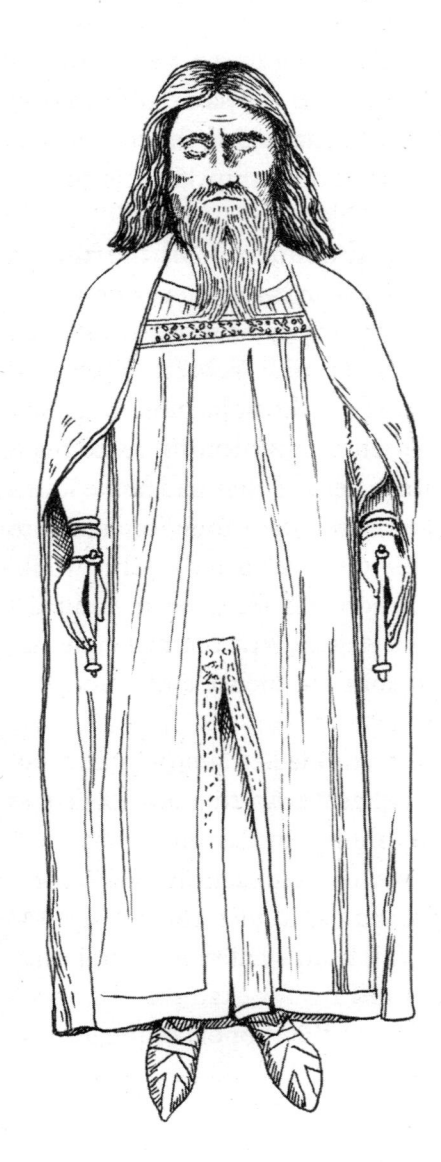

Edward III (from his effigy). One of our greatest kings – so successful that we don't often talk about him. We pay much more attention to those monarchs who were political failures than those who were successful.

powerful earls and barons. Unsurprisingly, those earls and barons hate the king's friends. In 1321 civil war breaks out. Edward's opponents are defeated the following year at the battle of Boroughbridge in North Yorkshire, and he rules for a short while without opposition. Even his archenemy, Roger Mortimer (who is no connection to me, by the way), surrenders to him and is safely locked up in the Tower of London. But Roger escapes from the Tower in 1323 and, three years later, teams up with Edward II's wife, Queen Isabella. Together they raise a small army in the Low Countries and invade England. Parliament agrees to depose Edward II in favour of his son, Edward III. Faced with the prospect of being deposed, Edward II abdicates in January 1327. He is not like his Norman ancestors; he is certainly not a king who can simply do what he wants and get away with it.

Jump forward to 1399, when another king – Edward II's great-grandson, Richard II – is facing widespread opposition. Victory in that year's metaphorical 'general election' goes to the Lancastrian Party, headed by the future Henry IV. What happens next is a reversal of the sequence of events of 1327. First Richard II is forced to abdicate and *then* he is deposed. If his abdication were the critical act marking the end of his reign, there would be no need for Parliament to depose him. But they *do* depose him. What's more they debate whether Henry of Lancaster should replace him or whether another member of the royal family should be king. Richard's own plan is that his uncle, Edmund, duke of York, should be his successor. Parliament does not agree. When asked whether they would rather have the duke of York, the MPs all shout 'No!' So what about the duke's eldest son, Edward? 'No!' And his other son, Richard? 'No!' and in that way, Parliament elects Henry IV as king.

Over the thirteenth and fourteenth centuries, therefore, kings go from omnipotence to subjection to the will of Parliament. By 1400 Parliament can remove kings from power and appoint their successors. Unfortunately, this does not save us from being ruled by the cruel and vindictive Henry VIII in the sixteenth century but it is a big step in the right direction.

L IS FOR LITERACY

One of the biggest modern misunderstandings of the Middle Ages is the belief that only the clergy can read and write – that if you want to have something written down or need something read to you, you'll have to find a priest. This is more or less true in the eleventh and twelfth centuries. If you are caught doing something heinous in the twelfth century but can read a chapter from the Bible, you are deemed to be a priest and can't be hanged. However, by the fourteenth century, literacy and the priesthood no longer go hand in hand. Thousands of laymen can read and write.

As educational incentives go, you might think that *not being hanged* takes some beating. But in the fourteenth century it is not the fear of the gallows that causes so many ordinary people to have their sons taught to read and write. It is rather the financial rewards on offer to the literate. In short, if you can read and write, more and more doors are open to you and, for a few people, great wealth awaits.

There are several stages to this development. One comes in the 1190s when the chanceries of both England and France are reorganised. Henceforth, copies of all outgoing royal letters are kept on official rolls. Hundreds of clerks have to be employed to keep a copy of every word of official business sent out across the Angevin Empire, which extends to all the lands in France ruled by the kings of England by virtue of their being dukes of Aquitaine and Normandy and counts of Anjou. Over the next few decades, bishops start to create registers of all their official actions. Then in 1272 Edward I inherits his father's throne while abroad on crusade. When he returns as king, he discovers that many royal estates have been given away. So he orders a survey to be made of what has happened to them. Manorial lords suddenly find themselves being investigated by royal officials as a result. They in turn take note of the legal power of the written record and start to create their own manorial court rolls and put together surveys of their estates. If something is written down, you have evidence that can be used in court. Thousands of clerks are needed to perform all this work. Large sums are spent on their salaries. A quill pen and a piece of parchment is the great start-up opportunity of the late-thirteenth century.

In the early fourteenth century clerks and scribes attend grammar schools, where they learn Latin as well as how to read and write in that language. Thus we can make a rough estimate of the proportion of the population that is literate by looking at the records of those giving testimony in Latin. For example, in 1320 Thomas de Cantilupe, a deceased bishop of Hereford, is being considered for sainthood. To be successful, the late bishop's supporters need to provide evidence of miracles performed by him. Many of those who provide that evidence do so in Latin. The majority of clergymen do, obviously, but of the laymen, 17 per cent of townsmen use Latin and 7 per cent of the countrymen, indicating some level of formal education. No women who give evidence offer a Latin response because none of them has attended school. These figures broadly correspond with what we know from other sources about literacy. By 1400 about 6 per cent of the male population of England can read and write. In towns, one in four men is literate, and in rural areas, one in twenty. But almost no women are. Not until the sixteenth century do women learn to read and write in significant numbers.

M IS FOR MONEY

Many twelfth-century people don't use cash. Instead, they depend heavily on barter and what they can grow themselves. The balance shifts substantially around 1190. Hundreds of markets are established. Suddenly people everywhere need money. In my home county of Devon, for example, there are only four markets in 1086. By 1300 there are about a hundred. And markets can't function without money. If you want to buy milk and the only way you can pay for it is by barter – by offering, say, a lamb in exchange – you are either going to go home with an awful lot of milk (if the milk vendor wants a lamb) or the milk vendor is going to have to find an acceptable form of change for your lamb. The development of markets and money thus go hand in hand.

In 1300 you will find your purse contains a number of silver pennies and groats (a groat being worth 4d). Two hundred and forty pennies weigh a pound and are a pound sterling in value but there is no coin larger than a groat. Groats are physically four times the size of each penny. People also cut groats in half to make 2d coins; they also cut pennies into halves and quarters to make halfpennies and farthings (a farthing is literally a 'fourthing' of a penny). These are the only coins in circulation. No sixpences, no shillings, no crowns, no guineas. As you can imagine, it is not easy to pay someone £40 for a *destrier* – a specially bred war horse – in pennies. Groats are relatively rare in the early fourteenth century because they are not minted between 1282 and 1351, so you will probably have to amass 9,600 pennies to pay for your war horse. That's like buying a car with £1 coins today.

Edward III is the man who solves this problem. In 1344 he tries out a new coin, a gold leopard, worth 6s, to rival the Florentine florin and the Genoese ducat. It doesn't catch on as the gold in the coin is worth more than its face value, so everyone who receives one immediately melts it down. But Edward is not to be deterred. He has his moneyers produce gold nobles, worth 6s 8d or eighty pennies. This is much more successful – not least because one of the most common units of accounting is the mark, which is 13s 4d or two-thirds of a pound. Thus a noble is usefully one-third of a pound and half a mark. Half-nobles and quarter-nobles are soon added to the coins available. Edward III starts minting silver groats again too. For the first time in English history you have a whole range of denominations: nobles, half-nobles and quarter-nobles in gold, and groats, half-groats, pennies, halfpennies and farthings in silver. That's how things stay until 1464, when Edward IV introduces the gold ryal, worth 10s. Gold sovereigns, worth £1, are first minted in 1489.

For substantial sums, you'll need a banker. In the fourteenth century the Italians dominate the business. Companies such as the Frescobaldi of Florence and the Riccardi of Lucca lend money to Edward I. Later, Edward III uses the services of the Bardi and Peruzzi of Florence. Making use of bankers is only for the rich, of course. Ordinary people do not have bank accounts. But if you are a merchant importing, say, carpets and spices from Venice or Constantinople, or an English wool merchant selling to the manufacturing towns of Ghent, Amsterdam and Rotterdam, you don't want to have to travel abroad with hundreds of thousands of silver pennies – especially not when there are a lot of thieves along the way. Instead, you transfer your cash via a banker. So too do aristocrats. When the future Henry IV runs short of cash in Venice on his way to Jerusalem in 1393, he simply asks a local bank for a loan repayable by his wealthy father, the duke of Lancaster, in England. You could say this is the fourteenth-century equivalent of being allowed to play with his dad's credit card.

N IS FOR NATURAL PHILOSOPHY

How do you fly a medieval helicopter? That, as you may have gathered, is a trick question. Medieval helicopters don't fly. Except in the imagination.

In the notebooks of Leonardo da Vinci there is a drawing for what he calls an 'aerial screw', or helicopter-like aircraft. And Leonardo is born in April 1452 – six months before King Richard III is born, three years before Gutenberg first prints a Bible, and forty years before Columbus sails across the Atlantic – so he definitely counts as a medieval man. The fact his design isn't airworthy is not the point: the key thing is that the concept of a helicopter exists. I might add that Leonardo's notebooks also contain ideas for other sorts of flying machines, in which beating wings created both lift and propulsion, like a bird in flight.

Leonardo's helicopter design dates from about 1489. His

famous Vitruvian Man demonstrating the geometric principles of the human body dates from the following year. But we tend to think of him as a lone genius. The truth is rather different. Where does Leonardo get his ideas about flying from? Partly from his observation of nature, no doubt. But partly from other medieval thinkers. One he quotes is the thirteenth-century English friar, Roger Bacon.

Many people don't know the name of Roger Bacon. Some confuse him with his namesake, the sixteenth-century polymath Francis Bacon. That's not an inappropriate mistake because both men are great exponents of natural philosophy.

The simple explanation of natural philosophy is that it is 'science without the mathematics'. But natural philosophers don't think of themselves as scientists. They see their task as that of exploring the physical attributes of God's creation. Consequently, natural philosophers are more open-minded than we are in our science-powered world. Consider this passage by Roger Bacon:

> Ships may be made to move without oars or rowers, so that large vessels might be driven on the sea or on a river by a single man, and more swiftly than if they were strongly manned. Chariots can be built which can move without any draught animal at incalculable speed... Flying machines might be made in the middle of which a man might sit, turning a certain mechanism whereby artfully built wings might beat the air, in the manner of a bird in flight. Another instrument could be made which, although small, will lift or lower weights of almost infinite greatness... Again, instruments might be made for walking in the sea, or in rivers, even to the very bottom, without bodily danger... And very many things of this sort might be made: bridges which cross rivers without pier or prop whatsoever, and unheard of machines and engines.

This is astonishing coming from a thirteenth-century Englishman. But it shows the medieval mind is, in some respects, an open one. Their intellectual boundaries are limitless. Their belief in miracles means that all sorts of phenomena are conceivable. When we pour scorn on medieval people for what seems to be ignorance, we should remember they are just as clever as us and, in some respects, more welcoming of new ideas about the natural world. They are formulating the rules and systems of understanding that one day will inform *us*. And who is to say we could do it from scratch any better than them?

O IS FOR OLD AGE

How long do people live in the Middle Ages? Much depends on how wealthy they are. A good diet in infancy and youth means the rich are more likely to reach adulthood and so, on average, they live about five or six years longer than their less wealthy tenants. But most of the illnesses going around in the fourteenth century affect the rich as well as the poor. There are some exceptions: fewer rich people die of plague because they are able to leave towns for the country and thus avoid the infected rats and people. But half the population is dead by the age of twenty.

Yes, you read that correctly. Half the population is dead before the age of twenty.

Now, because of the ways that averages work, that doesn't mean life expectancy at birth is less than twenty. Some people do live long lives – well into old age – and that means that overall life expectancy is between twenty-five and thirty-five years of age, depending on which year you are assessing and how wealthy the individual. But it is true that, if you're over the age of twenty, by medieval standards, you are living on borrowed time. Of course, from where we are sitting, twenty seems no age at all. We certainly don't regard it as a full lifespan. But as I wrote under A for Animals, some things we take for granted have altered hugely over the last 700 years.

If you *do* live to twenty in the fourteenth century, you have a 50 per cent chance of making it to the grand old age of forty. In other words, three-quarters of the population are dead by forty. Four-fifths of the remainder die before they are sixty. Only one in twenty fourteenth-century people lives beyond sixty years of age.

I suspect that at this point you might be thinking, 'Well, today we don't have to cope with the Black Death.' If you are, take a guess how much the plague affects life expectancy at birth.

It seems counterintuitive but the deaths of almost half the population actually leads to an *increase* in life expectancy. The Black Death kills old, young and middle-aged people, as well as children, infants and babies. It is not fussy whom it kills. So while about half of those who come into the world in the 1330s only make it into their teens, the other half – the ones that survive to twenty – live longer. The reason is the better diet that I mentioned under F for Food. Quite simply, after almost half the population is wiped out, there is more food to go round the remainder, so more of them survive youth and eat well enough to fight off diseases in adulthood and, in the cases of women, produce enough milk to raise healthy infants. Prosperous farmers in Worcestershire who attain the age of twenty in the first half of the fourteenth century can look forward to an average of twenty-eight years more life; their successors in the second half can expect another thirty-two years.

It remains the case, however, that only 5 per cent live beyond sixty, and this remains constant over the whole century. Nevertheless, you will meet a few very long-lived people in the Middle Ages. St Gilbert of Sempringham – the founder of the English monastic order called the Gilbertines – is over a hundred when he dies in 1190. Even the plague-ridden fourteenth century sees some very old people. Sir Geoffrey de Geneville is born in 1226 and retires from military command at the age of eighty-two in 1308 so he can live out his last days in a monastery. He dies in 1314 at the age of eighty-eight. More remarkable still is Sir John de Sully. He is summoned to testify in a legal case in 1386 – and is allowed to send his evidence by a messenger due to his then being 105.

P IS FOR POETRY

Poetry is the principal secular literary entertainment of the Middle Ages. There are no novels as such, only 'romances' (tales of chivalric endeavour). No one writes secular plays. Travel books and historical texts exist and supposedly impart knowledge, although you may doubt how much of it is reliable, given John Mandeville's tall tales. It is rather in the poems that you most clearly glimpse ordinary people. And in the fourteenth century, these poems start to be written in English. Admittedly, it is not the easiest English to our ears but it is English – or Middle English, as we now call it – not French or Latin. And some of it is enormously entertaining.

One insight afforded by poetry is how people regard wealth and class. We might imagine them having very straightforward attitudes. Poetry, however, shows us their views are more nuanced. The anonymous author of *Winner and Waster* contrasts the virtues and vices of old and new money. His character Winner – a hard-working representative of the new rich – mocks an aristocrat from an old family, whom he refers to as Waster on account of his lavish spending and colossal waste.

> I am called Winner and I help the whole world
> For lords can learn through leading of wit.
> You who will readily save and refuse to spend
> Living on little, I love you the better.
> Wit goes with me and guides me well.
> When my goods gather, it gladdens my heart.
> But this wicked false thief who stands before you
> Thinks to strike and stint me and destroy me for ever.
> All that I win through wit, he wastes through pride,
> I gather, I glean and he soon lets it go,
> I pinch and I save, and he opens the purse.
> Why does this varmint not care about corn?

His lands all lie fallow, his looms are sold,
Down have fallen his dove-houses, dry are his fishponds.

And so on. But Waster responds

'Yes, Winner,' said Waster, 'your words are high,
But I shall tell you a tale that will vex you.
When you have tossed and turned, awake all the night,
Like all your neighbours who live thereabouts,
Having stuffed your wide houses full of wool,
The roof beams bending with the bacon flitches
    hanging there,
Silver pennies stuffed under steel-bound chests,
What should that wealth be if there were no waste?
Some would rot, some would rust, some would feed rats.
Stop cramming your chests, for Christ's love of heaven,
Let the people and the poor have part of your silver;
For if you would walk far and wide, and learn the truth,
You would weep at the misery of the poor.'

According to Waster, the old money spends and spends – supporting hundreds of people in each lordly household and handing out alms to the poor – while the hard-working Winner spends all his wealth on himself. It proves to be the profligate man who is the better friend to society.

Of course, you can't talk about poetry in the fourteenth century without mentioning Geoffrey Chaucer. No other book written at the time serves up more humour and fun than his *Canterbury Tales*, especially 'The Miller's Tale' and 'The Reeve's Tale'. We see Chaucer's characters playing all kinds of tricks on each other – not least attempting to seduce each other's wives and daughters. And we are given rare insights into the little details of life. Take this description of a poor woman's cottage in 'The Nun's Priest's Tale', for example:

Full sooty was her bower and also her hall,
In which she ate full many a slender meal.

Just those two lines give you an impression of what contemporary people think of two-room cottages with a fire in the middle of the living room. Another little detail is cat flaps. Not many domestic doors have survived, so unless you have been to visit one of the very few medieval houses with a cat's entry in the wall, such as Bradley Manor in Devon, it's only from 'The Miller's Tale' that you learn people cut holes low down in their doors for their cats to come and go, just as we do today.

Above all, it is the emotional side of life we discover in the poetry of the time. For instance, there is a manuscript in the British Library that contains four remarkable fourteenth-century poems, all composed by an anonymous writer from the north of England. The most famous is *Sir Gawain and the Green Knight*, which is rich in its descriptions of courtly life and love. But another poem in that volume is *Pearl*. The narrator of this poem describes a pearl in a gold clasp, which he has lost in a garden:

> So round, so radiant in each array,
> So small, so smooth her sides were,
> Wheresoever I judged gems gay,
> I set her singly above them all.
> Alas! I lost her in a garden,
> Through grass to ground she fell away.
> Wounded by love, by love forsaken,
> I mourn that pearl without a flaw.

And having drawn you into thinking he is describing a jewel, it is with a tender shock that you realise he is really talking about his infant daughter, who has died before her second birthday.

Although people often lose their children in infancy in the fourteenth century, the death of this little girl evokes a deep sense of loss in the poet. In the poem he sees his daughter, his Pearl, as a little queen in Heaven, and from the far side of a stream she speaks to him, telling him how through faith in God he can learn to accept her passing. But he still cannot resist going towards her, to hold her. And that is where the poet gets you, because in stepping forward to embrace her, he falls into the cold water of the stream and awakes to find himself lying on her grave.

Q IS FOR QUEENSHIP

What are medieval queens for? Obviously, they are the partners of kings and their prime duty is to produce the next generation of the royal family. In medieval times it is essential to have a line of succession: political stability depends on it. But it is worth asking what queens are for *other* than childbirth. After all, they are not like other aristocratic women. When Lord So-and-so goes off to court, he leaves Lady So-and-so behind to look after the household in his absence, with staff to carry out her instructions, just as in countless other private households in the country. But when the king travels, the court goes with him. His queen might remain in one of the palaces or castles or she might accompany him, but even if she remains, her role is limited. Officials are left in charge of the royal residences. Childcare is normally passed over to other women – wetnurses and guardians. When a fourteenth-century king goes abroad, he entrusts the guardianship of the realm to his heir or a near male relative, not his queen. (In this respect, the fourteenth-century is more sexist than earlier ones.) So it is fair to ask, what other purposes do queens serve?

There are several interesting ways to answer this question. For a start, no fourteenth-century English king marries an Englishwoman. Edward I first marries Eleanor of Castile and then Margaret of France. Edward II marries Isabella of France. Edward III marries Philippa of Hainault. Richard II first marries Anne of Bohemia and later Isabella of France. Henry IV is married to an Englishwoman, Mary de Bohun, before becoming king but she dies five years before his accession. The same pattern applies to the previous century: King John annuls his marriage to Isabella of Gloucester almost immediately on becoming king and marries a French heiress, Isabella of Angoulême, very shortly afterwards.

Queens are a diplomatic link with other kings and kingdoms. They bring with them foreign attendants and a large number of foreign relations – this is an age when third and fourth cousins are an important source of trust, information and support. Edward II's queen, Isabella of France, is given the task of negotiating a peace treaty with her brother, Charles IV of France, on her husband's behalf. Queens thus tie England into an international diplomatic network.

Edward III's queen, Philippa of Hainault, reveals another important role for queens, which is to play the 'soft side' of justice – in contrast to her husband's stern one. This is most clearly seen in the surrender of Calais in 1347, following an eleven-month-long siege. King Edward declares that he will hang the six burghers who surrender the town to him. In so doing, he presents himself as a ruthless king whom the French should never defy. But his queen then implores him to spare the lives of these six brave men and thereby allows him to show his forgiving, compassionate and lenient side. Without her pleading for their lives, he has no way of showing clemency without appearing weak. In such ways, queens can truly be the partners of kings, by highlighting their husband's non-martial attributes.

In the fourteenth century, a good royal marriage is part and parcel of a powerful reign. The strong and successful king, Edward I, is devoted to his first wife, Eleanor of Castile. After she dies in 1290 he has elaborate crosses erected at all the places where her body lies on its journey to burial in Westminster Abbey. In Edward II's case, tensions between his male companions and his wife result in his downfall. Edward III and Philippa remain together for more than forty years, until her death in 1369. Only after her injury in a hunting accident does he take a mistress – one of her ladies-in-waiting – and only then does the glory of his reign begin to fade. The unsuccessful Richard II never sires a child and does not seem to be interested in women. When his first wife, Anne of Bohemia, dies in 1394, he chooses a six-year-old French princess to be his next bride.

Why is a good royal marriage so important? We can never know the complete answer but I suspect the crux of the matter is that a successful king is a man who is able to love someone other than himself, who can listen to different points of view, and who respects people less powerful than himself, including women. In other words, the recipe for royal success is much the same as it is for the rest of us.

R IS FOR RELIGION

I once picked up a historical novel set in southern England during the time of the Black Death. One character declares 'there isn't a priest within four days ride from here'. That made me start calculating. Every parish has a priest, some more than one. Priests who die of plague are quickly replaced. There are priests in monasteries, friaries, colleges and hospitals. Lords have priests in their households, who act both as guardians of their spiritual wellbeing and as clerks in their bureaucracies. As a day's ride is a legal minimum of 20 miles, four days' ride amounts to an area of up to 20,000 square miles – 40 per cent of the area of England. Supposing you are on the coast, you can halve that. But even if you are located on a peninsula, such as Devon, a radius of 80 miles still includes the whole county and most of the adjacent ones. During the Black Death, there are at least 2,000 priests within four days' ride of any given point in southern England. This isn't the Wild West.

On the eve of the Black Death in 1348, there are more than a thousand monasteries and friaries in England and Wales. These are home to about 17,000 monks, canons, friars and nuns. To this total you can add the clergy who run a further 600 hospitals and 9,000 parish churches. Plus all the privately engaged priests, confessors and university college lecturers. Overall, about 2 per cent of the male population over the age of fourteen are in holy orders or preparing to enter the Church. Imagine this being the case in London today: a city of 9 million people would have about 90,000 priests. On every street you'd see someone in a cassock or ecclesiastical robe.

The friars would be preaching outside every coffee shop. Bishops would be travelling in limousines from Parliament to their palaces in the city.

This is a significant difference between the medieval world and our own. Spiritual salvation is the most important thing in many medieval people's lives. In the modern world, according to a series of polls organised by Gallup, only one-fifth of English people say that religion is important to them, compared to 99 per cent in most Middle Eastern countries. Were Gallup to conduct a poll in fourteenth-century England, they would find 99 per cent saying that religion is important to them here too. People might decorate the public spaces of their houses with wall paintings of a chivalric, secular nature, but their private chambers are adorned with religious scenes. Every great house has a chapel. Medicine is seen as less important in determining the survival or death of an ill person than divine judgement. Spiritual cleanliness matters more than physical cleanliness.

As you might imagine, anyone who does not subscribe to this way of thinking is seen as a danger both to himself and others. Atheism is out of the question. Creation exists so self-evidently there has to be a Creator. Not believing in God is like not believing in trees.

S IS FOR SEX

I don't want to give you the impression that all these priests mean that everyone is well-behaved and holy all the time. There's a good reason why so many priests are needed – a lot of people have quite a lot of confessing to do. And a fair proportion of it has to do with sex.

Judging by Chaucer's accounts of seduction and adulterous relationships in his *Canterbury Tales*, medieval society is just as obsessed with sex as we are in the modern world. Every town has its prostitutes. Many alehouses have a house prostitute – often the landlord's daughter. There are prostitutes in the royal household.

The extreme inequalities of life in an age when a day's work is worth less than a chicken mean that many women in towns and cities only manage to earn a living from selling sex. There are several legal cases of mothers trafficking their own daughters into the sex trade. Medieval men are normally on the lookout for teenage girls. A survey of prostitutes in fifteenth-century Dijon in France indicates most enter the trade before they are fifteen and almost all by seventeen. It is much the same in England. According to Chaucer, a thirty-year-old woman is merely 'winter forage'. Many young prostitutes are victims of gang rape: with the shame of what has happened to them, and it being common knowledge in the community that they have been deflowered, they have no chance of making a good marriage.

Medieval medical thinking about sex is based on that of the third-century writer, Galen, whose works state that women's wombs are 'cold' and need constant warming by 'hot' male sperm. In addition, according to Galen, if women do not regularly copulate, their 'seed' will coagulate and suffocate their wombs, thereby damaging their health. Therefore it is widely understood that women have a physical need to have sex regularly. Men are doing women a favour by regularly sleeping with them, even if they are not paying them. Not that the pleasure is always shared. Galen's works teach that a woman has to have an orgasm in order to conceive a child. It follows that, if a man rapes a woman and she becomes pregnant, she must have enjoyed the experience.

Medical misunderstandings are not the only reason for this. The Bible is often used to justify people's actions. The Old Testament includes many respectable men having many wives. The Book of Deuteronomy declares that if a king takes a town by force after it has resisted him, he is entitled to kill all the men and treat the women and girls as the spoils of war. Henry V reminded the people of Harfleur of this as he sat outside the walls with the English army in 1415. The Bible also blames a woman, Eve, for offering Adam the fruit of the forbidden tree. The Church Fathers extend the responsibility for that deed to all women. As Chaucer puts it, the Bible is 'a text wherein we find that woman was the ruin of mankind'. This underpins an awful lot of medieval sexism, and most women have no option but to put up with it. After all, very few of them are literate, so they can't draw up tracts complaining about the inequality.

Then as now, wealth is also a contributing factor. Rich and powerful men can seldom be held to account for molesting or seducing women. In *The Book of the Civilised Man*, written around 1200, the author Daniel Beccles tells young aristocrats that women 'want to be conquered by force, as if they were unwilling'. For many lords, sex is something of a sport. In his book recounting his secret pleasures and vices, *The Book of Holy Medicines*, the great military leader Henry, duke of Lancaster, talks about his love of eating salmon and piquant sauces, hunting and listening to the song of the nightingale, smelling the scent of roses and seducing girls. He says he especially likes having sex with peasant girls 'because they complain less'.

As there are few literate women in medieval England and morality is such a dangerous issue, you don't find many female expressions of sexual desire to compare with the duke of Lancaster's. But Chaucer writes one on behalf of women, in his prologue to 'The Wife of Bath's Tale'. Here he gives us a picture of a woman who marries five times and loves making love. It suggests that Chaucer has come across strong female characters who are not afraid of their desires and are not bound by convention. To give you a glimpse, the Wife of Bath recalls hardly weeping at all at her fourth husband's funeral, for she already has another mate lined up. He is Jenkin, a twenty-year-old clerk. She notices his legs as the requiem bell is being rung for her late husband. Although she is forty and gap-toothed, she is still eager for fun –

> For truly, I am all of Venus
> In feeling, and my heart is of Mars.
> Venus gave me my lust, my wantonness,
> And Mars gave me my sturdy hardiness.
> Taurus was my ascendant, with Mars therein.
> Alas, alas, that ever love was sin!

I always followed my inclination
By virtue of my constellation
Which made me so I could not withdraw
My Venus-chamber from a good fellow.
Yet I have Mars's mark upon my face,
And also in another private place.
For God so truly was my salvation
I never loved for the sake of discretion
But always followed my own appetite,
Though he were short or tall, or black or white.

T IS FOR TOILET PAPER

What do people do for toilet paper in the fourteenth century? According to *The Book of the Civilised Man*, a lord sitting on the loo in the late twelfth century will call for compressed mats of straw or hay to wipe his bottom. John Russell's *Boke of Nurture*, written in the early fifteenth century, tells us that the young servant attending his lord should make sure there is plenty of 'blanket, cotton or linen to wipe the nether end'. The 'cotton' in that list is not cotton as we know it but cotton wool. This is used frequently by the future Henry IV in the 1390s. Everywhere he goes in England he buys this luxury item to have something soft with which to wipe his 'nether end'. I suspect the various illnesses that afflict him leave him rather sensitive in this area.

Poor people use large leaves like dock leaves, moss and handfuls of grass as well as compressed straw. Several medieval chronicles mention that straw is used on the floor of latrines, probably to absorb some of the smell, and if there is no grass to hand, you might grab a handful of this. Coarse cloth is found in monastic latrine pits too. But how much spare cloth the poor have for this purpose is open to question. When many people only own one or two garments, old pieces of cloth are not that easy to come by. Especially if everyone else wants them for the same reason.

Proper absorbent toilet paper is introduced in the fifteenth century. Some noblemen's accounts refer to it being bought by the quire (twenty-four sheets), like fine-quality writing paper. However, it does not become a cheap option until the sixteenth century, when soft paper is made for wrapping all sorts of things. It is used in latrines after it has served its original purpose, like cloth and everything else of small value. But if you're visiting England in the fourteenth century, a hundred years is a rather long time to have to hang on.

U IS FOR URINE

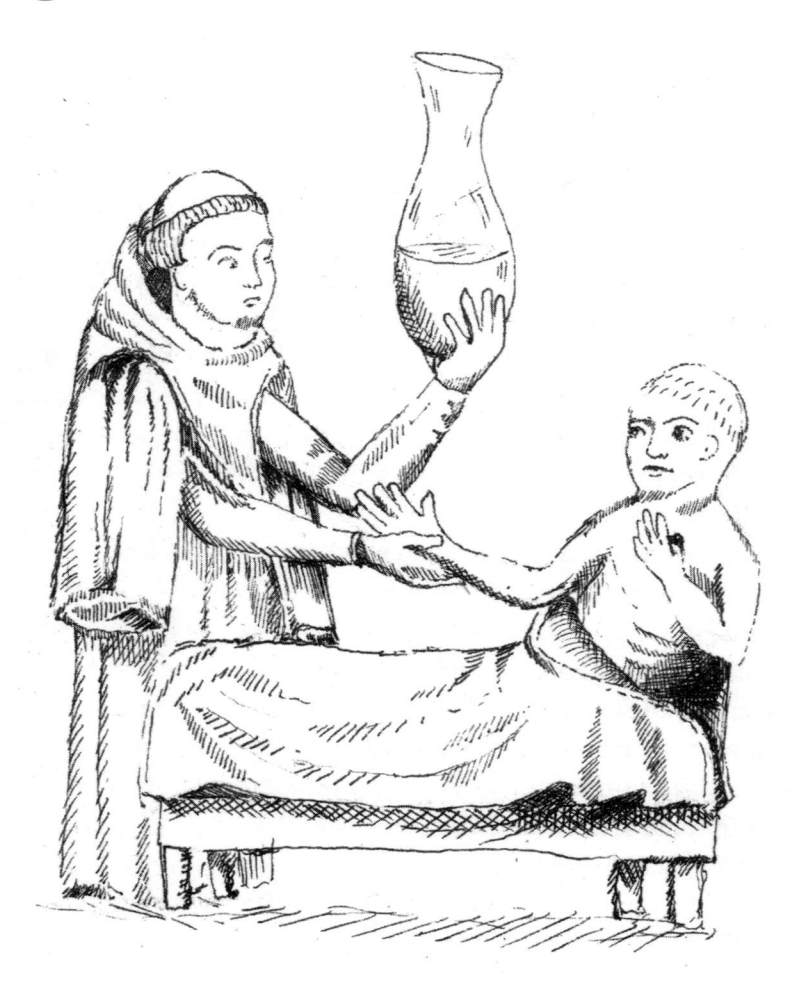

Today, none of us keeps vats of urine stored around the house. But until the nineteenth century it is collected and put to use in fulling wool and scouring cloth, as well as being employed in various dyeing processes. It is in demand because it's a natural and cheap source of ammonia, which is an alkali. People also use spots of it when removing stains from clothing. It becomes more efficacious when it is old, so people really do store vats of it for long periods of time. Thus, when you imagine the smells in an ordinary medieval home, along with the smoke and the traces of rotting offal in the rushes, add the smell of stale piss.

The point here is not to laugh at how gross life was in the past. It is rather that people in the pre-industrial age look at things that we think of as undesirable in different ways. In the 1960s the sociologist Mary Douglas famously observed that there is objectively no such thing as 'dirt' but rather what we call 'dirt' is simply 'matter out of place'. A good example is manure: in the garden, it is definitely in the right place; in the middle of your living-room carpet, it is dirt. This is why medieval people keep hold of things that neither you nor I would want lingering around the house. In a world created by God, everything has its 'right place'.

Usefulness is the key. Or sustainability, as we might call it today. Medieval people keep old ashes from the hearth to make potash, which is used for scouring pots and pans with handfuls of straw. They also use potash for making lye (in which you wash your hair, even though it is strongly alkaline). It is also a key ingredient of liquid soap (in which you clean your clothes). Likewise, medieval people will eat all manner of offal that we would throw away. Apples are kept carefully for a full year; if they turn rotten, they are pressed to make cider. Nothing is wasted. Bones are boiled for their marrow. Fat is stored in dripping pans. Skins from all sorts of animals, including goats, dogs and cats, are made into gloves. Fallen boughs and sticks are put aside for firewood. The heat that remains in an oven after the bread has been baked is used to make small cakes. 'Waste not, want not' is the motto by which everyone lives unless they are rich enough to be a 'waster', and even the wasters let their castoffs and rubbish be used by other people. Almost nothing is thrown away except broken pottery and the cloth used to wipe your 'nether end'.

V IS FOR VIOLENCE

As we have already observed, the Middle Ages are famous for their violence. The very definition of a castle is the defensive feudal residence of a lord and his family and retainers. Why do the rich feel they need to live in such a militaristic setting except to be prepared for violence at all times? By the fourteenth century, some lords also have ordinary manor houses; they do not live in castles all year round. But still most noble families maintain a castle as their chief residence – and continue to do so until the abolition of private armies in 1504.

One of the purposes of this A–Z is to stress how medieval society is much more than just violent. That said, I would not be giving you the full picture if I did not alert you to the fact that many aspects of daily life are just plain bloody. Today we tend to compartmentalise violence into three categories – warfare, crime and abuse – and thus separate them from what we consider normal. Medieval people cannot do this. Warfare and abuse are part of their normality. Much of the violence they experience is not only not criminal but a by-product of the power structures inherent in the criminal system itself. Therefore, with a view to revealing the range of discomforts that people have to put up with, here is an A–Z of violence within my bigger A–Z of medieval England. You will never complain of a bad day at the office again.

THE A–Z OF MEDIEVAL VIOLENCE

A *is for Arms and armour*
While shining armour is expensive – the best-quality steel plate from Italy and Germany is very costly indeed – every man and boy over the age of fifteen is expected to equip himself with arms for keeping the peace. According to the Statute of Winchester, anyone with even £2-worth of land must be able to lay his hands on a sword, bow and arrows and a knife. If you have chattels worth more than 20 marks (£13 13s 8d) or income of £10 from land (which is the equivalent of a small manor of about 1,500–2,000 acres), by law you need to possess a helmet and chain-mail shirt as well.

B *is for Bows and arrows*
Not only are men required to own a bow and a sheaf of arrows but also they have to learn how to shoot them. From 1363 it is compulsory to practise archery every week. At the same time, men are prohibited from playing football – so that they can concentrate on their archery.

C *is for Chivalry*
Chivalry is literally the behaviour expected of a knight. You should honour the Church, be brave in battle, respect female virtue, be faithful to your word, and be merciful to the vanquished. As you may guess, it is more frequently encountered in romance than in daily life.

While knights are often genuinely brave, they tend only to respect the Church if it is to their advantage. Women's virtue is rarely respected. Knights are not above lying and cheating. And victors in battle are far more likely to be merciful if the vanquished man is wealthy and can pay a hefty ransom.

D *is for Dungeons*

Prison is not normally seen as a punishment itself but rather as a place to hold people temporarily until they can be brought to trial and either hanged or released. There are exceptions. Most people locked up indefinitely are political prisoners of high rank, who are normally treated reasonably well. Perhaps the nastiest form of dungeon is the oubliette, from the French word *oublier* (to forget). This is an underground room with no door but a hole in the roof, through which you are dropped and promptly forgotten.

E *is for Evisceration*

If you are unlucky enough to be sentenced to be hanged, drawn and quartered (the legal punishment for men guilty of treason), between the hanging and the quartering you will also be eviscerated. First you will be cut down from the gallows while still alive, then your abdomen will be sliced open and your entrails removed. Your penis will also be cut off. These will then be burnt in a fire in front of you. Sir Thomas Blount experiences this painful end in 1400. As he sits in a bloody pool, watching his guts and private parts consumed by the flames, the executioner asks if he would like a drink. 'No,' he replies, 'because I have nowhere left to put it.'

F *is for the Flagellants*

As the Black Death rages across Europe, an ultra-religious group decide that they will take it upon themselves to atone for humanity's sins by going from town to town in rags lashing themselves over the back with whips until they are covered in blood. That says something about the medieval mind. Pain is not the problem but the solution.

G *is for the Glory of war*
Whereas we in the modern democratic western world tend to regard war in a negative light, medieval people see it much more positively. For noblemen, war is an opportunity to prove themselves and win glory. For lesser men, it is also an opportunity to make themselves rich by capturing a lord and ransoming him – again, winning glory. For the ordinary foot soldier, war offers the chance to plunder and rape on the path to defeating a hated foreign enemy, thereby lending the whole escapade a touch of glory. Although a handful of knights in the 1390s suggest religious reasons for being against war, it is only with the spread of cannon in the fifteenth century that anti-war views gain momentum.

H *is for Hunting*
Violence to animals is a pleasure for most medieval men and women. Whether hunting coneys with birds of prey, capturing birds with nets, pursuing wild boar, chasing stags and harts with hounds, or simply shooting deer with a bow, everyone revels in killing. There is no sensitivity at all to the suffering of animals. Pigs are bled to death as slowly as possible, for the sake of the quality of the meat. Bulls are baited with vicious dogs – much to the delight of the onlookers – again, due to popular beliefs about the quality of the meat.

I *is for Injuries*
Medieval people in all walks of life carry injuries. These may be old war wounds, scars from brawls and hunting accidents, lost limbs from surgical operations or, very commonly, work-related mishaps. Broken bones are common and bone setters are not always able to fix them. Perhaps the most common ailments of all are dental. By the time they die, most adults have lost at least four teeth, in many cases as the result of a fight.

J *is for Jousting*
You'd have thought that privileged young men from knightly families would be grateful for the chance of an easy life. But many of them

prefer the idea of riding at full tilt at each other with lances primed, intent on hitting their adversary and knocking him off his horse. The more dangerous the sport, the better. Women are keen to watch the spectacle too. Most popular of all is the 'joust of war', which is fought with sharpened steel lances (as opposed to blunted ones). Men are frequently killed as a result. Perhaps the height of bravado is reached in 1341 when twenty English knights challenge twenty Scottish knights to jousts of war at Berwick. The Scots agree – on condition that no one wears any armour.

K *is for Knives*
Everyone carries a sharp, pointed knife on their belt, mainly to cut food. However, this means that if someone makes them angry, they have the means to stab them. If someone insults you or your wife, or cheats at dice, or robs you, you might instantly reach for your knife and use it. This frequently happens where large numbers of young men are gathered. In 1340 Oxford is as violent as Dodge City at the height of the Wild West – with more than 100 murders per 100,000 adults each year.

L *is for Lithuania*
If you can't find a good battle to fight at home in England, why not go on a crusade to Lithuania? There you are guaranteed military action alongside the Teutonic Knights, fighting the last pagan people in Europe. Many English knights, including the future Henry IV of England, do exactly that. Many never return – which perhaps makes the rest of England a little safer.

M *is for Murder*
Given the ubiquity of knives, it may not surprise you to hear that the murder rate in fourteenth-century England – around twenty-three killings per 100,000 adults per year – is about twenty-five times higher than it is today. Still, most of England is far safer than other European countries, especially Italy, where the number of stabbings per head of the population is higher than anywhere else in Europe.

N *is for Needles*
During this period, we often encounter the name 'Mortimer' in connection with glamorous events: battles, tournaments, rebellions, escapes from the Tower of London, and so forth. Somewhat less glamorously, one Roger Mortimer of Edvin Loach in Herefordshire is prosecuted with his two sons in 1397 for kidnapping a man and pushing needles into his testicles. As if all the problems of living in the fourteenth century weren't enough, men feel they have to treat each other in such a cruel manner. Roger Mortimer has nothing to do with me, I hasten to add.

O *is for Outlaws*
In the early part of the century, gangs steal, rape and murder throughout England. They are often composed of family members, including brothers, sisters and children of the ringleader. It is not unusual for gangs to be the kin of the lord of the manor. Even if they are caught and brought before a judge, juries of local men are too fearful to find them guilty. Thus organised crime is a real problem for those responsible for maintaining law and order. Yet by the 1370s their exploits are being celebrated in Robin Hood stories. The romance lives on.

P *is for the Pillory*
The pillory is the raised pair of wooden boards with sockets in which to trap your head and hands. The stocks are the version that hold you by the legs. Both are used to punish people publicly for serious misdemeanours. People caught selling bad meat are often pilloried, with the offending meat burnt beneath their faces. Merchants selling bad wine may well end up in the stocks with the wine poured over them. Not to mention all the abuse, rotten matter and stones hurled at them by their victims as they stand or sit there, trapped.

Q *is for Quarters of men*
The 'quartering' bit of 'hanging, drawing and quartering' involves the decapitation of a hanged and eviscerated traitor. The body is then cut in half at the waist, and hacked in half vertically, through the chest and through the pelvis. The head is normally placed on the

gatehouse of London Bridge; the quarters are sent around the kingdom to warn people of the punishment meted out to traitors. Thus children in major towns and cities grow up inured to the sight of hunks of men's corpses decaying and stinking above the city gates.

R *is for the Rich*
A large proportion of the violence in medieval society is perpetrated by wealthy men. When the law is slow and inefficient, and the king distant, local lords can bully their tenants and neighbours – and no one can do anything about it. You are more likely to be a rapist and a multiple murderer in the fourteenth century if you are rich than if you come from the lower classes.

S *is for Sieges*
In a medieval conflict, one side generally besieges the towns and castles of the other. This has a huge impact on the surrounding area, with soldiers – sometimes encamped for months – stealing from those who live nearby and spreading diseases such as typhus ('camp fever'). But for those inside a besieged settlement, things are even worse. Every man, woman and child may be called on to resist the intruders, even if just by throwing rocks at them. And of course every man, woman and child is vulnerable if the enemy wins.

T *is for Torture*
The good news is that torture is against the law in medieval England. In 1308, when the king of France urges Edward II to torture the Knights Templar, Edward proudly refuses on the basis that Englishmen 'don't do that sort of thing'. Or words to that effect. On that occasion, the French pope grants special dispensation to allow the English to use torture just this once. Now for the bad news: Englishmen often use torture anyway. And not just to extract confessions from politically important people. You've already heard about Roger Mortimer and his needles. Let me give you another example. One Newcastle woman accused of murder begs not to be imprisoned while awaiting her trial because the gaoler has threatened to rape her and pull

all her teeth out once he has her in his power. As I said in the introduction to this A–Z of violence, people have to accept the abuse of the criminal system as part of their daily life – and that includes the illegal use of torture.

U *is for Unifying force*
Some kinds of violence have a silver lining: they can unify people. The English see more than half a century of domestic peace because Edward III focuses all their efforts on fighting the Scots and French. The previous reign was anything but peaceful. It is ironic that a man can be a peacemaker and a warmonger at the same time but when the defence of the realm is a king's prime responsibility, it is often the case.

V *is for Vitriol*
Violence begins with attitude. And it begets more attitude. For example, the English have been fighting the French on and off since the Battle of Brémule in 1119. After that, you wouldn't describe relations between the two kingdoms as cordial. Here, for example, is what the fourteenth-century poet Laurence Minot has to say about our ancestral enemies. 'France, womanish, pharisaic, embodiment of might, lynx-like, viperish, foxy, wolfish, a Medea, cunning, a siren, cruel, bitter, haughty: you are full of bile.' Come on, Laurence, tell us what you really think.

W *is for Wives, abuse of*
In English law, a husband can beat his wife as much as he pleases as long as he doesn't kill her. He may rape her with impunity too. What we would call abuse is day-to-day reality for many women.

X *is for eXecutions, public*
Roughly one-third of those arrested for a serious offence are hanged. Noble traitors might be beheaded instead. The key thing is that all these killings are performed in public, in front of large crowds. Generation after generation grows up with the idea that justice is brutal. And if *justice* is so violent, why should normal life be any different?

Y *is for Youth*
The fact that half the population

is dead by the age of twenty, and three-quarters by the age of forty, means that most people in fourteenth-century England are young. People assume leadership roles at a very young age, whether they are lords leading diplomatic embassies and military expeditions or aldermen in charge of towns. Hence the leaders of society are often prone to rashness, bravado and hot-headedness. Young men especially act on impulse and only think about the consequences when it is too late. This goes some way to explain the higher levels of violence in medieval society. It is perpetrated by those in positions of responsibility.

Z *is for Zealousness*
Perhaps the hardest thing to understand about medieval violence is that men *want to fight*. They are eager to prove themselves in battle. As we have seen, if there are no good fights to be had at home, they'll joust with sharpened lances. If tournaments aren't enough, they'll go and fight abroad as a mercenary or crusader. The whole attitude is exemplified by Sir Giles d'Argentein at the battle of Bannockburn in 1314. When he is ordered to retreat, he shouts, 'I am not accustomed to fleeing a battle – and nor will I now!' and promptly charges into the midst of the Scottish army. Some men define themselves in terms of violence and courage to the extent that they would rather die than be seen shirking a fight.

After the foregoing litany of violence and slaughter, we should remember that the fourteenth century is relatively civilised compared to previous centuries. Back in the tenth and eleventh centuries, there is no conception of chivalric behaviour. The twelfth century sees massacres that are rarely seen in the fourteenth. It is in that century that Henry I has all the moneyers in England punished by having their hands cut off. Trial by battle, which is introduced by the Normans to resolve legal disputes and involves two champions fighting each other – sometimes to the death – is very rare in the fourteenth century.

Don't get me wrong: fourteenth-century society is still dangerous. But with a murder rate of twenty-three deaths per 100,000 adults per year, it is not as dangerous as, say, twenty-first century El Salvador, Honduras, Venezuela or Jamaica – to name just four countries with homicide rates in excess of forty per 100,000. But I should add that these statistics are *peacetime* homicide rates. If you are in fourteenth-century England and find yourself caught up in one of the (almost incessant) wars with the Scots or the French, the casualty rates are far higher – in some cases, thousands per 100,000 combatants. Neither do the figures include executions. While I maintain we are wrong to think of the Middle Ages as primarily violent, it would be even further from the truth to think of it all as sweetness and light.

But back to the main A–Z...

W IS FOR WOMEN

Generally speaking, the more violent a society, the more sexist it is. Chroniclers might praise a knight who chivalrously defends the honour of a maiden but romance and reality are only distantly acquainted. Men don't just have the legal right to beat their wives; there is a legal framework for women to be regarded as second-class citizens.

According to medieval English common law, a married couple is a single entity represented solely by the man. It follows that a married woman cannot give evidence in court against her husband, no matter what terrible things he has done to her. She cannot disobey him or even allow anyone into his house without his permission. Making the right choice of husband is thus crucial for a girl's chances of happiness. Unfortunately, that decision normally falls to the bride's father, whom she has to obey until she marries and is handed over to the control of her husband. She is trapped – and will remain so until she becomes a widow. And if she runs away...? Well, such is the violence and sexism in medieval England, that is no escape.

Women in the fourteen century cannot receive a proper education to set them on an equal footing with men. A few enlightened families employ private tutors to educate their daughters but not many and, of course, they have to be rich. Almost all medieval Englishwomen are illiterate. They cannot go to university or practise any of the professions; they are debarred from most positions of responsibility. Technically speaking, widows can hold certain official posts – two noblewomen serve as sheriffs in the thirteenth century – but this does not happen in the fourteenth.

Having said all that, things aren't quite so simple. Because women cannot get an education, they can't write the sources that we use today to study the past. What they think about their lives is largely a blank to us. Moreover, certain aspects of medieval society are to women's advantage. If a man's wife gives birth to a child by another man, the husband legally has to accept the baby as his own, even if that baby will be his heir. Nor can a man legally leave his wife. Even if he runs away, he will find himself still married. Moreover, he will have forfeited his good name. He will be in a strange town with no property and no protection, and no right to run a business in that place. There is a risk that in focusing on the *legal* inequality of the sexes, we end up studying the law and not the people. So much depends on status. Wealthy women are respected. In their husband's absence, they are in charge of the household, so they can tell the servants what to do. When a merchant dies, if he leaves a widow she is expected to carry on his business. In the case of the aristocracy, the men owe their position to their military responsibilities. When the king goes to war, so do they, risking hardship and death. Their womenfolk do not. Instead, they enjoy all the privileges of high rank but none of the responsibilities.

There are a few remarkable women who don armour and lead their husband's retainers into battle. One is Agnes of Dunbar – Black Agnes, as she is otherwise known, on account of her fearsome reputation. In 1338 Edward III needs to capture Dunbar Castle in East Lothian quickly so he can proceed with his invasion of France. He despatches his most trusted and capable commander, William Montagu, earl of Salisbury, to storm the castle. Montagu takes 4,000 men with him. Unfortunately for them, 4,000 men are no match for Black Agnes. She stands on the battlements and yells defiantly at them. They pound the castle gates with a battering ram and smash the walls with boulders thrown from trebuchets. She doesn't move or shut up. When a stone smashes into the battlements near where she is standing, she merely takes a cloth and demonstratively starts to dust the stonework. Eventually the English troops drag her brother, the earl of Moray, before the walls and threaten to kill him unless she surrenders the castle. To which she replies that they should go ahead and kill him, for she is his heir and will become the countess of Moray if they carry out their threat. After five months of listening to Agnes shouting defiance, Montagu and the survivors of his 4,000-strong army give up and return to England.

X IS FOR XENOPHOBIA

Medieval England does not have a good track record when it comes to welcoming foreigners. This is not entirely surprising: there is a long-lasting and deep-seated caution when it comes to strangers. It begins way back in the ninth and tenth centuries. Warriors from Norway and Denmark (whom we collectively refer to as Vikings) suddenly arrive by ship and kill and plunder their way across the country. When the Normans show up in 1066, the English don't exactly hang out the bunting for them either. People do not live by the coast for fear of piracy. So when the Jews come here after the Norman invasion, keeping themselves to themselves and not intermarrying or mixing with the local people, there is a great deal of suspicion. At times, this turns into open hostility. Suspicion of the Jews – and envy of their money-making abilities – results in Edward I expelling them in 1290.

Things are slightly different for the aristocracy in the thirteenth and fourteenth centuries. Dozens of foreign aristocrats come to live in England following Isabella of Angoulême's marriage to King John in 1200 and Eleanor of Provence's marriage to Henry III in

1236. The sons of those aristocrats marry English heiresses and their daughters marry English noblemen. By the 1300s most high-ranking English lords have French and Italian cousins. They like to hear news from abroad. And they generally welcome their third and fourth cousins when they visit. Their kinsmen are assets: they can be expected to offer shelter, support and protection in return when they go abroad themselves.

Many English towns and cities have significant foreign populations in the fourteenth century. As a rule, communities of merchants and workers are valued for the wealth they generate and the services they render. But as long as they retain their foreign identities, they are never properly assimilated. At the end of the century, the process of denization is introduced, whereby foreigners can give up their original nationality and effectively become English. Still, when citizens grow restless, frequently they take out their anger on foreign communities. During the Peasants' Revolt in 1381, for example, the English peasants decide to kill all the Flemish weavers in London, most of whom are just as poor as they are.

As we can see, there is a whole spectrum of foreign relations in the fourteenth century. At one extreme, an Englishman might cordially call on his French kinsmen and stay with them in their castle, knowing that he might yet inherit it. At the other, you have Laurence Minot's attitude to the French, mentioned above. 'France... cruel, bitter, haughty: you are full of bile.'

Y IS FOR YOUR ANCESTORS

People often ask me if I am descended from Roger Mortimer, the first earl of March, the chap who dethrones Edward II. It's a fair question, given that we share the same surname. However, Roger Mortimer's male line dies out in 1425. Nevertheless, he and his wife Joan de Geneville are common ancestors of all the English-descended English people on account of their eight daughters.

Similarly, Edward III and Queen Philippa are also now common ancestors of the English people. So, if you come from English stock, there is a less than 1 per cent chance you are *not* descended from Edward III and Queen Philippa – and that calculation is based on the assumption that there has never been any adultery. Now this might come as a shock, but there has been quite a bit of that over the centuries, spreading those royal genes even further.

The logical implication of this is that all the ancestors of the above-mentioned medieval characters are also common ancestors of the English people. The ancestors of Roger Mortimer include the princes of Gwynedd and William Marshall, the greatest knight of the Middle Ages. Joan de Geneville's ancestors include the long-lived Geoffrey de Geneville and a long line of French aristocrats. The ancestors of Edward III include all the ruling houses of Europe. The history of the kings of England prior to 1377 is the collective family history of the English people. If you are English, you are descended from Edward III, Edward II, Edward I, Henry III, King John – sorry about that – Henry II, the Empress Matilda, Henry I and William the Conqueror. Through Henry I's wife, Matilda of Scotland, you are descended from the kings of Wessex, including Alfred the Great. Through William the Conqueror, you are descended from the dukes of Normandy and Rollo the Viking. Through Queen Philippa's ancestors, you are descended from the counts of Hainault; through Queen Isabella and her ancestors, the kings of France; through Queen Eleanor of Castile and her ancestors, the kings of Castile; and through Queen Eleanor of Provence and her ancestors, the counts of Provence. The good news is that we all have proverbial blue blood. The bad news is we are all descended from Fulk Nerra, the eleventh-century count of Anjou, who has his wife burnt alive in her wedding dress when he suspects her fancy has strayed to a strapping young tenant of his.

My reason for saying this is not to flatter you with your royal ancestry but to illustrate that, however strange, brave and cruel medieval England might appear, you are descended from many of the strange, brave and cruel people who make it thus. You are also descended from many of the merchants and peasants – even some of the churchmen, not all of whom are always as celibate as they are supposed to be. These people are your ancestors, whether you like it or not. And just as they survive the Black Death and all the many wars of the time, so we too are adaptable to misfortune. As a picture of what the English are really like, this reveals more than you can possibly get in the snapshot that is a single lifetime. Everything you have heard about so far is in some way or other, your inheritance.

Z IS FOR ZENITH

What is the zenith of fourteenth-century England? What reaches its absolute pinnacle in this period? You might think plague, murder, famine and warfare – just as Barbara Tuchman implies in the title of her famous book, *A Distant Mirror: The Calamitous 14th Century*. But that is like saying that bombs, machine guns and rationing are the high points of World War II. No, I prefer to see the high point of World War II as the crushing of Fascism and the end of the Holocaust. We miss the point if we only focus on the negative. Better to accentuate the positive.

The great thing about the fourteenth century is this: despite all the plague and famine, we survive. You and I are here – surely that is something to celebrate? For that reason alone, we should be in awe of our fourteenth-century ancestors. Besides, you've already heard enough about medieval misery. It is only right we should go out on a high. And in all of medieval England, there is no higher point than the top of a cathedral spire. So my Z is for the Zenith of cathedral building.

There are nineteen cathedrals in fourteenth-century England relating to seventeen dioceses: Canterbury, Rochester, London, Chichester, Winchester, Salisbury, Bath, Wells, Exeter, Worcester, Hereford, Lichfield, Coventry, Lincoln, Ely, Norwich, York, Durham and Carlisle. How many of those are in ruins today? Only Coventry, due to it being bombed during World War II. And, of course, London's cathedral – St Paul's – dates to the seventeenth century, having been rebuilt after the Great Fire. The rest are all substantially medieval. The same cannot be said for medieval castles, most of which are now in ruins, even though there are hundreds more of them. The cathedrals have lasted. That's not just down to luck. Their survival is due most of all to their builders – not just because they made buildings of such physical strength and durability but because they made buildings that we wish to preserve on account of their beauty. Their legacy is timeless. Almost no one believes that we could do better ourselves, even if we were to pull them all down and start again. In that sense, medieval cathedrals display a sort of perfection.

Most cathedrals take a long time to build. The majority assume their basic form before 1300. But the fourteenth-century makes an enormous contribution. Take the spires. When that of London Cathedral – Old St Paul's – is completed in 1314, it stands 489ft above the ground. Just imagine working on that, climbing up ladder after ladder through the wooden scaffolding poles and boards, so high above the city. Even taller is the central spire of Lincoln Cathedral, which reaches up to 525ft when it is finished. That makes it the highest structure on Earth – taller even than the Great Pyramid in Egypt. Salisbury Cathedral spire is not quite as tall but it still stands today at more than 400ft, despite having been built in the 1320s. I doubt there is anyone alive in the twenty-first century who could construct a 200ft stone tower with a 200ft spire on top that will last for 700 years without using any structural engineering, computers, calculations, steel scaffolding or power tools. Somehow, fourteenth-century masons and carpenters can build on that scale without these advantages. It is an amazing achievement. We should be proud to be descended from them.

The fourteenth century also sees the nave of Exeter Cathedral completed, with the longest continual medieval vault in the world. If you don't know it, go and see it. It is the greatest example of Decorated architecture anywhere. When you visit, look at the windows. Not just the glass but the stone tracery too. Almost every single window is different, and some of the designs are astonishing, especially the great west round window.

Other fourteenth-century wonders include the unique octagon of Ely Cathedral and the great perpendicular east window of Gloucester Cathedral. Perhaps greatest of all are the soaring arches in the naves of Canterbury Cathedral and Westminster Abbey, designed by Henry Yevele, who dies in 1400, the same year as Chaucer.

That's something to think about. In an age of misery and war, some people can spread their wings and take flight.

Undeniably, there is much that is terrifying about the Middle Ages. But as in the modern world, there is genius too. There is inspiration, vision, skill and courage. And if you know where to look, you can find gentleness and compassion – for example in a man's tender expression of grief after losing his little girl, his pearl. This is what I hope you take away from the fourteenth century: the recognition that, despite all the suffering and difficulties of medieval life, we can work together to create spires that reach halfway to heaven, build networks of markets so that people can be fed and clothed, and find ways to express our deepest feelings about the world and each other – and that all of these things will last.

PART TWO

A TO Z

OF ELIZABETHAN ENGLAND

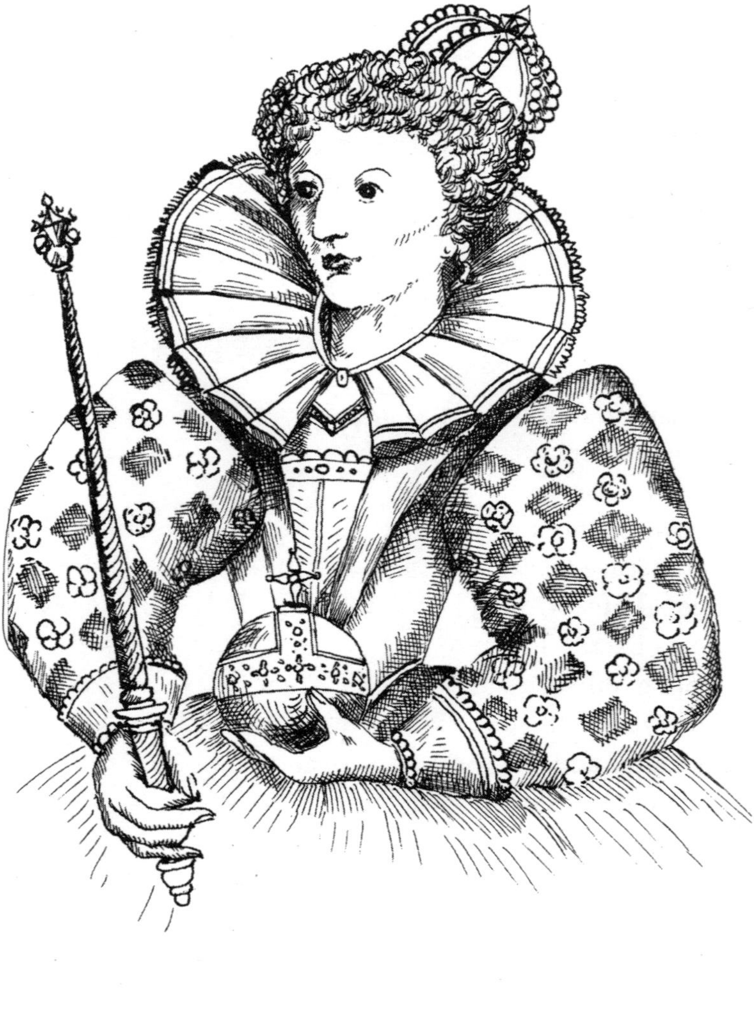

ELIZABETHAN ENGLAND

1558–1603

For many of us, the reign of Elizabeth I, from 1558 to 1603, is the golden age of English history. It is the time of Shakespeare, explorers such as Drake and Raleigh, and that extraordinary woman, the queen herself. But at the start of her reign, Englishmen and women are full of doubt about England's place in the world. As one government official puts it:

> The queen poor, the realm exhausted, the nobility poor and decayed. Want of good captains and soldiers. The people out of order. Justice not executed. All things dear. Excess in meat, drink and apparel. Divisions among ourselves. Wars with France and Scotland. The French king bestriding the realm, having one foot in Calais and the other in Scotland. Steadfast enmity but no friendship abroad.

That's not exactly a golden age he's describing. And then, right at the moment he says these things, the twenty-five-year-old queen herself causes a deep unease across the realm when she indicates that she intends to follow in the footsteps of her father, Henry VIII, and once more tear England away from the Roman Catholic Church. Later generations look back on Elizabeth's break with Rome as a moment of glory but, at the time, people don't know what to think. Will God approve? Five years later, half the magistrates in the country still have not sworn the required oath acknowledging the queen to be the supreme governor of the Church of England. It has to be said that England at the start of Elizabeth's forty-five-year reign is very far from seeing its 'golden age'. It is fearful, inward-looking and still largely medieval.

The stages whereby all the anxiety gives way to outward-looking confidence and self-justification are many and gradual, but one of the most significant turning points in the whole process is the defeat of the Spanish Armada in 1588. This military victory separates the unsteady first thirty years of Elizabeth's reign from the glorious last fifteen. Ironically, Elizabeth herself is in far better physical shape in the earlier period. Yet England sees its apogee when she begins to lose her teeth and hair, and everyone has stopped speculating about her possible marriage partners. Thus the first point in my A–Z of Elizabethan England has to be…

A IS FOR THE ARMADA

GOD BLEW AND THEY WERE SCATTERED

In England, we grow up with the impression that the defeat of the Spanish Armada – a large invasion force – is a battle for the security of the realm, like the Battle of Britain. We tend not to think of it in terms of a *medieval* battle. But it is important to see it that way because it has more in common with a medieval battle than a modern one.

What's the difference, you might ask? A modern battle is simply an earthly conflict. A medieval battle involves heaven too – or at least the possibility of divine intervention. Victory and defeat have deep religious symbolism, reflecting God's judgement. As mentioned above, England isn't full of raving Protestants in the early part of Elizabeth's reign. Many of her subjects worry that Henry VIII's break from Rome in 1533 is a huge mistake; they are not at all sorry when Mary restores the Catholic faith on her accession in 1553. Now, with Elizabeth on the throne, there is great uncertainty as to whether we should remain a Catholic country or go our own way. Has the queen done the right thing in choosing the latter course? This is why it really matters in 1588 that a Protestant English fleet decisively defeats the Armada of Catholic Spain: it reassures as well as safeguards the realm. Even better, the wind is partly responsible for the victory, like a divine breath of air on the English side. The English see this as a sign of God's approval of their religion. The defeat of the Spanish Armada thus opens the door to a newfound spiritual and cultural confidence in England, as well as reminding the rest of Europe that England has a navy worthy of their respect.

B IS FOR BREAKFAST

As 'a full English breakfast' these days is such a national tradition, it might surprise you to hear that it is only in the sixteenth century that the English start to eat breakfast on a regular basis. And it is not a 'full English' even then (the 'full English' being an early twentieth-century invention). Historical novelists who describe medieval characters sitting down to breakfast every morning are making a mistake. Before 1500 you might eat breakfast before setting out on a long journey or going to do a full day's work at harvest time, if this is one of the customs of the manor. You might also eat the occasional breakfast if you are taking part in a *jantaculum* (the Latin word for a ceremonial breakfast) in an aristocratic household or in a civic ceremony. But the vast majority of people in medieval times do not eat three meals a day. They eat two. The main meal, dinner, is eaten in the late morning, starting at 10:30 or 11 a.m. The lesser meal, supper, is normally eaten five or six hours later.

Why do we start eating breakfasts in the sixteenth century? It is a consequence of people working in towns and increasingly having to regulate their lives according to the hour of the clock. Whereas in the Middle Ages people organise their own time or follow the directions of the official in charge of their manor, in the sixteenth century townsmen are employed for a set number of hours each day. An Act of Parliament passed in 1514 notes that some workers do not deserve to be paid because they spend too long over their breakfast or dinner. This same Act declares that between mid-March and mid-September, workers should start work before 5 a.m. and continue until after 7 p.m. During the rest of the year, they are to work from dawn until dusk. These long hours are obviously incompatible with the traditional two-meal day. People now eat something before they go to work – normally just bread and butter with some ale or beer. Then they have one meal around midday, which in Elizabeth's reign they might call 'luncheon', before returning to work. At the end of the day, they have supper at home.

Not everyone makes this transformation at the same time. Aristocratic and gentry households stick to two meals a day for decades. So too do university colleges and country dwellers. This is still the case in 1577, when William Harrison notes in his *Description of England* that merchants and townsmen rarely eat before midday and have their evening meal at 6 p.m., whereas the rural folk and nobility still eat both meals earlier. If you visit England at the end of Elizabeth's reign, you will find people in towns on the three-meal cycle with which you are familiar, while those in the countryside still observe the older two-meal day.

C IS FOR CRUELTY

Although Elizabethan England is a 'golden age' with regard to literature, architecture, music and geographical exploration, it is also a 'golden age' of many things we should not be proud of, such as bear-baiting, wife beating and child abuse. The cruelty of Elizabeth's realm should put most people off wanting to visit. Especially if you are a woman or a child. Or a bear.

Let's start with the animals. Bear-baiting is so popular that Queen Elizabeth recommends that all the foreign ambassadors and dignitaries who come to London should go to see the bear-baiting theatres in Southwark, on the south side of the River Thames. She herself visits several times. But, as far as we know, she never goes to the Globe Theatre next door, to see one of Shakespeare's plays. She is not alone in loving the spectacle. Several contemporaries describe the fights with fascination and relish. They are clearly entranced by the froth foaming around the bear's mouth and the blood matted in its fur as it fights the vicious dogs that assail it over and over again, as it stands chained to the spot. The bear tosses the dogs with great blows. Men stand around the ring with pairs of long sticks with which they catch the dogs to break their fall, so they can go back into the attack.

Bears are not the only animals made to suffer. Bulls are similarly baited with dogs: chained to the spot and forced to fight. The dogs repeatedly try to bite the soft flesh around the bull's neck while the bull furiously tosses them away on its horns. Cock fighting too is hugely popular. People love the spectacle of these animals sparring to the death. They place large wagers on the outcome. Money, chance and blood together are a spellbinding combination in Elizabethan times. When it comes to stag hunting, Robert Laneham, writing in 1575, declares it 'pleases more of the senses than anything else' to see an animal in full flight from the hounds that are about to rip it apart.

This cruelty pervades society to the extent that it is widely believed that a man is morally bound to beat his sons. The thinking here is that being soft on them is irresponsible because it risks them growing up wild and unfamiliar with discipline, so they might commit a crime and be hanged.

The pillory gives ordinary Elizabethan men and women the chance to display their cruelty. We sometimes laugh at the mock-ups of pillories in pub gardens, seeing our children put their heads and hands playfully through the holes in a plank meant to hold them there. In reality, men and women who are pilloried often have their ears nailed to the wood while rotten matter and stones are thrown at them. And when they are removed from the pillory, their ears are cut off. In one case of poisoning in 1559, a man and a woman not only have their ears cut off but their hands too. Sometimes being pilloried proves fatal.

Then there is the cruelty towards women in particular. You only need to look at the records of the church courts – the courts that deal with morality – to realise how extreme this is. Women are regularly humiliated for adultery and castigated for unmarried pregnancies even though a number of these sexual relationships are non-consensual. It is naturally assumed that a man employing a young female servant will use her for sex. Of course, if she gets pregnant, that is deemed to be her fault and she will be dismissed. Unfortunately, that pregnancy may end her chances of making a good marriage as well as finding other employment. There are relatively few options open to a woman in such a position – and, as we noted with regard to the medieval period, none of them is good.

The rule that a man may legally beat his wife with impunity as long he does not actually kill her shows you how different Elizabethan society is from that of the twenty-first century. And it is not just uneducated brutes abusing their wives. When the physician Simon Forman suspects his wife of adultery, he writes in his diary that he has to hit her two or three times until she will listen to him – as if it is *her* fault that he has to resort to violence. And he prides himself on being a good husband.

On top of all this domestic cruelty there is state-sponsored torture. You might recall that England is unusual in the Middle Ages in that its laws and customs do not permit torture. This changes during Elizabeth's reign. From about 1580 the court known as Star Chamber starts to authorise the use of torture against Catholic priests and their helpers. Several accounts survive written by men who endure immense suffering in the Tower of London. Some mention the use of thumbscrews. There is also the Little Ease – a room 4ft cubed – in which you are placed and left for days, unable to straighten out or stand up. There is the rack, on which the body is slowly pulled apart, dislocating bones and causing immense pain. And then there is being suspended by ropes around your wrists. After a few hours of incremental agony you pass out – whereupon your torturer will lower you to the ground, wake you up by pouring cold water over you, and then haul you up again. *That's* the real torture: the coming to and realising the agony is about to start all over again.

When I hear people talk about progress, I often think to myself that they have a very rosy picture of the world. Progress in the sixteenth century means turning from a world in which we prided ourselves on *not* torturing people to deliberately causing someone as much pain as possible. If you cast your mind back to the start of the last section and that quotation from the film *Pulp Fiction* – 'I'm gonna get medieval on your ass' – to be accurate, Marcellus Wallace should have declared 'I'm gonna get Elizabethan on your ass'.

D IS FOR THE DEATH PENALTY

This is also a bit of contrast with the 'golden age' picture of Elizabethan England. The good news is that people no longer have to worry about being boiled to death. That law is repealed in 1547 – and replaced with being burnt at the stake. It is generally considered that burning people to death is more humane than boiling them.

There are five ways in which you can be executed in Elizabeth's reign. Being burnt at the stake is the standard punishment for poisoning and heresy. Although Catholics are not burnt in Elizabeth's reign, Anabaptists and other supposed heretics are. Burning is also the standard punishment for women found guilty of treason. This can be petty treason – murdering your husband or your employer – or high treason, which includes plotting to kill key members of the royal family and damaging the coinage system. As a result, women are burnt at the stake for clipping coins as well as killing their abusive bosses or spouses. Witchcraft, it should be noted, is not considered heresy in England, so although witches *are* burnt alive on the Continent and in Scotland and Ireland, they are merely hanged in England and Wales.

Hanging is by far the most common form of execution. A conviction for the theft of anything worth more than a shilling is normally enough for you to end up swinging on the end of a rope with a crowd jeering at you. Violent assault, rape, sodomy and a plethora of other crimes also merit the same punishment.

Hanging has its variation in the sentence of being 'hanged, drawn and quartered'. This is the punishment meted out to male traitors. The 'drawing' relates to the victim being dragged to the gallows on a hurdle. It does not mean having your entrails removed – a common misunderstanding, due to a mistake in the *OED* – although, as we have seen with regard to medieval evisceration, that does happen too.

Beheading is the most common punishment if you are an important lord or lady found guilty of high treason. You are required to kneel down and place your head on a block so an axeman can hack it off. If you are lucky, he will succeed with a single blow. If not, you might be kneeling there while he smashes his axe blade into your shoulder or the back of your skull. And then pulls it out and has another go. Some people endure three or four such erratic blows before they die.

Beheading is also the standard punishment if you live in the Yorkshire town of Halifax. Anyone found guilty of a felony there is meant to have his or her head cut off by the Halifax gibbet. You may know this machine better as a guillotine. Its use in Halifax can be traced back to the thirteenth century – half a millennium before Dr Joseph-Ignace Guillotin causes a twinkle in an executioner's eye. At least twenty-three criminals are executed in Elizabeth's reign in this way. Interestingly, whereas Dr Guillotin proposes the use of the machine that now bears his name because he thinks it quicker – and thus more merciful – than other forms of execution, that is not why the people of Halifax use it. Their reason is collective responsibility, so no one is labelled with breaking the biblical injunction *thou shalt not kill*. In theory, all the good men of the town are supposed to pull together on a rope to remove the peg holding up the heavy blade, thereby collectively taking responsibility for the act of justice. Criminals are allowed to move to try and dodge the blade as it comes down but, as it descends very rapidly, they are more likely to have their head cut in half than escape.

The fifth and final form of judicial killing is *peine forte et dure* – which may be translated as 'strong and hard punishment'. This is the fate you will suffer if you refuse to enter a plea of guilty or not guilty in court. It involves you being pinned out flat, with your hands and legs tied to stakes in the ground and a small rock beneath your spine. Then a board is placed on top of your chest and rocks and boulders slowly added until about seven or eight hundredweight lies on top of you. If you die in less than three hours, you are lucky. Some people are in agony for more than twelve.

The extraordinary thing about *peine forte et dure* is that you can only die in this way if you choose to – because it is always your choice whether to enter a plea or not. This gives rise to the obvious question, why on earth would anyone choose to die this way rather than plead guilty and simply be hanged?

One answer is to maintain control of family property. If you have an estate entailed on you and your descendants, and you are accused of treason and found guilty, the crown will confiscate your estate and you will be hanged, drawn and quartered or (in the case of women) burnt at the stake. Not only do you suffer a terrible death anyway, your sons and daughters lose their inheritance and, with it, their income and social standing. If you do not enter a plea, the trial cannot go ahead, so you cannot be found guilty. In this case, the family estate simply passes to the next generation. Hence this form of execution is chosen by some very brave souls who wish not only to defy the government to the very end but also to ensure their family can carry on the fight after their death. Famously, Margaret Clitherowe of York also opts to be pressed to death in 1586 so that her young children won't be tortured by Elizabeth's agents to discover the whereabouts of the Catholic priests she is hiding.

E IS FOR EXPECTATION OF LIFE AT BIRTH

You might remember from the medieval A–Z that half the population in the fourteenth century die before they reach the age of twenty. One consequence of this high early mortality is that the streets are full of young people. That is still the case in the sixteenth century: there are five times as many under-sixteen-year-olds as there are over-sixties. Today those two sections of the population are about equal. The sad fact is that half the children in Elizabethan England never have the chance to grow up.

How does life expectancy in Elizabethan times compare with the Middle Ages? Only a little better. Although famine is less common, day-to-day poverty is not. Inequality is as bad in 1590 as it is in 1290. If you want to visit England when the working class are less deprived than at any time before the late-nineteenth century, you want to turn up in about 1470. That's when the real wages of the average worker are at their maximum. Put out of your mind any idea of constant progress in this regard: the relative wealth of the poor is more like a sine wave than a straight, upward-moving trend. As a result, if you are born in the 1560s, you can expect to live to twenty-eight. If you can hang on for twenty years, however, and are born in the 1580s, then you can expect to live to forty-one. It doesn't sound that great but, in truth, that's as good as you're going to get for the next 300 years.

F IS FOR FISH

In the Middle Ages, the Catholic Church attempts to control people's diet. You are not permitted to eat meat on Wednesdays, Fridays and Saturdays. After the initial break with the Roman Catholic Church, that restriction regarding Fridays and Saturdays remains in place. And in Elizabeth's reign, her secretary of state, Sir William Cecil, reintroduces the no-meat rule on Wednesdays to try to help the English fishing industry.

That point in itself is just worth dwelling on. We talk about government interventions in our lives today but just imagine the current environment minister declaring that no one is allowed to eat meat on a Wednesday – no beef, pork, lamb or chicken, nor any bacon, burgers, kebabs or sausages at home or in any pub or restaurant – in order to help the British fishing fleet. People would be up in arms! And that is exactly what happens in 1563.

At first, the observance of non-meat days isn't a problem. It is orthodox practice – just as it is in the days of the old Catholic Church. People are not unhappy with this situation. But gradually William Cecil's fish-Wednesdays fall by the wayside. People enjoy eating meat – especially beef roasted on a spit. Fridays and Saturdays continue to be observed as non-meat days – as does Lent – for some years. Only after the defeat of the Spanish Armada does the habit of exclusively eating fish on Fridays and Saturdays fall into abeyance. People by then are confident they can eat meat throughout the week and God will not punish them. You could say that in many people's lives, the shift from Catholicism to Protestantism that starts in 1559 with the establishment of the Church of England, is only complete when Protestantism proves victorious in 1588.

G IS FOR GLASS

Elizabeth's reign is when many ordinary people first put glass in the windows of their houses. Before that, lords and ladies have glass in the private chambers of their principal residences but lesser mortals have to do without. They generally live in dark, single-storey hall houses with windows that are closed with shutters and thus open for much of the day. Draughts are inevitable. You will also notice that the windows are normally small, to limit the wind that can enter and so help reduce heat loss. These allow in very little light.

Imagine walking around a poor person's house in 1558. Even in daytime, you'll be feeling your way. You are constantly walking in shadows. Hollywood films might show sixteenth-century interiors with banks of candles in every room but that's for the benefit of the cameras and the dramatic spectacle. In reality, people don't live like that. Candles are not cheap – especially beeswax ones – so even the wealthy don't use more than necessary. They certainly don't leave lots of them burning in a room that is otherwise unoccupied. There is not only the cost to think about but also the risk of burning the house down. When you walk from one room to another in an Elizabethan house, you will carry a light with you. Rather than candles, the poor use rushlights – which are trimmed rushes dipped in fat and held in a metal holder – but they don't use more of these than they require. In short, without glass, ordinary houses are dark by day as well as by night.

For the working man, who is outside for almost all the daylight hours, this doesn't matter all that much. However, for those who are indoors by day – womenfolk, infants, servants, the infirm and the elderly, as well as indoor workers, such as wool combers, spinsters and weavers – it matters a great deal. Living in half-light means that they are much more sensitive to textures than colours. You can see this reflected in the descriptions for different kinds of cloth. Linen isn't just 'linen' – it is buckram, canvas, lockram, holland, cambric or lawn. The differences lie in the way these things feel as well as how they appear. Woollens too aren't just 'wool'; they are scarlet, broadcloth, scammel, kersey, russet, frizado, frieze, kendal, cotton, flannel, worsted, serge, bay or says.

When the middling sort start to fit glass in their windows in Elizabeth's reign, it makes a huge difference. They can now do their needlework indoors or read by natural light. They also want more colour around their homes. As it happens, this is just when more and more dyes are imported. We have brazilwood from Asia, which gives an orange-red colour. We obtain kermes from the Mediterranean and cochineal from Latin America, both of which yield vibrant shades of red. These new dyes can be mixed with traditional ones such as woad (blue) to provide different violets and pale purples. Putting a glass window in the street-facing window of your house doesn't just impress the neighbours, it allows everyone to see the colours of the cushions and soft furnishings with which you might now furnish your hall. It also seems healthier: the more sunlight that enters your house, the more hygienic it's supposed to be, according to the thinking of the time.

This is even more the case at the top of the social scale. There's a famous saying, 'Hardwick Hall – more glass than wall'. If you visit Hardwick Hall in Derbyshire, built by Bess of Hardwick in the 1590s, you will see that it does indeed have a whole array of large windows. But the same could be said for almost every great Elizabethan house. Holdenby House in Northamptonshire, built in 1583, has twice as much glass as Hardwick. The glass pane might be ubiquitous today but for the Elizabethans, it is a demonstration of wealth, health, convenience and luxury.

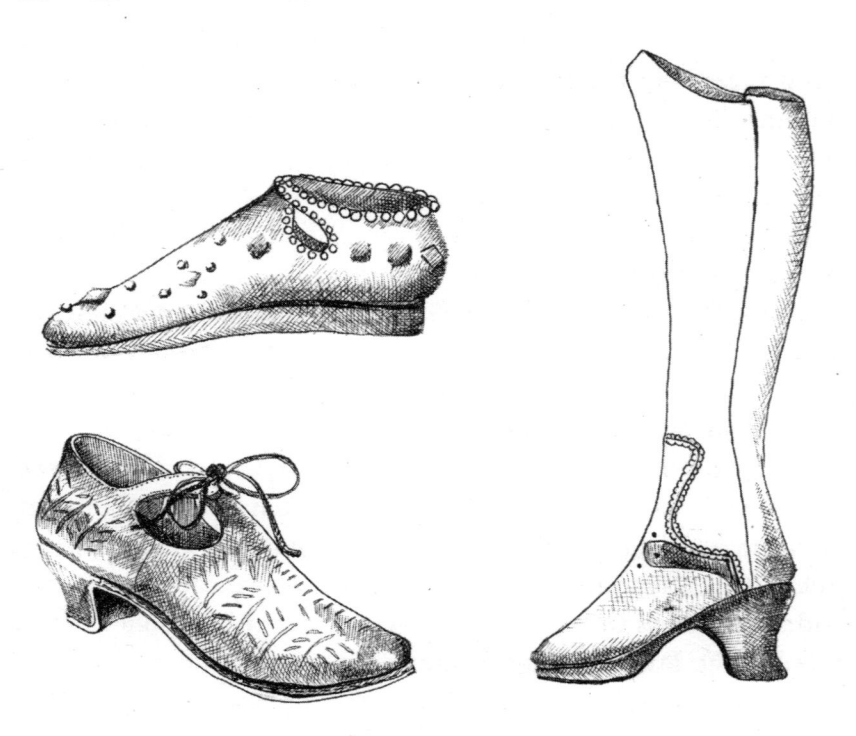

H IS FOR HEELS

Prior to Elizabeth's reign, shoes and boots do not have raised heels. They are all flat. The idea to build a heel into a shoe comes from cork soles, which are increasingly used in the sixteenth century. The problem is that cork soles do not wear down evenly. Often the heel goes long before the rest of the sole is worn out. So shoemakers start building up the heel at the back to compensate, resulting in a cork sole being wedge-shaped. If you look at ladies' funeral effigies from this period, you will notice that, by the end of the reign, the fashion is to cut away the cork heel and replace it with a solid wooden one. The queen herself purchases her first pair of 'high heels', as she calls them, in 1596 when she is sixty-three.

I IS FOR ILLNESSES

We've moved on from the medieval Black Death by the time of Elizabeth's accession. No more do we have onslaughts in which almost half the population drop dead over the space of seven months. Nevertheless, plague is still an extremely dangerous disease. This is especially the case if you visit a major settlement. In a small town such as Stratford-upon-Avon, which has a population of about 1,550 people, plague kills about 13 per cent when it strikes. A medium-sized one like Exeter with about 8,000 inhabitants, normally loses around 15 or 16 per cent. Bristol, with a population of 12,000, sees just over 2,000 victims in 1565 and 1575, which is 17 per cent. However, if you visit London in a plague year, then watch out. In fact, don't go there. Avoid it like, er, the plague.

In 1563, when London's population is nearly 70,000 people, a total of 17,404 of them die from the plague. That's 25 per cent. So heavy are the losses that it becomes known as the Great Plague. The numbers are carefully gathered by the parish clerks of the city and published as 'bills of mortality'. When later outbreaks strike, the numbers increase in proportion to the number of citizens. In 1603, when the population is approaching 200,000, there is a new Great Plague. This time, there are at least 32,257 victims.

One of the interesting things about Elizabethan illnesses is that they illustrate how the landscape of illness changes over time. As the continued prevalence of the plague shows, Elizabethan people suffer from diseases that do not affect us. Moreover, they experience plague in a different way from their medieval predecessors. It is deadly but not quite *as* deadly. We must suspect that either the plague has changed or the people have – perhaps as a result of having greater immunity – or both.

Plague is not the only example of a disease that varies with regard to its deadliness over time. Malaria is a big killer in the low-lying areas of England in the sixteenth century. One Elizabethan writer on Kent, William Lambarde, astutely divides the county into two parts: the higher ground, where there is 'health but no wealth', and the marshes, which are excellent for grazing cattle but where there is 'wealth but not health'. Another good example is smallpox. This is regarded as a children's disease until 1562. An English courtier diagnosed with it the previous year declares airily that he 'has nothing to worry about'. Those prove to be his last words. The queen herself catches smallpox in 1562 and is severely ill: there are worries for the succession. She survives but many people who catch it at a later date do not.

A fourth example of a disease changing is 'the sweating sickness', otherwise known simply as 'the sweat'. It is first recorded in England in 1485 and then comes back several times, normally killing about 20 per cent of the population of any town it strikes. But in 1550 it makes its final appearance. Elizabethan people don't know that it won't return, however, so it still features in their consciousness and their prayers. Why does it not come back? No one knows. Some modern writers, believing they have the full palette of human diseases at their disposal, think it is dengue fever. But the truth of the matter is open to doubt. All we can be sure of is that the list of ailments that affect us today is not the same as those affecting people in the sixteenth century, and the ailments in question do not affect people living in different centuries in the same way.

Another terrifying disease I suggest you watch out for is influenza. Elizabethan people are only just getting to grips with this. It strikes in 1557, the year before Elizabeth ascends the throne, but the pandemic lasts for almost two years. To give you an idea of how deadly it is, in August 1557 the number buried across the country is approximately 50 per cent higher than usual; that figure then increases month by month until, in February 1559, the number buried is three times the usual figure. Not until June 1559 are things back to normal.

It is often remarked that the influenza pandemic that follows World War I kills more people than the four-year-long war itself. That is not true for the United Kingdom: the war accounts for about 880,000 fatalities whereas the 'flu just 228,000. But, percentage-wise, the 'flu of 1557–59 is twice as deadly as both World War I and the 1918–20 'flu put together. Excess deaths amount to about 5 per cent of the Elizabethan population.

J IS FOR JAKES

Jakes are latrines, loos, privies, garderobes, toilets or chairs of easement – to give them just a few of the names by which they are known. I have two reasons for mentioning them here. First, if you happen to be in an Elizabethan house, where to go will soon become a matter of the greatest urgency, with the result that the whereabouts of the nearest jakes will exceed in importance all other aspects of daily life. Second, if you are in an overcrowded conurbation or army camp, what you and your neighbours do with your faeces might prove a matter of life and death. Excrement is one of those little details about the past that are hugely important but which, for reasons of politeness and taboo, historians consider beneath them. If you don't mind my saying so.

Let's start with the stuff of ribald humour, particularly the standing joke that people in this period empty their chamber pots out of the window over the heads of anyone who happens to be passing by. I'm not saying this *never* happens but, even if you don't hit anyone, it is against the 'law of nuisance'. Householders are expected to keep the street outside their houses clean. If you cause an obstruction or if you empty filth into the street, you are expected to clean it up or you will be fined by the civic authorities. You also need to remember that chamber pots are quite a novel invention in the sixteenth century. Not everyone can afford one. They are modest status symbols. So if your servants were to chuck the contents out into the street, they would embarrass you as their employer because your household would be showing a flagrant disregard for the law of nuisance. As for the commonly repeated notion that the word 'loo' is a corruption of the French word *l'eau* and that it comes from the warning *gardez l'eau* as people empty the contents of their chamber pots into the street, this too is codswallop. The word 'loo' is not recorded as having its modern meaning before the very end of the nineteenth century. In fact, the first unambiguous use of the word 'loo' in the modern sense appears in a book published in 1940 by the upper-class writer Nancy Mitford. She is definitely not the sort to empty a chamber pot into the street.

Older than chamber pots are close stools and you will still come across these in Elizabethan England. They are for the better-off. They consist of a wooden box with a velvet-covered seat that has a hole in the middle; beneath this hole is a basin that can be removed and emptied. However, the contents will often be retained to show your physician, so he can monitor your wellbeing. He might also ask you to urinate into a glass flask so he may assess the colour, aroma and viscosity of your urine, again for the benefit of your health.

For the urban poor, going to the loo is a serious concern. The problem is the cost – we're not just talking about spending a penny. Imagine you're living in a five-storey townhouse in London and sharing it with four other families, all of whom are struggling to get by on an unskilled labourer's wages of 4d per day. The latrines – wooden seats above a shaft – are designed to allow excrement and urine to fall into the cesspit in the basement. Imagine how much matter builds up in that cesspit over the course of a year from twenty or thirty people constantly using it. All that soaking, stinking matter has to be shovelled into barrels and carried up through the residence. And it has to be done by night – inevitably resulting in some spillage. But it is the cost that is most off-putting. One cesspit in London, which is emptied over two nights in 1575, contains 16 tons of excrement. Emptying that lot costs £2 4s – the equivalent of 132 days' work for an unskilled labourer, or twenty-six days each for the five families. That house of thirty people might have to have that much shifted every two years. When you have barely enough money to feed your family, the prospect of having to spend 4 per cent of your wages on emptying your cesspit is a depressing one. You'd far rather use the town facilities – presuming there are some – or if not, cast your excrement into the nearest river.

Into this miasma steps the great Sir John Harington, godson of Queen Elizabeth and the inventor of the water closet. In his book *The Metamorphosis of Ajax* – 'Ajax' being a pun on 'a jakes' – he describes how you might build your own flushing loo. The one he constructs at his house near Bath has a stone bowl and a bronze sluice. Using his design, you can build your own for just £1 10s 8d. It sounds like a bargain, compared to the expense and smell of emptying a cesspit. The only drawback is that you need your own supply of running water. And that is a whole other issue.

K IS FOR KISSING

How many of us have never been kissed? Not many. And how many of us don't care whether we will ever be kissed again? Very few. We are physically and emotionally programmed to want to be intimate with our fellow human beings – or at least some of them. But if I were to ask, have you been to the moon, the answer would be no. Similarly, if I asked if you have fought a pitched battle, very few people would answer in the affirmative. Yet these things are considered of huge historical importance and considered far more interesting and significant than being kissed. I am not saying for a moment that the moon landing and fighting battles are inconsequential – far from it – but I *am* saying that the things we all do on a regular, routine basis, such as eating, making love, going to work and raising our children are all far more important than school-based history leads us to believe. In placing such a heavy emphasis on the unusual, we tend to overlook the little things that unite us all. We ignore the universals that are the fundamental bedrock of who we are.

Back to Elizabethan kissing. What about it? Isn't it just the same as modern kissing? I am not sure about technique but I cannot help but notice that almost every foreign writer who comes to London during Elizabeth's reign describes the practice of kissing strangers. If a gentleman knocks on the door of a townhouse and it is answered by a woman – be she a maidservant or the wife or daughter of the householder – the gentleman should take her by the arm and kiss her full on the lips. How on earth do the English acquire a reputation for being stand-offish? Today we would call this sexual assault. In Elizabethan times it is considered a sign of good breeding. The foreign writers who remark on this practice emphasise how strange it seems to them. But they all go on to say how much kissing goes on in London.

Alessandro Magno is one of these writers. He is a Venetian who comes to London in 1562. He doesn't just refer to the kissing on the doorstep. He notes that, at dusk, the boys and girls of the city will often head out beyond Moorgate and 'play' in Moorfields, the area just to the north of the old city wall where on sunny days the washerwomen take their baskets to dry clothes on the grass and bushes. Magno explains that the most popular game among them is for the boys to try and trip the girls up and pin them down on the ground – not letting them get up until they have paid the forfeit of a kiss on the lips. He ends his account of their shenanigans with the observation: 'they kiss a lot'.

I should add though, by way of warning, that Magno visits England in 1562, which is just before the Great Plague of 1563 – the outbreak that kills off 25 per cent of the population. So I recommend you think twice before you embrace this practice of kissing strangers.

L IS FOR LITERACY

Even today, Elizabethan schools survive in their hundreds up and down the country. But they do not represent the full extent of learning. It is very easy to overlook the role of self-education, which starts to become a major factor contributing to literacy. In particular, you cannot ignore the importance of translations of the Bible into English.

We are often told that the invention of the printing press changes the world. This is not really true – at least, not in its simple sense. First, it matters how many people can read. Printing would have been almost useless in the early eleventh century. Second, it matters *what* you print. Early printed books are expensive and in Latin. They don't differ from manuscripts that much. Thus the press does not cause an overnight educational revolution – especially not in England. Even when William Caxton starts printing books in English at Westminster in 1476, the take-up of the new technology is surprisingly slow.

What *does* cause a revolution is the publication of the Bible in the vernacular. Almost the entire print run of the first Bible printed in English, William Tyndale's *New Testament* of 1526, is bought by the bishop of London so he can burn every copy. However, Tyndale's revised 1534 edition spreads covertly and quickly. After the appearance of Miles Coverdale's Bible in 1535, people increasingly have access to the word of God in their own language. In 1539 copies of the newly published Great Bible are placed in parish churches up and down the country. Many wealthy people acquire one of their own. You don't need the intervention of a priest to understand what it says because it is in your language. What's more, you have a good incentive to learn to read it for yourself. If you can buy or borrow a copy, you can study the means whereby you might obtain everlasting life. Male literacy rates rise from about 10 per cent in 1500 to 25 per cent by 1600.

So much for the men. What about the women? The problem girls face is that almost all schools are exclusively for boys. The few educational opportunities open to females in the sixteenth century are lost with the Dissolution of the Monasteries, which eliminates all the nunneries. But this point in time – around 1540 – is where the English Bible comes into its own. Unlike schools and schoolmasters, a book doesn't care about the sex of the person learning from it. In that respect, although the Bible may be full of sexism, its availability in English is truly egalitarian. Female literacy increases as a result. In 1500 less than 1 per cent of women can read and write. By 1600 more than 10 per cent can. Most teach themselves to read using a Bible. But having learnt to read that work, they can go on to read anything else they want. By 1600 cookbooks are produced in cheap editions aimed at women. For just 4d you can buy a volume incorporating all the recipes you need to impress your dinner guests. Or you might buy a book of religious consolation written *by* women *for* women. Or a book of poetry by women such as Isabella Whitney, the first published English poetess. You are no longer restricted to reading texts composed by men for other men.

M IS FOR MUSIC

People are confused by the Protestant revolution. They don't know what music they can play anymore. One moment they are in church, listening to the most wonderful Catholic polyphony, and the next there is silence. Music is not mentioned as an aspect of religion in the Bible so the reformers consider it secular and forbid it. If you go to church, the only music you will hear is the psalms – because the psalms *do* appear in the Bible.

This is another reason why the defeat of the Spanish Armada is so important in our history. Afterwards you see a great rise in cultural confidence. Italian madrigals (unaccompanied secular songs for many voices), are introduced into England by way of a book, *Musica Transalpina*, which is published in 1588, just before the Armada, so it is true that this change is happening anyway. But as soon as Protestant England has proved victorious, there is a newfound assurance in the performance of secular music in private houses. More music is published too.

What you will *not* hear is arguably the greatest piece of choral music ever written by an Englishman, namely Thomas Tallis's 'Spem in alium' ('Hope in another'). It is composed around 1570 and consists of forty parts in eight separate choirs. The reason you won't hear it is not because of the music itself – which is like lying on a warm beach and having wave after wave of sound breaking over you – but because its text is a Catholic one. Not only is Tallis himself a Catholic, the music is commissioned by the Catholic duke of Norfolk for private performance. For this reason, unless you know the duke – who is beheaded for treason in 1572 – you will have to wait until the next century for a performance, when the music will be given different words.

The late sixteenth century is when the Italian Andrea Amati and his sons develop the modern violin, viola and cello. It is unlikely that any of their instruments make their way to England at this time – although Andrea does make a number of violins for the French court. Instead you will hear the older viol and viol da gamba, which differ in having longer necks, more strings, sloping shoulders and flat backs. In public, official groups of town musicians called 'waits' play loud instruments such as the shawm, cornet and horn, as well as drums. You will also encounter bagpipes on a regular basis. In 1587 one visitor to London notes that the city 'is so full of unprofitable pipers and fiddlers that a man can no sooner enter a tavern than two or three cast of them hang at his heels to give him a dance ere he depart'. In private, the wealthy might learn to play a keyboard instrument such as the virginals, spinet or harpsichord. Queen Elizabeth herself plays the virginals. She also plays the lute. It is not an easy instrument to master, so there is definitely an element of 'soft power' in the queen demonstrating her accomplishments in this way.

The new enthusiasm for secular music prompts the greatest composers of the day to compete for attention. Madrigals are composed by the hundred. So too are airs – solo songs for accompaniment by a lute – after John Dowland makes the form popular in 1597. Two men in particular compete with each other in a sort of Elizabethan 'Battle of the Bands'. John Wilbye is a sober, careful composer of madrigals who never offends his patron and grows old in retirement. His rival, Thomas Weelkes, is the nearest thing you'll find to an Elizabethan rock 'n' roller. He is as famous for his drunkenness, blasphemy and all-round bad behaviour as he is for his music. On one occasion during evensong at Chichester Cathedral he stands on the edge of the organ loft and urinates on the dean of the cathedral, who is standing below.

N IS FOR NAVIGATION

Every time I hear the *Our Island Story* vision of the history of Great Britain, I am reminded of the widespread understanding that we have always been great sailors because England occupies most of an island. In reality, we produce mediocre mariners until the start of the fifteenth century. Then English fishermen start sailing off towards Iceland to plunder the huge shoals of cod that can be found there. By 1497 the men of Bristol are experienced enough in Atlantic navigation for a Genoese captain, John Cabot, to choose them to help him sail to Newfoundland, in modern Canada. But still the English aren't leading the way. All the tracts of navigation published in English before 1558 are translations of works written in Italian, Portuguese or Spanish. William Bourne's *Regiment for the Sea*, published in 1574, comments on how just twenty years earlier English sailors deride those who used plans and calculations of the height of the Pole Star to establish their position. Old-fashioned navigators do everything by personal experience.

This lack of navigational treatises is dramatically transformed during Elizabeth's reign. The English start to view navigation as a branch of natural philosophy – of discovering the physical properties and characteristics of the world. Mathematicians and explorers collaborate on such problems as how to measure the width of the Atlantic, how to measure the speed of a ship at sea, and how to measure more accurately the height of the sun, the Pole Star and the Southern Cross. There is a sudden increase in the number of technical devices that can be used for finding your way too. In just a few decades, the English go from being a backward nation in terms of navigation to being at the forefront of exploration.

Why is this? Religion is part of the explanation. Some people feel a spiritual obligation to discover more about God's Creation. The loss of Calais to the French is also an impetus. After the English lose their last foothold in Continental Europe in 1558, they look west and plan to build another 'Calais' on another continent, America. But the most important factor is money. In the 1560s John Hawkins demonstrates the rich pickings to be had by exploiting a triangle of trade: taking goods from Europe to African ports, selling them to buy enslaved people, taking those people to the West Indies and selling them to Spanish plantation owners in return for sugar, pearls and gold, and then bringing those riches back to Europe for sale at a profit. Francis Drake shows you don't even need to trade in slaves to get rich. When he returns from his circumnavigation of the globe in 1580, his newly renamed ship, *Golden Hinde*, is laden with bullion. He never admits how much money he brings back but the Spanish – from whom he has stolen most of it – estimate it to be £600,000, which is roughly twice the annual income of the English Crown. When Thomas Cavendish returns home from his circumnavigation in 1588, he is so rich that the sails of his ship are dyed imperial purple and his men are all wearing gold chains around their necks.

As a result of this prosperity, many people want to go to sea to make a fortune. A good number of them take advantage of the recent advances in English navigation. If you have read James Clavell's 1975 novel *Shogun*, you'll be familiar with the story of John Blackthorne, an English navigator who sails with a Dutch fleet to Japan and lands there in 1600. It is based on the true story of Will Adams from Gillingham in Kent. From 1600 until his death in 1620 Adams lives at the court of Tokugawa Iyeasu, the shogun of Japan. He writes back to London from Japan and takes up a position working for the East India Company (established in 1600). As a result, Elizabeth's successor, James I, writes a letter to the shogun, Tokugawa. It is all a far cry from the backwardness of English navigational science at the start of Elizabeth's reign.

O IS FOR ORAL HYGIENE

How should you brush your teeth in Elizabethan England? The answer is more complicated than you might imagine. Just think about the reasons *why* you clean your teeth. You probably do so because you want to preserve them, so they don't fall out. You might add that you don't want them looking bad either. Elizabethans know about tooth decay – some are aware that sugar damages their teeth, for example – but overall they don't know how to prevent it. Their priorities are how their teeth look and how their breath smells. And their ways of achieving success aren't all bound up in one fluoride, whitening toothpaste with multisyllable ingredients. They think about the problems of appearance and smell separately.

Probably the most important oral-hygiene matter to Elizabethans is the smell of the breath. Elizabethan books and plays hardly ever mention bodily odour but they frequently mention foul-smelling breath. Therefore it is only natural that they place a high priority on making their breath smell sweet. For this, they chew cumin seeds or aniseed. As for making the teeth look white, some recipes enjoin readers to use a tooth cloth – a strip of linen – with a mixture of water and rock alum. Alternatively you might use your tooth cloth to apply a dentifrice. This is normally made of spices and herbs: one recipe calls for 'savoury, galingale and wood of aloes'. Or you might apply a 'tooth blanche', made from powdered cuttlefish bone. After rubbing the cuttlefish bone into your teeth, you should wash your mouth out – first with white wine and then with spirit of vitriol. Just in case you don't know, 'spirit of vitriol' is sulphuric acid. Your teeth might not go white but the rest of you will.

P IS FOR PERSONAL CLEANLINESS

Undoubtedly the most famous line to do with sixteenth-century personal hygiene concerns a remark about Queen Elizabeth herself. The Venetian ambassador, writing to his superiors back in Venice, supposedly declares that 'she has a bath once a month, whether she needs it or not'. It sounds like a statement commenting on how rarely she washes. Unfortunately there are a number of variations on the statement, such as that she has a bath every two or three months, 'whether she needs it or not'. Now, I have looked for the original source and so far I have failed to find it, so I can't be sure it says she has a bath every *month* or every two months or some other interval. The thing is, when people start using quotations like this, they tend to adapt the original to suit their own ends, and it is much funnier if you say Elizabeth 'takes a bath every *year*, whether she needs it or not' than every month. Nevertheless, I believe that the original is out there somewhere, and the reason why I am so confident is that I know what the Venetian ambassador is driving at, and it is not what you think.

Elizabethan people don't habitually immerse themselves in large amounts of water for several reasons. The first is the cost. There is a firewood shortage, so heating up water is expensive. In a town, just obtaining that much water is difficult. It has to be brought to your house by a water carrier, normally hauling it on his or her back. Very few people are rich enough to be able just to turn on a tap. For those living in a rented room on the fourth floor of a London house, that water has also to be carried up the stairs and, after it has been used, back down again… Is it worth it, just for a bath? No. You don't do this if you're in a rented room. It's an awful lot of effort and money for something that might make you ill. And that will cost you even more in physicians' fees.

Since syphilis came along and infected all the women working in the London bath houses in the early sixteenth century, bathing has been associated with immorality and disease. And rightly so. Although you're not going to catch syphilis simply from immersing yourself in water – it's the bath attendant who gives you that, having allowed an earlier customer to have his wicked way with her – you are vulnerable to all manner of other diseases. You don't know where your bathwater has come from. You don't know what impurities are in it. Nor do you know what poisons might have been put in it. Although people do not yet know about germ theory, they do have a rudimentary grasp of 'the seeds of illness' being conveyed into the body through its orifices and the pores of the skin. Putting yourself in such a vulnerable position as sitting in water is therefore dangerous to your health. Bathing and disease go hand in hand.

So how does this affect Good Queen Bess and her monthly baths? Just as the body can absorb *bad* things through the skin and orifices, so too it can absorb good things. Most people understand the virtue of medicinal baths. On a day-to-day basis, they merely wash the parts that show and rub down their bodies with linen towels or 'rubbers' to remove grime and sweat. But if the need arises, they know they can go to a physician who will prescribe a medicinal bath. It is made with the best-quality, cleanest water – ideally rainwater that has fallen on to the roof of your own house – which has then been boiled and had the necessary medicinal ingredients added. This is what the Venetian ambassador means when he says the queen has a bath every month 'whether she needs it or not': the queen bathes in hot water regularly *even when she is not ill*. In fact, Elizabeth carries a bathtub on her progresses around the country for just this purpose. Far from being a statement about how rarely she washes, it is an acknowledgement of a higher degree of cleanliness than the Venetian ambassador and his superiors back home are used to.

Q IS FOR QUEENSHIP

What makes a great queen? That is a very interesting question in the context of the late sixteenth century. It is much easier to say what makes a great king. A king needs to abide by his coronation oaths – to deliver justice for all his people, to protect the Church and to defend the realm. That means he needs to keep control of his legal system – and intervene, if necessary – and work with Parliament in delivering good laws. Most of all, he needs to be victorious in battle. How can a sixteenth-century queen do any of these things? She cannot be seen to administer justice because her sex prevents her from professing an understanding of the law or intervening in it. The Church too is biased against her sex. She cannot be a strong military leader because she cannot lead her troops in battle. How then can she defend the realm? How can she possibly rule like a king or be a great monarch?

Elizabeth herself draws up the blueprint for successful female monarchy. Every European queen since 1600 owes her something. It is Elizabeth who demonstrates how important it is to be *seen* to be queen. To be fair, it is her half-sister, Mary I, who pioneers this. If you read *The Diary of Henry Machyn*, a Londoner who records the events of the city from 1550 to 1563, you will see that Mary takes every opportunity she can to hold a procession through the capital. She regularly displays herself and all her courtiers to the citizens, to keep them both loyal and subservient. Elizabeth sees this but realises it is not enough simply to be seen in the capital. She undertakes processions – or, rather, progresses – through the whole country. Except she does not go anywhere that is dangerous, where Catholic tendencies still run strong. She does not risk a progress through the West Country, for example. But travelling around the country with hundreds of carts and carriages, and perhaps thousands of men, she repeatedly reminds the public of her personal status. Those people living in the areas that she does not visit learn soon enough what awe she strikes wherever she goes. You could say she weaponizes her royal presence.

Then there is the money. Elizabeth keeps control of the purse strings. A king might have been required to lead his army on the battlefield in medieval times but now, when battlefields are so dangerous because of guns, kings are no longer expected to risk having their heads blown off. What matters instead is appointing the right commanders, having enough intelligence to know how to defeat the enemy, and having enough money to equip a large army. Elizabeth takes care of all these things. What's more, although she has many advisers – and many of them are extremely valuable to her – no single individual is allowed to dominate. She plays off her privy councillors against each other so that no one can claim to be in the ascendant. In this, her first-rate education serves her admirably. Even if a foreign diplomat spouts Latin at her – presuming she will not understand, being a woman – she can reply fluently in Latin and put him in his place. Lastly, she does not succumb to the pressure to marry, so she never becomes subservient to a man. She remains an unbridled, untamed figurehead for England. My own opinion is that she is the only truly great monarch we have had since Edward III. And just as Edward III was described 300 years after his death as 'the greatest monarch that, perhaps, the world has ever known', so I would venture that Elizabeth is his female equivalent: the greatest queen of historical times.

R IS FOR RELIGION

If you're Catholic in England, life gets worse at roughly ten-year intervals. Obviously the Elizabethan Settlement of 1559 (the queen's arrangements for the Church of England after her accession) is not good news for Catholics. It makes quite a lot of their divine service illegal. Things deteriorate in 1569. The Northern Rebellion – an armed Catholic insurrection led by the earls of Northumberland and Westmorland – is defeated. It is followed in 1571 by the pope excommunicating the queen, thereby obliging every Catholic in England to do what he or she can to remove Elizabeth from the throne. This makes all Catholics traitors in the eyes of their compatriots. The year 1580 sees the arrival of the Jesuits: militant priests serving the Catholic minority and looking to convert more people to the Catholic cause. Within a year, there are more than a hundred of them in hiding, often protected by Catholic noblemen and members of the landed gentry. The government responds with a crackdown. This is when the regime of torture starts. This is also when prominent Catholics start to make priest holes in their houses. Practising Catholics in England become very, very scared.

Catholics experience yet further persecution in 1593. New legislation forbids them from travelling more than 3 miles from their homes without permission from a magistrate. They aren't allowed to send their children to school. Saying Mass will incur a year in prison and a fine of 200 marks (£133). Just *hearing* Mass will cost you half that sum. If you contrast that with thirty years earlier, when most magistrates in England refuse to recognise Queen Elizabeth as the head of the Anglican Church, you can see the Catholic cause has sunk a long way. It is astonishing. We think of our faith as something that is unchanging. We will cling to our beliefs until we die. But during Elizabeth's reign, the faith of the entire nation is turned upside down in one generation.

S IS FOR SEX

The records of the Elizabethan church courts – in which you can be tried for adultery, bigamy, incest, harbouring a prostitute and a mass of other moral crimes – show that sexual intercourse outside marriage is very common. During Elizabeth's reign, more than 15,000 people in Essex are indicted for sexual offences – mostly adultery – which is more than a third of the adult population of the county. I know what you're thinking: it's *Essex*. But I have to tell you that an even greater percentage of Yorkshire people are accused of fornication of some sort or another. Up and down the country, people are flouting the seventh Commandment with joyful abandon.

You might be wondering, how do people know what their neighbours get up to behind closed doors? The system works like this. Those living in small communities keep an eye on each other. They observe who goes into and who comes out of each house. And if a man is noticed entering Widow Smith's house at dusk but is not seen to emerge, suspicions are aroused. Sometimes the constable will be summoned to find out what's going on. Are they in separate beds? Does Widow Smith even have a separate bed for her guest? If the archdeacon's official is informed, he will despatch an apparitor to summon both parties to a court hearing. To clear their names, each of the accused will have to bring along between six and nine compurgators or, in the case of Widow Smith, between six and nine compurgatrices. But it can be a long way to your archdeaconry court, and if you are the man accused of fornication with Widow Smith – or if you are Widow Smith herself – you'll have to pay all their travel expenses, including perhaps an overnight stay at an inn. That will be a prohibitive amount of money for a poor widow.

Where I live, on the edge of Dartmoor in Devon, it is 25 miles each way to my archdeaconry court in Totnes. Perhaps I don't have six friends who will come that far, giving up at least two days of their time, to swear that I am as pure as the freshly fallen snow. But if my co-accused can persuade the right number of compurgatrices to turn up and swear that nothing improper took place between us, she will be found innocent and I will be found guilty by default. I will probably be humiliated in my parish church or in the marketplace for three successive weekends. I will be ordered to wear a white robe and carry a white wand and confess my sin publicly. I will be made to parade around the church while my erstwhile lover sits in the pews, no doubt feeling rather ambivalent about the whole spectacle. Just such a situation occurs in 1579, when Henry Packer is found to have behaved immorally with a widow. According to his testimony, he sleeps in a separate bed but hears her moaning in the night. He goes to her to find out if she is all right and she asks him to warm her feet. She then falls pregnant from having her feet warmed. Her friends swear to her innocence in the matter. His, however, do not.

T IS FOR THE THEATRE

You could hardly expect me to talk about Elizabethan England and not mention the plays of William Shakespeare. And yet you don't really need me to. You already know about them. If you don't, you can see most of them for yourself whenever you want. Rather, it is the other playwrights I think I should talk about here. So completely does Mr Shakespeare dominate our thinking of the Elizabethan and early Jacobean theatre that he has pretty much blown every other writer of the period out of the water, with one or two exceptions. Given this pre-eminence, we can hardly limit ourselves to the years of Elizabeth's reign: Shakespeare is undoubtedly the king when it comes to drama, and he lives until 1616. So, to give you a few glimpses of what else is going on, here is a little A–Z of plays *not* by William Shakespeare that were performed in London during his lifetime.

THE A–Z OF PLAYS NOT BY SHAKESPEARE

A *is for The Alchemist*
'Fortune, that favours fools,' are the words with which Ben Jonson begins this comedy, published in 1610. While a London gentleman is absent, his servant and two accomplices use his house as a base for gulling people into believing they can make their wishes come true through magic. It is a satire on the follies of men and women and the foolish things they will do to advance themselves in society. There are dozens of other plays along similar lines but this is reckoned one of the best.

B *is for The Blind Beggar of Bednal-Green*
Written in 1600, this play tells the story of a young woman who catches the attention of several suitors, all but one of whom are put off by the fact her father is a beggar. But guess what – he's really a wounded veteran knight in disguise. The play's author, John Day, is an alumnus from Cambridge, from where he is expelled for stealing a book. Ben Jonson describes him as a 'rogue'. Jonson should watch out: Day kills a fellow playwright with a rapier. He's not exactly a man with whom you want to have professional differences.

C *is for Cupid's Whirligig*
The Devonian playwright, Edward Sharpham, publishes this comedy in 1607. Coincidentally Sharpham is also described as a 'rogue' by Ben Jonson. He has a strange start in life: when he is sixteen his mother sues Thomas Fortescue for using witchcraft to kill her first husband and make her fall in love with him.

That's a pretty good background for a writer – although perhaps not a recipe for a happy life. Sharpham has worse to come, however: he dies of plague in London in 1608.

D *is for Dr Faustus*
Christopher Marlowe's masterpiece, written in 1593, has it all: good and bad angels, a doctor who sells his soul to the devil, conversations with characters from history – including Helen of Troy, with whom the doctor has a love affair – and, of course, the unforgettable demon, Mephistophilis. The writing is superb. It is one of the very few plays of the period that ranks alongside Shakespeare's greatest works.

E *is for Edward II, the Troublesome reign of*
Another play by Christopher Marlowe, his fifth, written about 1592. Marlowe enjoys being outrageous, saying things like 'all they that like not tobacco and boys [are] fools'. This is dangerous because sodomy is punishable by hanging in the wake of the 1533 Buggery Act. But Marlowe is not afraid. He finds a suitable character for his subject of male love in the character of Edward II, whom medieval chroniclers accuse of being too fond of his favourite, Piers Gaveston, and whom medieval propagandists accuse of sodomy in October 1326 in order to disempower him and remove him from the throne. People still sometimes refer to Edward II as England's only openly gay king. That is testimony to the power of Marlowe's writing: it has nothing to do with the sexual behaviour of the historical Edward II.

F *is for Friar Bacon and Friar Bungay.*
Robert Greene's play, written about 1589, concerns a woman wanting her own way in marriage. The heroine is Margaret of Fressingfield, the love interest of Prince Edward, son of Henry III. The prince sends his friend Earl Lacy to help win her heart and, naturally, Earl Lacy and Margaret themselves fall in love. Edward then makes plans to kill Lacy. When Margaret finds out what the prince intends, she says: 'Thinks King Henry's son that

Margaret's love / Hangs in the uncertain balance of proud time? / That death shall make a discord of our thoughts? / No! Stab the earl and 'fore the morning sun / Shall vaunt him thrice over the lofty east, / Margaret will meet her Lacy in the heavens.'

G *is for Greenes Groats-worth of Wit, Bought with a Million of Repentance*
This is not actually a play but a tract by Robert Greene satirising the state of the London literary scene in 1592. Various real but anonymised characters come in for criticism – most famously William Shakespeare, who is described as 'an upstart Crow, beautified with our feathers, that with his *Tiger's heart wrapped in a Player's hide*, supposes he is as well able to bombast out a blank verse as the best of you: and being an absolute *Johannes factotum* [Jack of all trades], is in his own conceit the only Shake-scene in a country'. Greene dies a few days before publication. Shakespeare definitely has the last laugh.

H *is for How a Man May Choose a Good Wife from a Bad*
Thomas Heywood's very dark comedy, published in 1602, is the story of Arthur, who acquires a poison in order to murder his wife so he can marry a prostitute. The poison he is given is actually a sleeping potion. Nevertheless, he is found guilty of murder. Only when he is about to be executed does his wife throw off the disguise she has been wearing since she woke up and save him. Frankly, when he has already tried to *kill* her, I think she should have waited until he was dead before revealing her true identity.

I *is for If You Know Not Me, You Know Nobody, or the Troubles of Queen Elizabeth*
Another work by Thomas Heywood. This one mixes up Elizabethan history and a play about a haberdasher called Hobson, whose apprentices run rings about him as they spend time in taverns and with prostitutes. Heywood sensibly waits until 1605 before publishing it, by which

time the Virgin Queen is dead. I am not sure she would have approved.

J *is for The Jew of Malta*
The prologue of Christopher Marlowe's third play, written about 1590, contains the famous line: 'I count religion but a childish toy, / And hold there is no sin but ignorance.' That sets the tone for what follows. Barabas, the Jew of the title, shows very little religious faith but kills, plots and poisons most of the other characters. He switches loyalties repeatedly before receiving his come-uppance at the end, being boiled in a cauldron in a fiery pit that he intends for someone else.

K *is for The Knight of the Burning Pestle*
This remarkable lampoon of old-fashioned chivalric virtue by Francis Beaumont is first performed in 1607. It begins with an interruption by a London merchant in the audience. He gets up and declares indignantly to his fellow audience members that he does not want to see any more plays to the discredit of London or its merchants. The play includes a quotation from Shakespeare's *Henry IV Part One*, which the merchant's servant recites to show he too can act. Unfortunately, Beaumont's inventiveness did not save the play from being a box-office flop. As the publisher admitted in 1613, the audience did not appreciate the fine irony.

L *is for The London Prodigal*
The first edition, published in 1605, has a title page that declares it is by William Shakespeare. It is not: it sounds nothing like Shakespeare. It is about the prodigal son of a London merchant. The merchant disguises himself as a servant and gains employment in his son's household so he can spy on his son's profligate behaviour. Its chief interest for Devonians like me is that one of the prodigal son's love rivals, Oliver, speaks in Devon dialect. This is the first time Devon dialect appears in print. Interestingly, the following year, the real Shakespeare employs Devonshire dialect in the character of Edgar in his *King Lear*. Perhaps the great man contributes the

dialect element of *The London Prodigal*? Perhaps the real author of *The London Prodigal* helps Shakespeare with the Devonian bit of King Lear? Or maybe both authors have a mutual friend from Devon?

M *is for The Merry Devil of Edmonton*
Another anonymous play assigned to the pen of William Shakespeare, published in 1608. It begins with a spirit, Coreb, coming to take the soul of a renowned scholar, Fabell, off to Hell. But Fabell uses the magic he has learned to trap Coreb in a chair. He then forces Coreb to grant him seven more years' liberty on Earth. I like that twist on the theme of unavoidable fate. As Fabell says, 'Man, striving still to find the depth of evil, / Seeking to be a God, becomes a Devil.'

N *is for Northward Ho*
This satire on London society is written by Thomas Dekker and John Webster in 1605. It is a response to *Eastward Ho*, a play written earlier the same year by Ben Jonson, George Chapman and John Marston, which in turn is a response to Dekker and Webster's *Westward Ho*, written in 1604. What about the obvious fourth directional instalment, *Southward Ho*, you may ask? There is no such play – only a Western film of that name, released in 1939, starring Roy Rogers and Trigger. Not quite the same.

O *is for Oberon, the Faery Prince*
We all know the name Oberon as the king of the fairies in Shakespeare's *A Midsummer Night's Dream*. Here the fairy king is the central character in a masque, performed at Westminster in 1611. It is the work of a 'dream team': the text is by Ben Jonson; set design by Inigo Jones; and the music by Alfonso Ferrabosco. The prince of Wales plays the part of Oberon. His mother, Queen Anne, dances on the stage. And part of the set includes a crag which opens up to reveal two live polar bears. What an extravaganza!

P *is for The Parliament of Bees*
The title page of the first edition describes this as 'an

allegorical description of the actions of good and bad men in these our days by John Day'. More of an extended set of dialogues in verse than a play as such, it also features Oberon, king of the fairies. Composed between 1608 and 1616, the text includes a message 'from the book to the reader' which says: 'In my commission I am charg'd to greet / And mildly kisse the hands of all I meet… / For my next heire, who with Poetick breath/ May in sad Elegie record my death. / If so: I wish my Epitaph may be / Onely three words, Opinion murdered me.'

Q *is for the Queen of Carthage*
I have to confess the full title of this play by Christopher Marlowe is *The Tragedy of Dido, Queen of Carthage*, but both the letters T and D are already spoken for in this A–Z – both by other plays by Marlowe. This one is his first, written in or in about 1586. It deals with the love story of the legendary queen deserted by Aeneas, as told by the Roman poet Virgil in his *Aeneid*. Although neither as memorable nor as original as his later plays, it nevertheless marks a significant benchmark in Marlowe's career and is thus an important moment in the history of English drama.

R *is for The Roaring Girl*
Moll Cutpurse is the 'roaring girl' of the title of this play by Thomas Middleton and Thomas Dekker, written about 1605. Moll's character is based on that of a real London woman called Mary Frith. Mary dresses in male attire, smokes a pipe, swears like a trooper, jumps overboard when about to be taken to America, and is the doyenne of all London petty criminals. The play is yet another example of the agency of a clever woman with boundless, unpredictable charisma. When Moll Cutpurse is thought to be of easy virtue because she is wearing men's clothes, she fights and beats the man who is so rash as to presume this. While society might have been legally weighted against women, some do triumph over the adversities stacked against them – and seem all the more glamorous as a result.

S *is for Sir Thomas More*
When an author runs into difficulties with a play – whether these be problems with the authorities over its contents or its literary clumsiness – he might call on his fellow playwrights for help. Anthony Munday hits both types of problem with his *Sir Thomas More*. At least five other writers come to his aid. The heavily annotated original manuscript survives with sections written by Henry Chettle, Thomas Heywood, Thomas Dekker and William Shakespeare. As the manuscripts of all of Shakespeare's own plays are lost (presumably destroyed in the Great Fire of London, if not before), this fragmented play contains the only known literary passages in his own hand.

T *is for Tamburlaine the Great*
Christopher Marlowe's second play is written in two parts in 1587–88. It is one of the principal inspirations for the great histories and tragedies that follow over the next twenty years, including those by Shakespeare. It is dripping with memorable speeches and quotable lines, from 'Accurst be he that first invented war' to 'Virtue is the fount whence honour springs'.

U *is for Usher*
The full title of the play is *The Gentleman Usher*, written in 1602–3. Its author, George Chapman, is famous for translating Homer's *Iliad* and *Odyssey* into English. He also completes Marlowe's unfinished poem, *Hero and Leander*. Small wonder that he is an excellent writer of plays too. The leading character in this comedy, Bassiolo, insinuates himself into the life of Prince Vincentio, to such an extent that the prince urges him to call him Vince and embraces him in a homoerotic manner and lies with him on the floor. Bassiolo also helps Margaret, his master's daughter, write a love letter to Vincentio in a very amusing scene. All the social norms are questioned, from sexual propriety to social hierarchy.

V *is for Volpone, or the Fox*
Ben Jonson's comedy, written in 1606, concerns a Venetian nobleman and the question of the inheritance of his estate.

All the Italian characters have the Italian names of animals. The play includes three English characters too: Sir Politic, Lady Would-be and Peregrine. It is in their company, discussing 'quacksalvers' or 'fellows, that live by venting oils and drugs' that Volpone utters the memorable insult: 'These turdy-facy-nasty-paty-lousy-fartical rogues...'

W is for A Woman Will Have her Will

This is the original title of William Haughton's first play, a comedy written in 1598. A rich Portuguese moneylender, Pisaro, intends to marry off his three half-English daughters to three wealthy foreigners. The daughters, however, want to marry Englishmen. In the end, they prevail. Along the way, there's a lot of cross-dressing and disguise. Interestingly, the real spaces of London – specific streets, the cathedral and the Royal Exchange – also feature for probably the first time on the English stage, making the setting one that all Londoners recognise. The play is renamed *Englishmen for my Money* when it is finally published in 1616.

With the letters X, Y and Z, I have a bit of a problem: I can't find any plays from Shakespeare's lifetime that begin with these letters. So, I ask myself, what would Shakespeare do in such a situation? His advice would probably be to cheat. Make something up. Be inventive. 'But Mr Shakespeare,' I reply, 'Clio, the muse of history, does not allow historians the same latitude with the past as she does playwrights.' 'But what alternative do you have? You can't reasonably end the alphabet with a W.' Ah, but in that word 'end' I have my answer. I know a play where the title ends with an X...

X is for The Phoenix

Thomas Middleton's comedy, first performed in 1604, shows the duke of Ferrara in old age exhorting his son and heir, Phoenix, to go out into the world to see what men and women are really like. Phoenix, wise despite his youth, chooses to stay incognito in his own kingdom with his faithful servant Fidelio. In so doing he uncovers a world of sins: marital abuse, the abuse of the law, selfishness, lust, adultery, attempted incest, justices accepting bribes and attempted murder. At the end, of course, Phoenix reveals himself to his father, and all the malefactors are punished.

Y *is for The Spanish Tragedy (because it ends with a Y)*
Thomas Kyd's best-known play, written in the 1580s, is one of the most influential literary works of all time. The characters are members of the Spanish court and the Portuguese embassy in the wake of Spain's forced annexation of Portugal. Andrea, a dead Spanish officer, is present on stage throughout, along with the personification of revenge. Revenge and rivalry are the principal themes of the play, which sees the deaths of Horatio (Andrea's best friend); Horatio's father and mother; Bel-Imperia (Andrea's and Horatio's sweetheart); her servant; and the sons of the king of Castile and the viceroy of Portugal. With the ghost of a victim, a play within a play and writing that is occasionally raw with real grief, many of the hallmarks of English renaissance drama are here on display. It leaves an indelible mark on Shakespeare and all his tragedy-writing contemporaries.

Z *is for Zweno*
I cannot find a play that begins or ends with a Z. However, there is a character, Zweno, in *Fair Em*, a play written about 1590 and sometimes said to be by William Shakespeare although it most definitely is not. It is perhaps the most inaccurate piece of historical fiction ever. The play contains two plots: one in which William the Conqueror travels to the court of Zweno, king of Denmark, to woo his true love and is beguiled by another woman, Blanch, into accepting her instead. The Fair Em of the title is supposedly the daughter of a Manchester miller who is courted by three men and is deceived by her favourite but accepts the love of the one who remains true to her. At the end, her father is revealed not to be a miller but a wrongly banished knight, whom William the Conqueror pardons.

As you can see, the golden age of the English stage is much more than the thirty-seven plays of William Shakespeare. In addition to the fifteen playwrights named in my little A–Z, I could have mentioned George Peele, Philip Massinger and Thomas Nashe. Also, looking at these plays together, it is striking how daring the dramatic writing of the period is – daring, that is, in both theme as well as literary style. We see here the overturning of norms by the dozen. Women frequently take the lead and assume real agency. Homosexual closeness is displayed. Transvestitism is common and disguises even more so, leading to the upending of the social hierarchy. There is a wealth of creativity in the ways that writers break the 'fourth wall' and integrate their plays and audiences. The dominant themes might be love, lust and the desire for money, power and revenge, but within these themes there is a seemingly limitless capacity to surprise, entertain and draw attention to the deeper meaning of life.

One last thought on the matter of the golden age of English drama. Christopher Marlowe and William Shakespeare are almost exactly the same age: Marlowe was baptised on 26 February 1564 and Shakespeare on 26 April the same year. By the time Marlowe dies in May 1594, he has completed seven plays (counting the two parts of *Tamburlaine the Great* separately). Shakespeare has perhaps completed eight by then (*The Taming of the Shrew*, *Henry VI Parts I–III*, *Richard III*, *Titus Andronicus*, *The Comedy of Errors* and *Two Gentlemen of Verona*). Very few people count these among his finest creations and many would say that Marlowe's *Dr Faustus*, *Edward II* and *Tamburlaine the Great Parts I & II* match or exceed them all. Imagine, then, how we might think of this period differently if it were Shakespeare, not Marlowe, killed in that tavern brawl in 1594. Imagine too that Marlowe lives for another twenty years, writing better and better plays. It is extraordinary to think that of all the possible rivals to Shakespeare for the title of the preeminent playwright in the English language, the man who comes closest is his nearest contemporary. This is the measure of the greatness of the golden age of English drama. We have more than a dozen supremely gifted, original writers and not one but *two* out-and-out geniuses.

And now, having finished our theatrical interlude, let us return to the main A–Z…

U IS FOR UNDERWEAR

Does Queen Elizabeth I wear underwear? Obviously, she wears a chemise or smock and petticoats, like all sixteenth-century women but, to be specific, does she wear drawers? Most women don't. When dealing with bleeding, they wrap 'menstrual cloths' around themselves. But Queen Elizabeth's wax funeral effigy in Westminster Abbey sports a pair of woollen drawers. There is no doubt that Elizabethan *men* normally wear drawers (albeit made of linen, not wool) but do high-status women?

To answer this question we need to look further afield. Catherine de' Medici, queen of France, apparently wears woven drawers; she introduces them to the ladies of the French court in 1533, when she marries Henri, duke of Orléans, the future king of France. A decorated sixteenth-century pair are in the Metropolitan Museum of Art in New York. Looking at them, the embroidery starts to give away a few secrets. These garments are meant to be seen, even though they are not normally on show. This tallies with a few references in late-medieval Italian literature to courtesans wearing drawers. In short, as with Moll Cutpurse in the play *The Roaring Girl*, people presume that if a woman wears clothes like a man, she must be 'up for it', especially if the clothes in question are intimate and revealing. There is also the physical evidence from Lengberg Castle in Austria, where several linen brassieres and pairs of ladies' drawers dating from the start of the sixteenth century have been found, hidden under a floor. Such items are erotica. If you are an Elizabethan gentleman and you suspect your wife of having an affair with her dancing master, and you see her putting on a pair of drawers before going out to meet him in her carriage, you have good reason to be worried. It is ironic that these days we think of 'going commando' as the naughtier option.

This is a very long way of saying that I don't think Queen Elizabeth ever wears drawers. I think the woollen ones on her effigy are there for the sake of decency. They are brown and shapeless. They are *not* items of erotica – the merest glimpse would put you off sex for a month. But perhaps that's why she remains the Virgin Queen.

V IS FOR VAGABONDAGE

When we talk about Elizabeth I as Gloriana and England as experiencing a 'golden age', we have to remember that thousands of people are starving. Indeed, it is often said that the famine of 1597 is the last time that people starve to death in large numbers in the south of England (1623 is the last major famine in the north). Obviously that's not true for some other parts of the British Isles or other parts of Europe – people are still starving to death in their millions in France in the 1690s and in Ireland in the 1840s. But in England the 1590s are when that bitter suffering starts to come to an end. In 1597 the Old Poor Law is reformed in such a way as to make parish authorities responsible for the upkeep of destitute people in their locality. Rates are levied on the inhabitants, and the overseers of the poor in each place distribute alms as necessary. Together with a sophisticated market system, which means almost no one in the country is more than two hours' walk away from a market, food is circulated and made available to those who need it.

The catalyst for the 1597 Act for the Relief of the Poor is the desperation of the people. There are large numbers on the road. Whole gangs of orphaned children roam their neighbourhoods, begging and stealing because they have no other way of feeding themselves.

The root cause of the problem is population expansion. The number of people in England at the start of Elizabeth's reign is about 3.1 million; by the end, it is about 4.2 million. That is a rise of 30 per cent in four decades. Imagine if the population of England were to rise by that degree today: we'd have problems dealing with housing and feeding an extra 15 million people. But no one in Elizabethan England is collecting the relevant statistics so they do not know what is happening or why. No one is able to make provision for all these extra people. All they see is the consequences – the homelessness, the gangs of youths, the criminal activity, the increased dangers of robbery – and apply the old vagabondage laws with an extra degree of harshness. These date back to the late fourteenth century, when people started roaming the countryside looking for work in the wake of the Black Death. They are designed to keep people in their place of birth. But if there is neither work nor food for them there, what are they supposed to do?

Richard Carew, writing in 1600, says he does not believe any other English county has as many impoverished people as his native Cornwall. At the other side of the country, William Lambarde remarks on increasing numbers of homeless people in Kent. In Lancashire in 1597 a gang of twenty beggars is found to include twelve boys under fifteen and three under the age of five. In Stratford-upon-Avon in 1601 it is estimated there are about 700 homeless people sleeping in barns. In London it is said that 30,000 are living rough. And for all these people, the law is their enemy. If you're homeless and living outside your own parish it's *illegal* for somebody else to give you shelter. Householders can be fined £1 for looking after a homeless couple, even if they have done nothing wrong. If you see a cart trundling through the street with a half-naked man or a half-naked woman tied to the rear, being whipped by a man walking behind them, that is someone who has committed the crime of being homeless. Elizabeth's reign might be a golden age for many, especially when seen through the rose-tinted spectacles of patriotic hindsight, but if you're down and out on the streets of an Elizabethan town, it is an age of misery.

W IS FOR WOMEN

As you may already be aware, the idea of equality in Elizabethan England is about as common as the idea of travelling to the moon. It is considered to be about as natural too. Men regularly point out that women are not only smaller and generally weaker than they are but also suffer more diseases. Therefore God must have put men in charge for a reason. And the reason, they say, is because women are fickle temptresses. Did not Eve tempt Adam with an apple in the Garden of Eden? And was the result not Mankind being thrown out of Paradise? Most men don't think they need to say any more on the matter.

As a result, all the sex-related inequalities of medieval England are alive and well in Elizabethan times. It doesn't matter that there is a woman on the throne: this is still very much a man's world. A woman cannot vote or go to university. She cannot become a lawyer, ambassador or clergyman. She cannot become an alderman or the mayor of a town. There are very few schools for women. Even if a noblewoman inherits a title in her own right, she can't sit in Parliament. And all the legal disadvantages of marriage are still in force: a wife must do her husband's bidding and cannot give evidence in court against him; her property is legally his, and so on.

Having said all that, you cannot help but notice how every visitor from the Continent remarks on what freedoms Englishwomen have in comparison to women in Holland, Germany, Italy and France. Englishwomen can leave the house by themselves and go for walks or ride together with other women, unchaperoned. They can go shopping in the local market unaccompanied. They can go to taverns or alehouses and listen to music when their husbands are not present – although admittedly not by themselves, to avoid accusations of immorality. I don't know who first coins the phrase that 'England is a paradise for married women, a purgatory for servants and a hell for horses,' but it is certainly repeated by several foreign visitors in Elizabeth's reign.

Literacy is another reason to suppose things are gradually improving for women. Throughout history men have been able to presume that, if they write something, their audience will be exclusively male. The handful of medieval women who can read can't reach out to a supportive female audience. In fact, they are doubly compromised: if a woman writes anything in retaliation to the sexual prejudices of the day, only men will read it. Hence all the laws are written from a male perspective. But that is now changing. As mentioned previously, more than 10 per cent of the female population can read and write by 1600. This means they can respond to books by men without having to ask men to be intermediaries. Women can write their own books attacking men for their sexism. And women can write to entertain each other as well as defend their sex.

One woman who does all these things is Emilia Lanier, the fourth published poetess in the English language. In 1611, she produces *Salve Deus Rex Judaeorum* in which she takes issue with the widespread belief among men that God made them stronger in order that they should command women for their mutual benefit. She also hits back at the idea that the Fall of Man occurred because Eve tempted Adam in the Garden of Eden. Her argument – forgive me for paraphrasing – runs along these lines: 'If God created men to be stronger because he intended them to take responsibility for women – with the implication that it is God's will that women should follow their husband's commands – then, when Eve offered Adam the apple and *he accepted it*, he failed in that responsibility. Thus the Fall of Man was *his* fault, not hers.'

Touché.

X IS FOR XENOPHOBIA

There is a general misapprehension about Elizabethan England which is that as long as you're baptised in the Christian faith, you have a relatively easy time of things. This is a falsehood. The sixteenth century sees a growing fear of black people, especially those from sub-Saharan African. This isn't noticeable before the slaving missions; we don't find polemical or underhand racism in previous reigns. However, as the slave trade becomes normalised, so too does racist language and imagery. Robert Gainsh, writing in 1554 after one of the earliest English slave-trading expeditions, refers to black people as 'of beastly living... without a God, law, religion or Commonwealth... [among them] women are common for they contract no matrimony, neither have [they] respect to chastity'. In 1578, George Best puts forward the idea that black people are all the descendants of Noah's son Cham, who was cursed by God for having sex with his wife on the Ark. In 1584 Reginald Scot refers to the devil as having dark skin like a black man. By the 1590s, playwrights such as Christopher Marlowe and George Peele are describing black men being used as beasts of burden to draw rulers in their chariots. In 1596 the Privy Council gives permission to a German trader to buy black people in England and ship them abroad – a ruling based purely on the colour of their skin.

I find it difficult to escape the conclusion that the rise of this racist packaging is part and parcel of the Christian guilt for profiting from the slave trade. Or perhaps 'guilt' is not the right word. Perhaps a better expression is 'denial of humanity'. By emphasising the lack of Christian values among black people and denying them full human status, these writers are trying to justify buying and selling human beings. That certainly will go down well in those gentlemen's houses where enslaved black people are kept as servants. Denying humanity legitimises any amount of cruel behaviour – at home and abroad – including lending out black females for sexual experimentation among one's friends, as attested by several parish registers.

Sometimes, when confronted by the shallowness of our cruelty, I fear we do not deserve to call ourselves *homo sapiens* – 'wise man'. In promoting war, tolerating social inequality and advocating racism – and in our selfish desire to enrich ourselves even at the risk of destroying our own world – we prove ourselves unworthy of that title *sapiens*.

Y IS FOR YOUR ANCESTORS

In the course of this short A–Z, we've covered some horrific things: cruelty to animals, women and children; the 'Heinz 57 varieties' of the death penalty; low expectations of life at birth; nasty illnesses; poor standards of cleanliness; torture, sexism, misogyny and xenophobia. It hardly makes a glossy travel brochure for Elizabethan England. It is therefore all the more remarkable that society pulls itself out of this pit. Does it not amaze you that amidst all these terrible sufferings, we thrive and produce the most magnificent music, build stunning architectural masterpieces, learn to read and write on a scale never previously seen, and produce some of the greatest literature known to humanity?

I wonder if some of the suffering contributes to the achievements. It is as if the will to conquer adversity leads us to triumph in other walks of life. I am sure you know the famous Orson Welles joke in the film *The Third Man* – that 300 years of war and bloodshed in Italy gives us Michelangelo, Leonardo da Vinci and the Italian Renaissance, whereas 500 years of peace and democracy in Switzerland produces the cuckoo clock. Welles was clearly a better raconteur than a historian – you would not consider an army of sixteenth-century Swiss pikemen exactly a symbol of peace – but the general idea that a people can face calamities and turn them to their advantage is not only inspiring but perhaps true. In England, we have a century of the Wars of the Roses, religious division and persecution, appalling crime and homelessness, plague, starvation and infant mortality and what do we end up with? The plays and poetry of William Shakespeare, Christopher Marlowe and many other writers whose works will be admired for as long as the English language is spoken.

Y is therefore for 'your ancestors' because it is *your* ancestors who face all these terrors and make this remarkable transition. You might not be descended from William Shakespeare or Christopher Marlowe but you are descended from people who know them. Your ancestors laugh at their jokes and watch open-mouthed as their heroes speak of human life and suffering. Depending on how old you are and how many of your ancestral lines arise in England, you have perhaps 12,000 ancestors alive in this country in Elizabeth's reign. That's an awful lot of relatives to call on if you do find yourself visiting. But your existence depends on every single one of them. They suffer and survive. Among them are those who commit injustices and exploit their fellow men and women. Also among them are the victims of those injustices. In their descendants – in you – they all now make their peace.

Z IS FOR ZENITH

What cultural achievement of Elizabethan England stands comparison with the cathedrals of the Middle Ages? I don't think anyone would give me any credit if I did not say it is the zenith of English literature. Shakespeare's plays and sonnets in particular are the pinnacle. It's not his plots or even his stories that hold me, still less his history. It is his use of words: his monologues, especially his meditations on life.

Isn't it incredible that a man who knows so few of the changes that society has experienced in modern times can speak so fully and eloquently for us? It suggests that our fundamental characteristics have not changed hugely since his time. Ask almost any reasonably well-educated person if they know any Shakespeare and they will start quoting any number of lines from *Hamlet* ('Brevity is the soul of wit', 'the rest is silence', 'Alas, poor Yorick', 'the Lady protests too much, methinks', or the soliloquy, 'To be or not to be'). Otherwise it will be *Macbeth* (either 'Is this a dagger I see before me?' or the soliloquy, 'She should have died hereafter'); *Romeo and Juliet* (either 'Romeo, Romeo, wherefore art thou Romeo?' or 'What's in a name? A rose by any name would smell as sweet'); *King Lear* (either 'I am a man more sinned against than sinning' or 'Nothing will come from nothing'); *Twelfth Night* (either 'If music be the food of love, play on' or 'Some are born great, some achieve greatness and some have greatness thrust upon them'), *Richard III* (either 'Now is the winter of our discontent' or 'A horse, a horse, my kingdom for a horse'; *The Merchant of Venice* ('All that glisters is not gold'); or *As You Like It* ('All the world's a stage and all the men and women merely players'). Just there we have seventeen quotations that almost everyone knows and lives by, more than 400 years after his death. What's more, this is true internationally. Wherever you travel abroad, you see advertisements for productions of Shakespeare's works in the local language. There can hardly have been a day in the last hundred years when there wasn't a production of one of his plays being staged somewhere in the world.

To my mind, Shakespeare's upbringing in the Midlands is part of the secret of his success. He is, in every respect, in the middle of things. He is neither from the north nor the south. He is both a provincial and a Londoner, spending most of his adult life in the capital. He is acquainted with the court but, in walking with kings, he never loses the common touch. He is educated but not to the extent that he speaks in tongues unfamiliar to the common man and woman. His success brings him financial rewards but not so much he can be reckoned amongst the gentry. I am sure that, in being away from his wife and children for such long periods, his passions induce him to have several romantic affairs – perhaps even many. He knows guilt and grief as well as anyone. His plays are not just tragedies but also comedies and histories – he sees all the elements of human nature. In so many ways, he stands in the very midst of human life and experience.

Shakespeare occupies a position in the middle of time too – neither wholly part of the old medieval world of lordly violence and royal tyranny nor wholly of the post-medieval world of parliamentary sovereignty, scientific discoveries and economic planning. He himself witnesses the last major famine to blight southern England before the Old Poor Law renders famine a thing of the past. He speaks of the natural, unfettered society to which we know society could easily return, if we were to see our economies collapse and the trappings of our modernity washed away. He thus remains a spokesman for both our own inner selves and for those of earlier, earthier times: a wizard like Merlin from the Middle Ages yet a man always on the brink of a Brave New World. This remarkable man really is 'for *all* time' as Ben Jonson says of him. And although he is not alone of his generation in achieving greatness in the written word, I imagine his works will outlast even the medieval cathedrals.

PART THREE

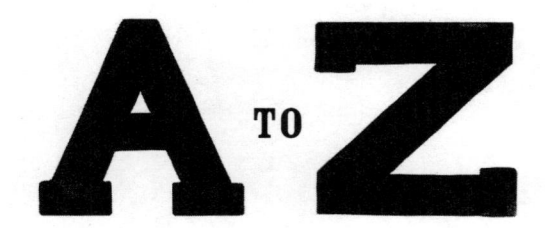

A TO Z

OF RESTORATION ENGLAND

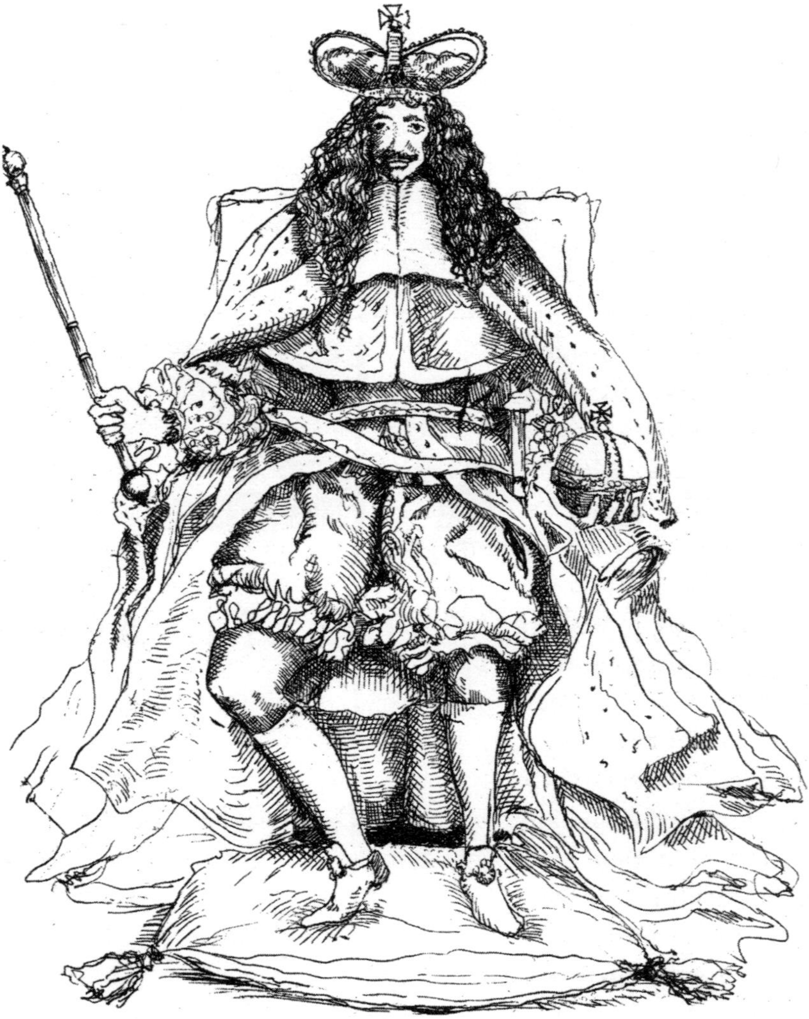

RESTORATION ENGLAND

1660–1700

The four decades from 1660 to 1700 are perhaps the most underappreciated in all English history. Popular history magazines regularly splash their covers with articles on the Romans, Anglo-Saxons, Vikings, Middle Ages, Wars of the Roses, Tudors, Civil Wars, Georgians, Regency, Victorians, Edwardians, World War I, World War II and the Swinging Sixties. But it is unusual to see banners carrying the names of the late Stuart kings, Charles II, James II and William III, or discussions of the Restoration of the monarchy itself, or its cultural and social achievements. I find this disappointing. As a researcher, I sometimes come across profound changes in the late seventeenth century that matter to all of us. Naturally, I want to talk about them. But often I am made to feel as if I have turned up on someone's doorstep campaigning on behalf of an unpopular political party. If it weren't for Charles II and his lust for women – and Samuel Pepys and *his* lust for women – the last forty years of the century would pass largely unnoticed.

How wrong this is! This is the age of iconic events, such as the Great Fire of London, the last Great Plague and the expansion of British influence in India, the West Indies and America. It sees the development of new ways of thinking – not least of which is Isaac Newton's pioneering efforts in mathematical science and groundbreaking movements in various forms of quantitative analysis. It is one of the most culturally stimulating periods in English history – from the mad antics of the rakes and the rebirth of English theatre to the introduction of champagne and fine wines, not to mention tea and the development of coffee houses. Nor should we forget that the Restoration of the monarchy in May 1660 marks the *end* of many things too. It sees the conscious turning away from failed experiments in government and old ways of thinking. It draws a line under the past and defines this period as something new. Thus we begin with...

A FOR ABOLITION

When Charles II returns to England as king in May 1660 there is near-universal rejoicing. The last twenty years have seen so much controversy and tension that no one looks back wistfully on the Commonwealth. In fact, I don't think the royal family has ever been so popular. Charles II literally comes to the rescue – to mend divisions and restore law and order. How many other kings can honestly say they have rescued their people? Most of the time, the boot is on the other foot.

The year 1660 is arguably the second most important date in English history, after 1066. It sees so much change at every level of society. The diarist and gentleman of letters, John Evelyn, refers to the previous troubles as 'a most bloody rebellion of nearly twenty years' and that is how it must appear to many men and women of his vintage. Laying aside the politics, society has been turned upside down over and over again. In 1642 all the theatres are permanently closed. It doesn't matter how respected Shakespeare is: the Globe Theatre becomes a block of tenements. Christmas is turned into a fast day in 1644. It is abolished altogether in 1647 along with Easter and Whitsun. That's a bad move, in my opinion. If you want to curry favour with the people, don't abolish Christmas. But that is what happens. If you are caught making plum pudding or mince pies in December 1648, or if you have holly and ivy around the door to your house, you can be reported to the magistrates. People who are not of a Puritanical disposition conjure up an imaginary figure to protest against this repression. He is portrayed as a man with a long white beard and called 'Old Father Christmas'.

Then we come to 1649. The monarchy is more than just abolished; it is literally decapitated. All the bishops are sacked too and so is the House of Lords. Some people might approve but I would urge you to be careful what you wish for. Violent revolutions rarely result in compromises or moderation. In this case, the consequence is an unleashing of severe moral judgement. In 1650 Parliament passes the Adultery Act. This makes it punishable by death to commit adultery. It sounds extreme but this is the thinking of the time. Hanging people is not seen as a moral problem but the *solution* to moral problems.

Just in case you yourself are a Puritan and reckon that this sort of legislation sends the right messages: think again. It is not just about messages. People die. Obviously, it is very difficult to prove a man guilty of adultery so those hanged in accordance with the Adultery Act are married women who are killed for having children conceived during their husband's absence. One such woman is Susan Bounty, from north Devon. Her husband, Richard, spends a long time away from home and when he returns unexpectedly to find her pregnant, he is more than surprised. But the new legislation allows him to get his revenge. He reports her to the magistrates who try her, find her guilty of adultery and sentence her to death. She is imprisoned for as long as it takes to give birth to her son and then she is dragged off to the gallows and hanged. And her child is given to her husband, the man who reported her. That amounts to a sickening vindictiveness that cynically takes advantage of the legal system. It is not justice.

The general thinking is that everything that is immoral should be regarded as a felony. *Conform with puritanism or die* is the message. Blasphemy becomes a capital offence as well. You would have thought that people would be up in arms, calling for an end to such draconian measures. But, if anything, people say the opposite. Some magistrates feel that there should be *more* women hanged for adultery, not fewer. This isn't just a repressive system: it is one built on fear. Everyone has to be seen to be living a morally irreproachable, pious life. It's a bit like living in communist Russia when people might snitch on you to the secret police – except the secret police in this case believe they have God on their side. Meanwhile the economy is in free-fall. By the time Oliver Cromwell, the Lord Protector, dies in September 1658, England is on its knees. There is no head of state. There are only generals and troops – and no one to pay them. If you think a country could get along fine without someone in charge, you only need to look at England in the year 1659 to realise that this is not the case. As John Evelyn writes in his diary,

> The army now turned out Parliament. We [have] now no government in the nation; all in confusion; no magistrate either owned or pretended but the soldiers, and they not agreed. God almighty have mercy on us and settle us!

Into this chaos steps Charles II. He is not a Puritan – he already has an illegitimate child of his own, James Scott, the future duke of Monmouth. Moreover, in many people's eyes, he is already the rightful king, having automatically inherited that position on the death of Charles I. But can Charles II be persuaded to return to the kingdom that killed his father? General George Monck is the man who tells him it is his duty. His country needs him. When Charles II sets foot on English soil, there is exultation up and down the land. Everybody breathes a huge sigh of relief. We have stable government once again and we have a king who's going to abolish puritanism forever.

Welcome to the Restoration – and the return of the king; the return of bishops; the return of playhouses – and the opening of a brilliant new chapter in England's history.

B IS FOR BUILDING

Prior to 1650, town houses are still timber framed. Normally they have the old jettied upper storeys leaning out over the street, like their precursors from the previous four centuries. Indeed, many of their medieval ancestors are still to be seen in the lanes and alleys of towns up and down the country. That's true of London too. If you do a whistlestop tour of the city centre just before the Great Fire in 1666, you'll see it is almost entirely wooden. There are a few new stone and brick buildings, of which the most striking is the grand Palladian portico added to the west end of Old St Paul's Cathedral, designed by Inigo Jones. Otherwise, the new developments are all in the area to the west of Drury Lane.

This focal point – known today as the West End – is all-important. Queen Elizabeth I forbids anyone from building here because she wants to keep the ordinary people a good distance away from her palace at Whitehall. After her death, James I and Charles I prove almost as nervous as Elizabeth about the prospect of ordinary people building in the vicinity of Whitehall Palace. But rather than ban construction outright, they sell licences to aristocratic developers and lay down architectural rules as to what a town house should look like. The standard that emerges is one of terraces of fine houses that collectively resemble great palaces. Each terrace is composed of harmoniously proportioned brick buildings with stone ornamentation and a balustrade on top. There are no jettied upper storeys reaching over the streets. And the streets themselves do not have drains down the middle to collect all the refuse but a camber in the centre, with gutters and pavements on the sides. All these new terraces are centred on the first such new development, Covent Garden Piazza, designed by Inigo Jones for the earl of Bedford in 1631. Modern town planning in England starts on this spot, with townhouses that the aristocracy vie for.

Then comes the Great Fire.

We will have a close look at what the Great Fire is like later, but for now suffice to say it destroys 13,200 houses and clears 436 acres of land. It doesn't touch the nascent West End but it devastates the old city. It clears away all the old halls of the livery companies, the Royal Exchange and about a hundred churches. And it presents town planners with the chance of completely rethinking the area. Christopher Wren and John Evelyn both draw up plans for a new street layout, making use of piazzas like Inigo Jones's Covent Garden Piazza. The problem is that, if you are a Londoner and you have just lost everything apart from the patch of ground where you used to live, the last thing you want is for someone to place a flashy new piazza for aristocratic housing on the still-smoking site of your old home. You don't sell that bit of land but hang on to it because it is all you've got. As a result, London is not rebuilt with piazzas and boulevards but along its old, medieval street plan.

The new houses planned after the Great Fire follow the idea of an idealised pattern, first formulated with regard to the terraces of the West End. Houses on a main street need to be four storeys high, not including the cellar or attic, and to have ground floors with a 10ft ceiling. They must have first floors with a 10½ft ceiling and bedrooms with 9ft ceilings and rooms at the top with ceilings 8½ft high. Lesser streets are to have three-storey houses with lower ceilings; alleys are to have two-storey houses with yet lower ceilings. This being the capital, of course, large amounts of money are available for the great rebuilding and it takes only a few years to complete. And since everyone of note at this period knows someone who lives in London, there is a sudden, widespread realisation of what a modern town can look like. Merchants and local leaders in provincial England can all see what *their* town could look like. It is no exaggeration to say that the Great Fire 'sparks' a revolution in urban design that rapidly spreads across the whole country.

C IS FOR COLD

If you are planning a trip to the late seventeenth century, I would strongly recommend packing thermal underwear. These are the coldest decades of what historians refer to as the Little Ice Age. In the twenty-first century, the average temperature for the three-month winter period – that is, December, January and February – is 3.7 degrees centigrade, day and night. In the winter of 1683 to 1684, it is minus 1.2 degrees. People call it the Long Frost. The sea is frozen for a mile out from the Kentish coast. No boats can get into any of the southern English ports until the end of February. John Evelyn and his wife sit up in bed once a week to read the European newsletters to each other. However, during the Long Frost, they don't have any deliveries for about six weeks. Then all six weeks' worth of newsletters come at once. Mr and Mrs Evelyn sit up very late each night, conscientiously reading them all.

In case the Long Frost doesn't put you off visiting Restoration England, consider this. Four of the twelve months of the year have their all-time lowest recorded temperature in this period. Remarkably, none of them is from the winter of the Long Frost. The coldest-ever average temperature for the whole month of March is 1674. The coldest-ever May is 1698. The coldest-ever July is 1695 and the coldest-ever September 1694. You will notice that three of those records are set in the 1690s. That's the same decade that sees repeated harvest failures across Europe on account of the cold weather. Ten per cent of the population of France dies. That's 2 million people. Ten per cent of Scandinavia perishes too, and 10 per cent of Ireland. Ten per cent of Scotland either starves or emigrates to England or Poland. When historians talk about this being the Little Ice Age, we are not just saying it's a bit nippy.

D IS FOR DRINKING

If anything makes up for the extreme cold of the late seventeenth century, it is the drink. Wine might be older than the *Iliad* and *Odyssey* but the wines that we know today originate in the late seventeenth century. So too do the hot drinks. They are not always drunk in the same ways that we drink them but the important point is that they are available. If you find yourself gasping for a cuppa after watching a Restoration drama, relief is at hand.

Let's start at the top of the drinks menu with champagne. These days only sparkling wine from the Champagne region of France can be called champagne. Thus it might come as a surprise to you to hear that it is developed in English wine cellars. The reason for this is that the Champagne region has a number of cold snaps, which mean there is often an unwelcome *petéance* or effervescence in the wine as the result of a second fermentation. Far from being the inventor of champagne, the real Dom Perignon is a master winemaker who tries to stop this effervescence and make champagne a still drink. It's more than a little ironic that he is now celebrated for what he would have considered the failure of his life's work.

How come it develops in *English* wine cellars?

If you store champagne in French wine bottles, when that second fermentation takes place, the bottles explode with the pressure. But English wine bottles are stronger. So when wine from the Champagne region is bottled in England and the English cold is allowed to replicate the chills of the Champagne region, the second fermentation in the bottle creates the fizz. In 1676 George Etheredge mentions 'sparkling champagne' in a drinking song in his play, *The Man of Mode*:

> At the plays we are constantly making our court,
> And when they are ended we follow the sport
> To the Mall and the Park,
> Where we love till 'tis dark.
> Then sparkling champagne
> Puts an end to their reign;
> It quickly recovers
> Poor languishing lovers,
> Makes us frolic and gay, and drowns all our sorrow;
> But, alas! we relapse again on the morrow.

As for other fine wines, this is also the age that sees the birth of the great clarets. The four famous first growths of Bordeaux – Chateau Haut-Brion, Chateau Lafite, Chateau Latour and Chateau Margaux – all have their origins in this period. The wines are finer than any previously known. The Pontac family, owners of the Haut-Brion estate, start importing extremely good clarets to England in the 1660s. Charles II is very fond of them. Pepys too has a taste of Chateau Haut-Brion in April 1663 and declares it 'a good and most particular taste that I never met with'. Soon afterwards, every English gentleman is trying them. The philosopher John Locke loves Haut-Brion so much he goes to France to visit the vineyard. But I have to say, it costs a fortune. An Act of 1660 stipulates that ordinary wine from France should be sold at no more than 8d per quart and Rhenish wine at no more than 1s. But the Pontac family charge 7s for a quart bottle of Haut-Brion at their fashionable London tavern, Pontac's Head – known simply as Pontac's to the cognoscenti.

The last type of alcoholic drink I should mention is spirits. This period is when brandy and gin take off in a big way. They're not controlled by the same legislation that puts duties on wine, so for a long time they're very cheap. Even the best French brandy costs just 1s per bottle. One writer notes how in 1670 all of Kent is drunk on brandy. Gin is even cheaper. We haven't quite reached the gin craze of the mid-eighteenth century, when it is said in London you can be drunk for a penny and dead drunk for tuppence, but we're well on our way. In case you're wondering, the Scots have started distilling whisky by 1700 but it has yet to come south of the border. Rum, distilled from molasses, is easily available, although it is still referred to as 'rumbullion' or 'kill-water'.

That's not the limit of what may be distilled by adventurous Restoration men and women. They develop the idea that distilling something gives you its essence, so they start distilling all sorts of supposedly nutritious and medicinal things. Ever fancied distilled snails? Distilled chickens? They are available. If I were you, though, I'd stick to the port that starts to be brought here from Portugal at this time. I can't guarantee that it tastes better than distilled chickens but I am prepared to give it the benefit of the doubt.

If it's something less alcoholic you want, you can choose from coffee, tea and chocolate. The first coffee house opens in Oxford in 1650, the first in London two years later. Then their numbers mushroom. By 1663 there are eighty-two coffee houses in London, and by the end of the century, about a thousand. Note that they do not admit women. Gentlemen pay a penny or tuppence for coffee, to read newspapers and financial reports, and to discuss anything and everything apart from religion, which is strictly forbidden in most coffee houses.

Women are much more likely to drink tea. This arrives in England in 1658. But don't put the kettle on immediately: it costs £10 per lb when it first goes on sale. Things ease up in 1660, when a London coffee-house proprietor called Thomas Garway decides that tea is the next big thing and offers it for sale at a loss, charging just 16s per lb. But then the government puts a tax on it. It remains expensive for the rest of the century. There are three types: Bohea, which is a black tea; Singlo which is blue-green; and imperial green-leaf Bing, the most expensive of the lot. These are all drunk without milk in this period, although some people add sugar. Sir Kenelm Digby recommends adding egg yolks. Despite the cost, it becomes the non-alcoholic drink of choice for ladies of quality. Of course, the porcelain teapot and dishes are also expensive because they are imported from China.

Chocolate is a great secret in the early seventeenth century, closely guarded by the Spanish and the Portuguese. But in 1655 the English take control of Jamaica and capture the cacao trees, the cocoa beans *and* the secret of chocolate. So from the 1660s onwards you can have chocolate for breakfast in London. It comes in the form of a cake that you break up into pieces and dissolve in hot water. You might have it with sherry or port or even with egg yolks, as Pepys does. It's considered to be good for you, clearing out the system after you've been drinking the night before. Unsurprisingly, Pepys often has it for breakfast.

E IS FOR EXPLORATION

In May 1662, Charles II marries Catherine of Braganza, the daughter of the king of Portugal. This opens the door to the establishment of a new empire. She brings with her as part of her dowry two important ports: one on the north coast of Africa, Tangiers, and the other on the southwest coast of India, 'Bom Bahia' – literally, 'good bay' in Portuguese, better known to us as Bombay, or Mumbai. Tangiers does not last long in the cabinet of English territorial curiosities but Charles II hands over Bombay to the East India Company, which then establishes its eastern headquarters there. This stronghold allows the English traders to exploit India and the Far East. Not only does Charles II grant them the port but also the rights to mint their own money, make war, defend outposts with fortifications, and exercise jurisdiction in legal matters. The long-term results are both unpalatable and extraordinary – a cultural mélange that in retrospect is as obnoxious as it is educational and empowering. But whatever your thoughts on empires, there is no doubt that the establishment of the English as a major force in Eastern trade and culture reaches a new level in this period.

To illustrate some of the more positive aspects of exploration in the late seventeenth century, let's focus on two widely-travelled men to give you a glimpse of how geographical knowledge is obtained and circulates in the most unexpected quarters.

The first fellow is William Dampier from Somerset. In 1669, aged eighteen, he becomes an apprentice seaman. That is an odd thing to do for a young gentleman in the seventeenth century. But so too is studying soil types and recording the prevailing winds on his mother's farm. After a short spate in the Royal Navy, he is engaged on a sugar plantation in Jamaica but soon leaves that and sets out for Mexico. Unfortunately, he falls in with pirates. This is the more questionable side of his exploits, to say the least. As the years pass, he becomes more experienced in running a ship until in 1686 he decides to move on. He joins the captain of the *Cygnet*, sailing across the Pacific to Guam. He describes all the plants he sees, and becomes the first Englishman to write about breadfruit, bananas and plantain. In early 1688 his ship becomes the first English vessel to land on the coast of Australia. What does a thirty-seven-year-old ex-pirate do in such circumstances? He decides to spend six weeks sketching the local flora and fauna, of course. He also becomes a full-time adventurer, undertaking extraordinary feats such as canoeing 130 miles across the open sea to Sumatra. After exploring much of southeast Asia, he returns to England in September 1691, now aged forty. It is largely an accident that he has circumnavigated the globe over the last twelve years but, nevertheless, he thereby becomes the third English captain to do so, after Francis Drake in 1580 and Thomas Cavendish in 1588. He publishes a narrative of his exploits, entitled *A New Voyage Around the World*, in 1697.

Dampier's book makes him a celebrity. Famous people and men of letters, such as Samuel Pepys, John Evelyn and Hans Sloane, want to meet him. But having read that he has consorted with pirates, the gentlemen of the Admiralty are equally keen to have a little chat. Dampier manages to get out of that pickle and soon heads back out to sea. He ends up inadvertently circumnavigating the world a second time. And as if to prove that, once lightning has struck twice, it is bound to do so again, he circumnavigates the world yet again a few years later. On the third trip he rescues Alexander Selkirk – the man who becomes the model for Daniel Defoe's *Robinson Crusoe* – after the poor chap has spent seven years on the island Juan Fernandez in the South Pacific.

I have to admit, Dampier isn't the easiest of men to get along with. He is court martialled for cruelty and many people think he is better at navigating perilous seas than managing personal relationships. However, he is an incredibly resourceful and courageous student of the planet. Unlike most people, he is prepared to risk his life to satisfy his curiosity.

Another man who travels to the ends of the earth to satisfy his curiosity is Shen Fu-Zong. He is a Chinese convert to Roman Catholicism who visits England in 1687. By then he's already spent four years in Europe at the instigation of the Jesuit missionary and sinologist, Philippe Couplet. The two men have been working together on a translation of the mighty Latin edition of the works of Confucius, published in Paris in 1687. On arrival in England, Shen meets various luminaries and men of letters in London, before going to Oxford to work on listing the Oriental collections of the Bodleian. He helps the librarian to catalogue all the Chinese books, almanacks, tables, trinkets and other things that explorers have collected. Shen's hope is to take his knowledge of Europe back to China. To this end he leaves England the following year. Sadly, he doesn't fulfil his dream, dying in 1691 in Mozambique on the way home. Nevertheless, his visit is an indication that curiosity about the world is not just a Western phenomenon.

F IS FOR FIRE

People are somewhat careless with the matches in the late seventeenth century. You've heard of the Great Fire of London, which breaks out in Pudding Lane on the night of 2 September 1666. Within four days, 13,200 houses have been destroyed, displacing 80,000 people. The temperature in the heart of the conflagration exceeds 2,000 degrees centigrade. Eyewitnesses talk about the terrible roaring and crashing as the fire tears through the city, destroying everything in its path. But that's just one of *ten* major fires mentioned in Pepys's diary for the 1660s. On top of all those conflagrations, you'll want to avoid the Little Fire of London, which destroys 600 houses in Southwark in 1676. In fact, you can go around the whole country like this, listing the towns that have major fires. Some places are totally obliterated. Southwold in Suffolk, for example, is completely destroyed in 1659, and Bungay, also in Suffolk, in 1688.

In 1675, a few days after the Great Fire of Northampton has destroyed four-fifths of the town, the travel writer Thomas Baskerville drops by. When he reaches the remains of the town centre, he finds one small inn still standing amidst the devastation. It is appropriately called 'The Last' because its sign is a shoemaker's last. Baskerville notices that, above the door, there is a sign reading, 'I have sought after good ale over the town and here I have found it at last.' But he cannot help wondering how this building alone has survived. It is only made of lathe and plaster: it too should have been incinerated. So he goes inside. There he finds the innkeeper in his leather apron, who tells him that when the fire broke out, the regular drinkers decided to help save the pub. Together they hoisted hogsheads of beer out of the cellar up on to the roof and gradually poured the liquid down the walls to cool those parts that were likely to catch. This is surely a major landmark in the annals of English firefighting. In Northampton in 1675 a bunch of men take it upon themselves to fight fire with beer – and win.

G IS FOR GRAND DESIGNS

You might have heard of the long-running TV programme, *Grand Designs*, in which the presenter accompanies an optimistic couple on their quest to build an original and architecturally inspiring new home. The couple concerned nearly always run out of money. Often they fall out with their contractors; sometimes they discover that something terrible such as subsidence affects their site. The camera then dwells on their despondent faces as they contemplate the water-filled muddy hole in the ground into which they have poured their life savings. But imagine an episode of *Grand Designs* set in Restoration England.

Some of the most ambitious building projects ever undertaken date from this period. Many a lord gazes in the rain at a muddy excavation in much the same way that participants in *Grand Designs* do. As Lord Townsend remarks, when his brother writes to say he is coming with his family to visit him at Raynham Hall, 'I should be very glad to see him if I had any rooms to lodge him but I have taken down so much of my house and have so many workmen in that part of it which is standing and furnished that I have at this time only two spare beds in all my house.'

Why are so many grand homes being rebuilt in this period? In short, money and excitement. The rich are growing richer and they want to flaunt their wealth. As for the excitement, architects are beginning to see new, wider horizons ahead of them. Think of it this way, medieval houses are always one room deep. It is difficult for medieval people to conceive of anything else because how will they light the rooms otherwise? In Elizabethan times, architects envisage houses that are two rooms deep, looking out from either side of a central wall, like Robert Smythson's design for Hardwick Hall. But despite that innovation, most great houses in 1660 are still only one room deep, built around a central courtyard. Light is seen as healthy and precious, so you want the maximum amount of it in every room. Only after 1663, with the development of the 'double-pile' house – two blocks, one on either side of a central corridor – do the architectural possibilities reveal themselves.

Of all the grand houses from this time, the one we would probably most like to see being built is Chatsworth in Derbyshire, the first baroque country house in England. Its elegance seduces the soul. Indeed, it is difficult to think of any other house that so many people find as aesthetically satisfying. But the real reason it would make a great episode of *Grand Designs* is that its architect, William Talman, is a surly man who is frequently rude to his clients. Fortunately, his patron at Chatsworth, the earl of Devonshire (who becomes the first duke of Devonshire in 1694), is both patient and architecturally enlightened. The earl is so impressed with Talman's remodelling of the south front, completed in 1686, that he asks him to work his magic on the east front too, which Talman completes in 1696. No roof is visible: it is concealed by a balustrade. Columns are used at the edges of sequences of bays subtly to break up the lines of stone. It sits so well in its environment that you can be forgiven for thinking the entire valley has been designed to complement it. But that's not far off the mark: the landscape has indeed been modelled to bring out the best of the house. Nor are the gardens neglected. There are sculpted metal trees which, when a tap is turned on, sprinkle the grass with rain. As if it does not already rain enough in Derbyshire.

For the grandest of Restoration *Grand Designs* projects, however, we should consider St Paul's Cathedral in London. Here we might see in episode one the architect Christopher Wren surveying the old structure on the eve of the Great Fire and noting how it could be improved with a great dome on top – only for his colleagues to say that, no, the medieval pillars won't take the strain. Then comes the Great Fire in episode two, featuring the destruction of the cathedral and the city around it. Once again, Wren suggests pulling it down and building something with a great dome. Charles II insists on the old structure being restored. Only when a major section collapses in 1668 does the king relent and agree to the old cathedral being demolished. Wren then gets to submit the plans for his new cathedral, complete with its dome. But imagine the tension in episode three, as Wren tries to satisfy all the interested parties – from the bishop of London and other ecclesiastical dignitaries to the king. He is repeatedly forced to adapt his designs. Meanwhile he is designing new churches across the city. You can just imagine the presenter asking leading questions in episode four, such as 'So, Christopher, you're determined on this huge dome. Will your cathedral be the greatest in the world and, if so, do you think you'll go over budget? Will you even live to see it finished?' But the final episode is a satisfying and happy one. Wren lives to the grand old age of ninety-one, so he *does* get to see the building finished in 1711. It becomes one of the three greatest landmarks of London – along with Tower Bridge and Big Ben – which makes it one of the icons of the nation. And he himself is buried in the crypt. Directly beneath the dome is his epitaph in Latin, inscribed in a circle, reflecting the dome. It translates as: 'If you seek his monument, look around you'.

H IS FOR HEALTH – LACK OF

Today in the United Kingdom, life expectancy at birth is seventy-nine years for men and eighty-three for women. In the late seventeenth century, it is less than half that. For both sexes. A lot of that difference is down to infant mortality. This causes quite a few people to think that those low figures are not as bad as they seem. But let me put it this way: if you and your spouse have five children and lose two of them before the age of five, you certainly won't take any comfort from the fact that so many people die in infancy. Nor is the problem limited to the first five years of life. Just as in medieval times, half of the population die before the age of twenty-one. Suddenly those low life-expectancy figures seem horribly real. Tragically so. Everyone can expect to lose a parent early in life; everyone who has a child should be prepared to bury him or her. And this sad state of affairs affects the rich as much as the poor. Of the thirty-five legitimate children born to the royal family between 1660 and 1700, only three reach adulthood. Ninety per cent die before they are twenty-one.

The reason for so many short lives is, of course, the number of fatal diseases. Most feared of all is the plague. For the last three centuries it has returned with painful frequency. It spreads through the rat population, so the more crowded a settlement is, the more its inhabitants suffer. As we have seen, the Great Plague of 1563 kills 25 per cent of Londoners. Approximately one-sixth die in the Great Plague of 1603. In 1665, another Great Plague kills about 80,000 citizens in the space of eight or nine months, which is approximately 20 per cent of the city. Fortunately, that proves to be the last occasion on which large numbers of people die from plague in England.

Plague is not the only mass killer. In fact, because it is only occasional, it is not even in the top five causes of the death in the 1660s. This seems like an appropriate point at which to pause and introduce another mini-A–Z – this time, to ailments that might kill you in Restoration England. But we will focus on the period *after* 1670, when plague is no longer a feature of the landscape of illness. As you will see, I have based it on the Bills of Mortality that cover all the parishes of London and Westminster and their suburbs: 132 parishes, rising to 134 parishes in 1686. These are home to 475,000 people in 1670 and 575,000 in 1700.

THE A–Z OF DEADLY AILMENTS IN RESTORATION ENGLAND

A *is for Apoplexy*
Restoration people put brain haemorrhage and stroke in the same category and refer to all such sudden onsets of brain problems as 'apoplectic', whatever the cause. These normally account for about 0.5 per cent of all the deaths reported in the Bills of Mortality. Nevertheless, the idea you might be here one minute and gone the next is cause for widespread concern.

B *is for the Bloody flux*
We know this as dysentery, an intestinal disease caused by a bacteria or parasite. Symptoms include diarrhoea, nausea and vomiting. It is steadily declining in this period, causing 1.6 per cent of all deaths in the 1660s and just 0.1 per cent in the late 1690s. Still, not a nice way to go.

C *is for Convulsions*
Overall, this is the second most common cause of death as recorded in the Bills of Mortality and sometimes it tops the list (as it does throughout the 1690s). Modern science will tell you that 'convulsions' is not a disease itself but rather symptomatic of several different ailments such as epilepsy, brain tumour, stroke, meningitis or encephalitis. However, the old women of the parish who nurse the dying and examine each corpse do not have

the medical knowledge to tell the difference. It accounts for between 13 per cent and 16 per cent of all deaths.

D *is for Dental infection*
Almost 6 per cent of the population dies from problems arising from their teeth. This includes infants who have problems teething but, even so, this is astonishing: 'teeth' is normally the fourth or fifth biggest killer in London. More people die because of dental problems than they do from old age. There are dentists available, if you can afford one. There are cloves, alcohol and opium for the pain too. Dwale is a sedative composed of hemlock, opium and henbane, among other, less toxic things. In future, whenever you find yourself in a dentist's chair, staring at a bright light in the ceiling and listening to a dental drill while having your mouth drained of blood and saliva, think how lucky you are. The seventeenth-century equivalent is far worse – with or without dwale.

E *is for the Evil*
The Evil (or the King's Evil, as it is described in the Bills of Mortality until 1675) is another name for scrofula, which is a form of tuberculosis. It results in a swelling of the neck as the infected and swollen lymph nodes join together. It normally accounts for about 0.3 per cent of deaths in the urban population. People have believed since at least the twelfth century that it can be cured by the king touching the affected person or giving them a coin with his own hands. This superstition persists even in this period, although I am not sure Charles II really believes he has thaumaturgical powers. I suspect that, after the Restoration, it is just a way for a king to show how special he is compared to the ordinariness of a Lord Protector.

F *is for the French pox*
Many people are infected with the French pox – or syphilis, as we know it – especially in towns. However, relatively few die from it – about 0.3 per cent every year. More people probably die from the mercury treatments that sufferers are made to undergo by physicians.

G *is for Griping in the guts*
This is the fourth biggest killer on the fatality hit parade. It is probably a form of dysentery but I am not absolutely sure what makes it different from the bloody flux. One thing I do know is that it doesn't sound good. It leads to almost 10 per cent of the deaths in London each year. It also sounds like a particularly ignominious end – not the way you want to be remembered.

H *is for Hanging oneself*
You might say that this isn't an ailment but rather a free choice. Perhaps. But it also includes many people suffering from mental illnesses. So too does drowning, as some women prefer to throw themselves in the Thames rather than put a noose around their neck. On average, about 0.1 per cent of those who die each year hang themselves and probably a similar number throw themselves in the Thames. As a proportion of all deaths of those over the age of ten, at 0.4 per cent it is relatively low.

I *is for Impostumes*
An impostume is an abscess or a putrid swelling, so this is more of a symptom than a specific disease. It is slowly on the decline but even in the 1690s it is still associated with about 0.4 per cent of deaths in the capital, about the same number as suicides.

J *is for Jaundice*
It might surprise you to hear that jaundice can be fatal. It is a build-up of the residue from dead blood cells which normally are filtered out of the body. It makes the skin and the whites of the eyes turn yellow. Common in newborn babies, it is also associated with about 0.4 per cent of all deaths.

K *is for Kidney stones*
The initial symptoms of bladder and kidney stones are a constant pain in the back, blood in the urine, and a burning feeling when urinating. Pepys describes feeling these things prior to being 'cut' for the stone. He is so grateful to have survived the dangerous operation to remove his stone that he celebrates the anniversary as a holiday

every year and even has a box made in which he keeps the said stone. He is lucky that it is a bladder stone and not in his kidneys, which is far harder for a seventeenth-century surgeon to remove. His brother and aunt do not undergo the operation and both die as a result. On average, about 0.25 per cent of deaths each year are due to bladder or kidney stones, or infections following the operation to remove them.

L *is for Leprosy*

The most feared killer of the early Middle Ages is now a shadow of its former self. Only one or two deaths from the disease are noted in the Bills of Mortality each year.

M *is for Measles*

Measles is a contagious disease spread by a virus. We normally associate it with children today, but anyone can catch it, and in densely populated seventeenth-century London, an outbreak can carry off hundreds of people. Numbers of fatalities fluctuate considerably. In 1669, for example, just fifteen deaths in the city are associated with measles; the following year 295 are; and in the next, just seven.

N *is for Natal, Neonatal and maternal mortality*

Thousands of children born in the capital do not survive the first year of life. One-third of all deaths take place within the first two years and, in London, half before the age of ten. Maternal mortality normally accounts for 1.6 per cent of all deaths (male and female) – so at least 6.4 per cent of all females over the age of ten dying in any year do so as a result of childbirth.

O *is for Old age*

If nothing else on this list gets you, this one will. It is normally the sixth biggest killer in the Bills of Mortality, accounting for 6 per cent of fatalities. That in itself says something: 94 per cent of the population don't get the chance to die of old age. But what is 'old' at this time? That is down to the judgement of the 'searchers' – the women who go into the house of a dead person to ascertain a cause of death. Generally if you look over sixty, they are likely to say you are old. But if they themselves are in their forties, they may say you died of 'old age' in your fifties. Put it this way, in an age when half the population die in childhood, no one is said to have 'died before their time' if they make it to fifty.

P *is for Palsy*
Palsy or paralysis is another symptom recorded as a cause of death. It is uncommon in this period: only about 0.1 per cent of fatalities are associated with it.

Q *is for Quinsy*
This is an abscess between the tonsils and the wall of the throat. It is quite rare: normally fewer than twenty people die of it in London each year – less than 0.1 per cent.

R *is for Rickets*
The lack of vitamin D in children leads to a softening in the bones, stunted growth and skeletal deformities. Vitamin D is produced naturally in the body by exposure to sunlight, so rickets is particularly a feature of London's dense population. It is almost unknown in the early seventeenth century, as the overcrowding is not so bad and children regularly get outside. But in this period it is associated with between 1.5 per cent and 2.5 per cent of all deaths.

S *is for Smallpox*
After the decline of plague, smallpox is the most feared disease. It doesn't kill as many people as some other diseases – it is normally only the seventh or eighth biggest killer – but those who survive it are likely to be scarred for life with pockmarks. These are the residue of tens of thousands of pustules on their faces and bodies. A common reaction to seeing survivors is to shrink away in horror. From 1686 it is reported together with measles because the women who inspect the corpses are often unable to tell the difference between the two diseases. The number of fatalities varies considerably, depending on how rapidly the virus spreads. In a good year such as 1696, it results in just 1 per cent of all deaths; in a bad year like 1674, it may account for more than 12 per cent.

T *is for Tuberculosis*
Otherwise known as consumption, this is a bacterial infection of the lungs. Over the Restoration period as a whole, it is the biggest killer, being the cause of 18 per cent of all fatalities. By the 1690s it takes second place to convulsions. It is spread through the breath – especially when people cough, kiss or sneeze – and so is a particular feature of crowded urban living. It is not helped by congregations gathering in churches and singing lustily.

U *is for Ulcers*
This is not a category of fatal disease in the modern world but a symptom of an underlying problem. Nevertheless, in the Bills of Mortality, you will find a category for 'Sores, Ulcers, bruised and broken limbs'. These ailments account for 0.3–0.5 per cent of those dying in any year.

V *is for Vomiting*
Again, we regard this as a symptom rather than as a disease. Normally the number of fatalities each year is in single figures but in 1691, for some unknown reason, it hits forty. The very idea of vomiting to death is horrific. But, dare I say it, it is a fate that most of us can imagine – if we've ever had a particularly heavy night on the town.

W *is for Worms*
I was initially under the impression that this category in the Bills of Mortality included all manner of parasites, not just intestinal worms. And then I noticed an entry in the 1691 return that was for one person who died of 'being eaten up by lice'. Either way, we're talking about death by creepy crawlies. This is how between twenty and eighty people die in London each year.

X *is for eXecution*
As with hanging, you could say this is not an ailment as such. But since the Bills of Mortality account for *all* deaths, including accidents and intentional killings, it is interesting to see how few people in the London area are killed by the state in this period. In the 1670s the total is 176 for the whole decade; in the 1680s, 139; and in the

1690s, 260. That barely scrapes above 0.1 per cent of all deaths. More people die of worms.

Y *is for Young, diseases of the*
As we have noted, the majority of those featuring in the above causes of death are young. The seventeenth-century Bills of Mortality do not give specific figures for the numbers dying in each age group but the early eighteenth-century ones do. Using the figures from 1728, about 35 per cent of deaths in London are children under two; 9 per cent are between two and five; 4 per cent between five and ten, and 3 per cent between ten and twenty. That's a total of 51 per cent of all fatalities being young people. True, this is London, which is not kind to children. But still, it is much more than a sadness. It is an everyday mass tragedy.

Z *is for Zoonoses*
Zoonoses are diseases caught from animals. Plague is one, which we catch from the fleas that live on rats. Malaria is another, which we catch from mosquitos. You might associate malaria with exotic warm places but the fens of Lincolnshire and Cambridgeshire, the levels of Somerset and the marshes of Kent are exotic enough for it to be a major killer in the seventeenth century. It appears in the Bills of Mortality as 'ague and fever'. Although London is not one of its prime mortality zones, it still accounts for 13 per cent of all the deaths in the 134 parishes, making it the third biggest killer in the capital.

Setting out all these diseases like this makes everyone in the seventeenth century seem very vulnerable. And we have only here touched on twenty-six ailments. We haven't noted conditions like dropsy, which we know as oedema, a swelling under the skin due to the overproduction of watery fluid, which accounts for between 3 per cent and 6 per cent of deaths every year. Yet the citizens go about their lives as if everything were normal. There is perhaps a message of stoicism in this. In an age when most people don't make it to twenty-one, you've got to get on and live your life as if you'll be here forever.

I IS FOR IMMORALITY

In 1660, at the start of the Restoration, Cromwell's laws against adultery are still on the statute books. Charles II, 'the Merry Monarch', is the ideal antidote to that particular piece of legislation. As I've mentioned, he already has one illegitimate son. After he returns to England, he takes a number of mistresses, sometimes with a degree of overlap and not always with their husband's consent. Now, that is not unusual for powerful men in any age, especially kings, but Charles II does something wholly unexpected – something that his contemporaries see as utterly scandalous and extraordinary. He makes his principal mistress, Barbara Palmer, a *duchess* – the duchess of Cleveland, to be precise. He does the same for his next mistress, Louise de Kerrouaille, whom he makes duchess of Portsmouth. This is outrageous! There are perfectly respectable earls' wives up and down the country who have steadfastly been perfectly faithful to their husbands but who now find themselves outranked by women simply on account of these hussies having committed adultery with the king.

That's not the half of it. Charles makes his bastard sons dukes. His sons by Barbara Palmer – who is married to Roger Palmer, I should add – become the dukes of Southampton, Grafton and Northumberland. He creates his illegitimate son by Louise de Kerrouaille duke of Richmond. His son by Catherine Pegg is made earl of Plymouth. His son by Nell Gwynn becomes the duke of St Albans. It is as if Charles is trying to raise adultery itself to the front rank of the English peerage.

Charles is not the only immoralist in town. He is accompanied in his bad behaviour by a number of younger gentlemen who become known as rakes. They too show a clear and unbridled determination to cause moral outrage wherever they go. For example, in 1663 Sir Charles Sedley strips off naked and parades up and down the balcony of the Cock, a cook shop in Bow Street, London. As a contemporary puts it, he and a friend, Lord Buckhurst, 'play out all the postures of lust and buggery that can be imagined'. He then makes a highly blasphemous speech to the crowd below. He declares that he has 'a powder such as will make all the women of the town run after him', except that he doesn't use the word 'women', he refers to them by their sexual organs. Next, he takes a glass of wine, washes his private parts in it, and then drinks from it, toasting the king's health as he does so. Five years later, Sedley and Buckhurst are caught running through the streets of London at night naked from the waist down and staging a fight until they are arrested by the city guard. It's Buckhurst who lures Nell Gwyn away from the stage and takes her to bed before he hands her over to Charles II to be the king's next mistress.

The greatest rake of the lot is Lord Rochester. You will probably have heard of him as he is an exceptional poet. Every serious anthology of English verse that covers the seventeenth century contains at least one poem by him. But he is also capable of writing the rudest satires imaginable. Let me illustrate what I mean with his satire on Charles II. [A warning: what follows is very rude indeed…]

> In th'isle of Britain, long since famous grown
> For breeding the best cunts in Christendom,
> There reigns, and oh! long may he reign and thrive,
> The easiest King and best-bred man alive.
> Him no ambition moves to get renown
> Like the French fool, that wanders up and down
> Starving his people, hazarding his crown.
> Peace is his aim, his gentleness is such,
> And love he loves, for he loves fucking much.
> Nor are his high desires above his strength:
> His sceptre and his prick are of a length;
> And she may sway the one who plays with th' other,
> And make him little wiser than his brother.
> Poor Prince! Thy prick, like thy buffoons at Court,
> Will govern thee because it makes thee sport.
> 'Tis sure the sauciest prick that e'er did swive,
> The proudest, peremptoriest prick alive.

> Though safety, law, religion, life lay on 't,
> 'Twould break through all to make its way to cunt.
> Restless he rolls about from whore to whore,
> A merry monarch, scandalous and poor.
> To [Kerrouaille], the most dear of all his dears,
> The best relief of his declining years,
> Oft he bewails his fortune, and her fate:
> To love so well, and be beloved so late.
> For though in her he settles well his tarse,
> Yet his dull, graceless bollocks hang an arse.
> This you'd believe, had I but time to tell ye
> The pains it costs to poor, laborious Nelly,
> Whilst she employs hands, fingers, mouth, and thighs,
> Ere she can raise the member she enjoys.
> All monarchs I hate, and the thrones they sit on,
> From the hector of France to the cully of Britain.

As you can see, Rochester's satire is very rude indeed. It is also quite funny – as long as you are not Charles II. Unfortunately, Rochester one day accidentally hands this satire to the king himself. It does not go down well. Rochester is lucky to get away with simply being banished from court. Again.

If Lord Rochester were to draw up a curriculum vitae for a job interview at the age of thirty-three, the year of his death, it would not only contain the fact he has written some of the best lyric poetry of the century (as well as some of the rudest) but also the abduction of his chosen bride, serial adultery, confessions of sodomy (which is punishable by death), blasphemy (also punishable by death), atheism (punishable by excommunication), reckless courage in warfare, fighting an illegal duel, punching a royal servant in the king's presence, selling fake medicines, unlawful appearances on the London stage, and imprisonment in the Tower. On top of all that, he is the author of *Sodom*, the rudest play ever written. It is about a debauched king who encourages his sex-crazed subjects to indulge themselves in as much sodomy as they like. Just to give you a flavour of its lewdness, the key characters are King Bolloximian,

Queen Cuntigratia; Prince Prickett and General Buggeranthus. The maids of honour are called Cunticula, Clitoris and Fuckadilla.

Why am I telling you all this? Am I not just taking the opportunity to use rude words, like a naughty schoolboy?

There is more going on here than meets the eye. You can be forgiven for missing it, however, for the traditional historians who have told us about the rakes down the years have also missed it. Those historians were predominantly old Victorian men, intent on *judging* the past, often in the belief that they were considerably wiser and morally more upstanding than their predecessors. They portrayed the rakes as louts who, if they had not been the king's friends, would have been executed. But the rakes are not just louts. Like punks in the 1970s, there is a serious reason behind their antics – and it is one of severe disquiet. These men are aristocrats and gentlemen. They have all suffered under the supposedly moral Puritan government. Most of them have lost family estates. Most of them have spent twelve humiliating years in exile. Many of them have seen their fathers and brothers killed or executed in the name of the Puritan cause. They can see the hypocrisy of a system that facilitates unscrupulous men reporting their unfaithful wives so they are hanged for adultery. If King Charles and his fellow rakes are laughing now at puritanism, and taking every opportunity to pour scorn on it, it is a comparatively gracious response given what puritanism has done for them.

J IS FOR JUSTICE

'Justice is a relative concept in all ages and the seventeenth century is no exception.' I have used a variation of this line in almost all my books. And I stand firmly by it.

The fact is that the law is a massively cumbersome, slow-moving beast that takes a decade or more merely to turn its head. Lawyers are consequently always having to work with laws drawn up for the challenges of another time. But how should they apply statutes that were originally worded to send as many undesirable men to the gallows as possible, so they might be an example to others? As Lord Halifax puts it, 'Men are not hanged for stealing horses but that horses may not be stolen.' That phrase alone should strike terror into your heart. How does anyone work with a system that prioritises the protection of property and status symbols over the wellbeing of people?

The answer to that question, I am sad to say, is that they acquiesce. Except for the fact that, once in a while, a brave man or woman stands up and says, No! Enough. Fortunately, that is what happens in 1670, in a legal case in London.

The man who stands up and protests is called Edward Bushell. At the time it is permissible for a judge to lock up a jury without food, water or heat for as long as he wants until they reach a verdict with which he, the judge, is happy. And if he does not think they have reached the right verdict, he can lock them up again. Where's the justice in that?

Bushell's case is the result of two Quakers being accused of holding a nonconformist religious meeting of more than five people, contrary to the law. The jury – of whom Bushell is a member – have some sympathy for the Quakers and find them not guilty. But Quakers are a detested and persecuted group in 1670 and the judge is determined that they shall go to prison. So he threatens Bushell and his fellow jurymen with imprisonment until they return a guilty verdict. Bushell and the other eleven refuse. The judge has them locked up without food and water for two days. Bushell sues for a writ of habeas corpus and extracts from the Lord Chief Justice the concession that, henceforth, no jury can be imprisoned for reaching a verdict with which the judge does not agree.

This case is a clear step forward but don't imagine for a moment that justice has somehow miraculously arrived. Trials are still fleetingly short. Even if you're on trial for murder, you will probably not spend more than ten minutes in the dock. While a long trial in the twenty-first century might last months, few in the seventeenth extend beyond half an hour.

Perhaps the most worrying thing about appearing in the dock in a seventeenth-century court is that you're not allowed to have a lawyer speak on your behalf. The idea is that the judge should be able to ask questions which will tease out the truth. But there is no presumption of innocence, so you will have to defend yourself. If you are on trial for a felony, your life is literally on the line because if the jury deems you guilty, the judge has no option but to pass the legally required sentence – he cannot hand down a lesser one. This results in some boys and girls under the age of ten being hanged on account of thieving goods worth more than 12d – because that is the sum set down in Anglo-Saxon times as amounting to a crime worthy of the death penalty. I should add that, in the late seventeenth century, 12d is the equivalent of 2lbs of butter or ½lb of cherries.

As I said, justice is a relative concept in all ages; the seventeenth century is no exception.

K IS FOR KINGSHIP

When I was at school I was repeatedly told that Charles I was the last autocratic king of England – the last to wield 'absolute power', as my history teacher put it. I can remember thinking at the time, 'Well, if they cut his head off for treason, he can't have had *absolute* power, can he?'

There is something to be said for that youthful observation. There clearly *are* limitations on Charles I's power, even if he does not recognise them. You can see the roots of Parliament's ability to control the king way back in 1295, when Edward I acknowledges that he cannot demand extraordinary taxation without the assent of Parliament. In 1327 Parliament agrees to depose Edward II if he will not abdicate in favour of his son. In 1399 Richard is deposed without any choice in his successor. So Charles I's deposition is on the cards as soon as he decides to tax his people without the consent of Parliament. Moreover, what do we actually mean by 'power'? Traditionally we interpret this as referring to the control of the realm. But that is not the only interpretation. In some respects, Charles II, James II and William III are far more powerful than Charles I. They all command a navy that dominates the world's seas.

Having said these things, the Restoration kings do not rule on the same basis as Charles I. People might not mention the fact that Charles I had his head cut off but, in terms of elephants in the corner of the room – or elephants in the corner of the *realm* – they don't come much bigger. So in 1662, when Charles II is preparing to stand by his promise of religious toleration for all, to the great displeasure of English Protestants, he realises that things could go very badly wrong. He backs down and permits the penal laws against Catholics and other nonconformists to remain on the statute books. He also backs down on the only other occasion there is a serious rift between him and his ministers, over the same issue of religious toleration, ten years later. Although we think of Charles II as 'the Merry Monarch' and, as a French visitor to England at the time said, as being 'fonder of women than England and all the crowns in the world,' he is a subtle, pragmatic and flexible ruler. Crucially, he knows when to give way as well as when to press his case. He is also adept at employing what we would call 'soft power'. Like Elizabeth I, he sets a lot of store by being publicly *seen* as the monarch. He has wit and charm. He is an active patron of music and drama, and he has genuine interests in technology, anatomy and the Royal Navy. His personality is thus an important reason why the Restoration is a success – so much so that it has lasted into the twenty-first century.

James II does not have his brother's charm, pragmatism or flexibility. He believes that he has a divine mission to reconvert England to Catholicism. Within two years of succeeding to the throne, he has alienated the entire Protestant nation. Seven lords meet and agree to invite Charles I's grandson and granddaughter, William, prince of Orange, and his wife, Mary, to come to Britian to remove James. The elephant in the corner of the realm blows its trumpet once more. James knows what terrible fate might lie in wait if he tries to resist Parliament, so he tries to run away. He is caught but later permitted to go into exile into France, where he dies in 1701.

James II's successors are crowned joint monarchs as William III and Mary II in 1689. They are left in no doubt that they do not rule on the same basis as their grandfather. In fact, Mary does not rule at all. She *reigns* – and we call their joint reign that of William and Mary – but because in English law a married couple is a single legal entity represented solely by the husband, William rules over his wife as well as the kingdom. That said, he is made to sit through a speech in which he is told that he may not suspend any legislation that has been passed by Parliament. He may not maintain an army without Parliament's approval, nor may he authorise the use of cruel and unusual punishments. Nor may he object to Protestants bearing arms to defend themselves – so far as the law allows – and that he must allow them to petition him without fear of persecution, allow free and fair elections every seven years, and guarantee free speech in Parliament. William's acceptance of these terms is the basis of the constitutional monarchy in the UK today.

L IS FOR LONDON

London is by far the biggest city in the country. Its population in 1700 (about 575,000) is more than 10 per cent of that of the whole of England. What's more, it dwarfs the other large towns and cities collectively as well as individually. In 1377 the population of the capital compared to the ten next-largest towns is just 59 per cent. By 1600 the city has grown considerably: it is now 225 per cent of the size of the ten next-largest towns. But in 1660 it is a massive 417 per cent. It is almost the same in 1700, at 420 per cent. After that it starts to lose its dominance. In 1750 London is just 282 per cent of the ten next-largest places. In 1800, when the growth of the industrial towns of the north of England is well underway, it is down to 172 per cent. By 1861 it is just 136 per cent. Although Greater London's population today – about 9 million – is a larger percentage of the national total than ever, so many people live in the other large towns and cities that its dominance is less pronounced than it was, being about 160 per cent of the size of the ten next-largest places.

The important point is not the statistics themselves but the implications. Whereas we think of regional services spread out across the country, Restoration people think in terms of London. Everyone of note in Restoration England depends on the capital

– for buying and selling unusual, expensive and exotic things, for their private law courts, for their government and so forth. It is hardly surprising that one in six people spends some part of their lives in London. Nor is it a coincidence that this is when many transport innovations are made to improve access to the capital. Acts of Parliament are passed to facilitate the rebuilding of roads. Stagecoaches start to run regularly from the regional towns to London inns and back. People regularly start to use commercial horse hire, and the postal service is made more efficient. London compared to other towns becomes like a king in relation to his subjects: stately, rich and slightly mystical – and much more than first among equals.

M IS FOR MEDICINE

Most sane people, when faced with the prospect of travelling to the late seventeenth century, express concern about the medical care they are likely to receive. This is wise, especially considering the diseases mentioned earlier. Germ theory won't become widely accepted for another 200 years, so the best medical help you are likely to receive is the sage advice of someone like Dr Thomas Sydenham, who believes that the body can heal itself of many ailments if you create the right conditions for it to do so. Otherwise, the medical profession is still hung up on Galenic theory – a philosophy of medicine that has prevailed since Roman times. This holds that diseases are caused by miasmas that cause the four humours of the body – blood, yellow bile, black bile and phlegm – to be out of balance. When the best-qualified doctors are likely to cast a horoscope for the time of your infection and may even prescribe things such as 'the powdered skull of a man who has been dead for a year' as a remedy for epilepsy, you can be forgiven for thinking that medical knowledge is little more than witchcraft.

Such a reaction would be missing the point. This is the period when the medical profession takes off.

For many decades there have been well-paid lawyers in London and all over the country. There have been qualified physicians too since the previous century. Nevertheless, it is in the Restoration – particularly in the 1680s – that the idea of 'the professions' is fully realised. From now on, people want their lawyers, their clergymen and their doctors to be suitably qualified, socially acceptable, expensive, knowledgeable, successful and reliable. And in many respects, they are all of these things. Although you might be prescribed some awful medicines which will do you no good whatsoever, there are also some genuine medical breakthroughs. For example, a naturally occurring 'cure' for malaria is found in Latin America, in the form of Jesuit's Bark, or quinine. That is a huge step forward. Imagine how it would be if you were to discover a cure for cancer – growing on trees!

This isn't even the most important aspect of the development of the profession. If you are seriously ill in 1600 – so ill that you believe you are going to die – you send for a clergyman. Only about 5 per cent of sufferers tell their servants to contact a physician or surgeon instead. When you use the word 'doctor' in 1600, most people will think you are referring to a senior member of the Church of England with the degree of Doctor of Divinity – perhaps an archdeacon. If you pay for any medical intervention, it is more likely to be for nursing care provided by old women than medical expertise. But by 1680 a complete transformation has taken place. Many more people are paying for medicines than for nursing care. They have become obsessed with the idea that grips us: that if we are ill there has *got* to be some medical solution somewhere. As a result, almost three-quarters of those suffering a fatal illness pay for medical help. Physicians in the 1680s are often called 'Doctor' whether or not they have a medical degree: it is a mark of respect. Nursing care too has become semi-professionalised as women specialise in caring for the sick. Whereas in 1600 'nursing' means only wet nursing, now it means care for everyone who needs it.

This all adds up to the most extraordinary series of changes. In 1600 your best hope of medical salvation is putting yourself in God's hands. By 1700 it is by being in the hands of your fellow human beings – qualified doctors. I think this shift of hope – from the divine to the mortal – is one of the biggest social changes humanity has ever seen. Blind faith is gradually being replaced by professional expertise. In the late seventeenth century, God is increasingly expected to work *through* experts, not independently of them. As you can imagine, once the instrument of healing is seen as the doctor, not God, the divine element declines and the recognition of the doctor's skill increases. And this change in respect of our physical wellbeing is just the start. Where medicine leads, the rest of society will follow. The roots of the secularisation of society in the eighteenth century lie in the changing ways people think about their bodies in the seventeenth.

N IS FOR NOVELS

When it comes to picking up a good novel, you won't find a great selection at a bookseller or stationer's shop. The ongoing preoccupation with religion means that most seventeenth-century people are more interested in works of divinity. More than a quarter of the entries in the *Catalogue of All the Books Printed in England 1666–1672* are theological in nature. But a few novels do go on sale. One of the very earliest is John Bunyan's famous religious allegory, *The Pilgrim's Progress*, first published in 1678. If this is not your cup of tea, there are secular alternatives, such as *Tudor: a Prince of Wales* and *Capella and Bianca: a Novel*, both published in 1677. If you are really ambitious, like Samuel Pepys's wife, Elizabeth, you might try *Artarmenes, or the Grand Cyrus, an Excellent New Romance*. This is a ten-volume work translated from the French original of Madeleine de Scudéry and extends to almost 2 million words. If you invest in a set for your bedtime reading, you will probably never need anything else.

Great things often have modest beginnings and such is the greatness of later works of fiction that it is easy to miss the small but significant achievements of this period. When it comes to novels, we are so preoccupied with Daniel Defoe, Samuel Richardson, Jonathan Swift and Henry Fielding in the early eighteenth century that we forget the first professional female writer, Aphra Behn. She begins her career by composing poetry but, from her mid-twenties, she writes plays for a living, seeing more than a dozen presented by the two royal theatre companies in London. But she is best remembered for her novel *Oronooko, or the Royal Slave, a True History*, published in 1688. This tells the story of an African prince, Oronooko, who is trained for war. One day, during a fierce battle, one of his generals throws himself into the path of an arrow that otherwise would have killed Oronooko. The prince, in tribute to his fallen comrade, goes to see the man's daughter, Imoinda, a 'beautiful black Venus'. Of course, he falls in love with her. Unfortunately, her beauty is such that Oronooko's father, the king, also hears about her and makes her a part of his harem. Not to be dissuaded from the path of true love, Oronooko breaks into the building housing the royal harem and meets Imoinda. When the king finds out, he punishes Imoinda by selling her as a slave to a European trader. He tells Oronooko, however, that she has been executed. Later, Oronooko and his men visit a trader's ship and are tricked, becoming enslaved themselves. Thus Oronooko finds himself shipped against his will to Surinam in South America, where Imoinda has been taken. Their reunion, however, is marred by the terrible conditions they encounter. Eventually they and their fellow slaves revolt. The novel ends tragically with Oronooko killing Imoinda to save her from the torture she is likely to suffer after he has killed the cruel British officer in charge of the colony. Following a violent struggle with the authorities, he himself dies a traitor's death.

If you have grown up with the understanding that Restoration literature is all about theatrical comedies and metaphysical poetry, Aphra Behn's novel will come as a startling surprise. To begin with, there is the fact that it exists in the first place. All her life, she has experienced prejudice on account of her sex, with some theatregoers refusing to watch or comment favourably on her plays simply because she is a woman. Yet some men are angered by such misogyny and are determined to promote Behn and her works. Then there is the subject matter. She confronts the iniquities of slavery head on. She chooses a black African to be her hero. The British officers she casts as dishonourable, abusive and morally objectionable. She champions love over all – regardless of creed, colour, nationality, status, fortune or misfortune. That priority, of course, accords with our twenty-first-century sensibilities, making it appear just what any right-thinking person should think. But Behn is almost alone in saying these things. She is truly revolutionary. And in expressing her thoughts and sentiments in the way she does, she makes the novel a radical form of literature.

O IS FOR OSTENTATION

Who is the finest painter in England in the late seventeenth century? I imagine most people will reply with the name of the most successful society portrait painter of the day, Sir Peter Lely. He is the worthy successor of van Dyck, the Dutch artist who does for English portraiture what Inigo Jones does for our architecture. But ask a seventeenth-century crowd of art lovers and the chances are that they will say Antonio Verrio. Several diarists, including John Evelyn and Celia Fiennes, refer to him as 'the finest hand in England'.

Who is Antonio Verrio, you might ask? He is an Italian painter who moves to England in the 1670s and lives here for most of the rest of his life. He specialises in murals and ceilings, so his work does not end up on the walls of modern art galleries. Much of his career is spent working for Charles II at Windsor Castle, where he paints three staircases and twenty ceilings, as well as the King's Chapel and St George's Hall. It is work of the most exuberant style – and the king is thrilled with it. But unfortunately, a later king, George IV, has most of it destroyed. Just three ceilings survive at Windsor, besides a few fragments. Verrio also does a great deal of work for James II at Whitehall Palace, including painting the king's chapel and the queen's apartments. That all goes up in smoke with the rest of the palace in 1698. But you can still see some of Verrio's work at Hampton Court Palace (in the historic county of Middlesex) and Ham House (in historic Surrey). And if you have not been to Burghley House in Lincolnshire, you are in for a treat.

Verrio's work at Burghley includes an entire suite of rooms painted in the 1690s: the Drawing Room, the Great Drawing Room, the State Dining Room and the Saloon, also known as the Heaven Room. Beyond that is the Hell Staircase, which is also mostly by his hand. This is an image of the sufferings people experience in Hell, with the gate to the underworld being a giant cat's mouth. The Heaven Room, however, is his finest surviving piece. The subject matter is Venus and her lover Mars being caught in a net by her husband, Vulcan. The scene is witnessed by dozens if not hundreds of other gods, all very scantily clad as if they are all having one great big orgy. The fact that one of their number has just been caught *in flagrante* doesn't seem to bother them too much – it's all par for the course if you're an ancient god. It's also par for the course if you happen to be a Restoration earl or one of the rakes. But the amazing thing about this room – and the reason why I mention it in connection with O for Ostentation – is that it is all around you. The ceiling and the walls all form one coherent massive artwork, and you are at the middle of it. You too are a guest at this divine erotic party. It's par for the course for you too.

This sense of showing off and being outrageous with it is typical of the Restoration. There's a painting by Verrio called the Sea Power of Charles II which must be one of the most over-the-top royal portraits ever painted. Not even Elizabeth I has herself depicted in such a flamboyant manner. It is massive, about 8ft square. The image is a tumbling pyramid of horses charging through the sea, led by naked young mermen directed by a Poseidon-like figure, while bare-breasted young mermaids and giant goggle-eyed fish cavort around their stampeding hooves. Naked cherubs both swim in the surf and fly above the king, who sits in a giant scallop shell atop the entire pyramid, like a seventeenth-century kingly re-incarnation of Botticelli's Venus, surrounded by semi-clad beauties. In the background, English ships seem to be sailing off to the four corners of the Earth and angels trumpet the king's glory in the heavens.

Here we are just getting a glimpse of the exuberance of English Baroque decoration. It is manifest in the architecture that emerges at the end of the century and in artistry like the ironwork of Jean Tijou and the wood carvings of Grinling Gibbons. If you want an illustration of what is possible in iron, see the magnificent screen at Hampton Court Palace made by Tijou for William III, or the gates at Burghley and Chatsworth. As for Grinling Gibbons, his wood carving is so extraordinarily delicate it defies belief. One carved altarpiece is centred on a bird perched on a bouquet of roses, surrounded by garlands and topped with wreaths of foliage projecting from the background on which are perched two more birds, each with sprigs of laurel in their beaks. Another fine piece is a tied lace cravat intricately carved out of limewood. Many of Grinling Gibbons's mantlepieces have clusters of carved cherubs' heads with violins and flora. One example in a house on Tower Hill in London is so delicate that you can see the wooden flowers on the stems projecting from the fireplace vibrate as carriages pass in the street outside.

P IS FOR PLAYS AND PLAYHOUSES

As mentioned at the outset of this A–Z, the Puritans close the London theatres in 1642. The only performances that can take place after that are restricted to private ones behind closed doors. That's doesn't make for box-office success. However, in 1656, Sir William Davenant has a bright idea. If he adds *music*, he can legally advertise his drama as a recital. And that is what he does. He puts on a play at the Red Lion Inn in Clerkenwell, complete with stage sets and musical accompaniment by five of the leading composers of the day. Scenery and music are both novelties on the English stage. But the success of Davenant's project creates a new precedent for how a performance should look and sound. Both become permanent features of the English stage.

The real rebirth of English drama, however, does not take place until June 1660 when Charles II and his brother James attend a performance of Ben Jonson's *Epicene* at the Red Lion. From then on, they are both regular theatregoers. Indeed, it is the royal brothers who set the pattern for the London theatres for the next 150 years or so. The king grants only two patents allowing companies to put on plays in public. Thomas Killigrew gains the rights to operate the King's Company and Sir William Davenant the Duke's Company. In 1661 women appear on the London stage for the first time. Well-to-do people *love* the theatre and these new innovations of stage sets, music and actresses. If you walk at night past Killigrew's Theatre Royal in Bridges Street (subsequently renamed the Theatre Royal Drury Lane), you will see lines of lamp-lit horse-drawn yellow hansom cabs outside the theatre, their drivers waiting for the tide of theatregoers to pour out and call for a lift back to their town houses in the West End.

The richness of the theatre is astonishing. All the old writers are still popular. New folio editions of Shakespeare's works come out in 1663 and 1684; there are lavish new editions too of the works of Ben Jonson, and Beaumont and Fletcher. In addition, the Restoration sees a brilliant array of new playwrights. Aphra Behn is among them. So too are the poet laureate John Dryden and his successor in that role, Thomas Shadwell. Then there are the rakes, George Etherege, Sir Charles Sedley and Lord Rochester. The architect of Castle Howard, John Vanbrugh, is also an accomplished playwright. But the writer whose work has proved the longest-lasting of them all is William Congreve, the author of five comedies of manners, including *The Way of the World* and *Love for Love*. You might recall his lines, 'Music has charms to sooth a savage breast', and 'see how love and murder will out', and 'it is better to have been left than never to have been loved'. And 'Heaven has no rage like love to hatred turned, nor Hell a fury like a woman scorned'.

Q IS FOR QUANTITATIVE ANALYSIS

This doesn't sound like the most exciting subject, I know, but the introduction of quantitative analysis is one of the most important developments of the Restoration period. The reason is simply that you know something with greater certainty when you can measure it. For instance, if I were to sell you a sports car and you were to ask me, 'how fast does it go?' and I were to say, 'very fast,' you'd be none the wiser. However, if I replied, 'I did 123 mph in it on a racetrack last week,' you'd have a good idea how it compares to other cars and what I mean by 'very fast'. The importance of this shift from general impressions to specific quantities suitable for calculation can hardly be overestimated. Along with the shift from the divine to the mortal in respect of physical health, it paves the way for the Enlightenment of the eighteenth century – and for modern science and much of modern society thereafter.

The story begins way back in the sixteenth century, when the parish clerks of London start to compile the Bills of Mortality to measure the impact of the plague. In the early seventeenth century, the nature of these bills is expanded to give the cause of every death in all the parishes of the city and its suburbs. In the 1650s a London draper called John Graunt realises that, because he knows the population of all the parishes, he can work out the likelihood of dying from any ailment mentioned in the Bills of Mortality. He then goes on to work out the first life tables: charts showing life expectancy. He publishes his findings as *Natural and Political Observations Made upon the Bills of Mortality* in 1662. Thus the science of demography is born.

How do we know that 13,200 houses are destroyed in the Great Fire of London? Because the city authorities count them. Having developed the means to record and publish the casualties of plague, it is only natural that they do the same for the casualties of the Great Fire. Then, in the wake of Graunt's pioneering use of statistics, a man with the unusual name of Nicholas If-Jesus-Christ-Had-Not-

Died-For-Thee-Thou-Would'st-Have-Been-Damned Barbon enters the picture. He proceeds to do something almost as unusual as his name. He calculates the risk of buildings burning down and develops fire insurance. Insurance for ships and their cargoes has been around since the Middle Ages but this is the first time anyone has offered insurance for buildings and their contents. And because Barbon wants to save as much property as he can, so he can save himself large sums of money, he also invests in private fire brigades and fire engines.

As you can see, through life tables and fire insurance, quantitative analysis starts to affect people's lives in a practical way. And you don't need me to tell you that, once it starts, quantification is an unstoppable force. By the end of the century, Edmond Halley – he of Halley's Comet fame – is calculating accurate life tables, permitting life insurance to become reality. John Graunt's friend, Sir William Petty, pioneers what he calls 'Political Arithmetic', or economic quantification. In the next generation the astonishingly ambitious Gregory King draws up calculations for the population of the entire kingdom, including sections identifying which sectors of society are contributing to the economy and by how much and how many servants they are supporting. He draws up tables calculating land use, grain production, animal production, beer consumption, income from taxation and even future projections for the size of the population of the country in hundreds of years' time. He is completely inaccurate on this last point – due to his inability to foresee medical advances, improved transport and the development of artificial fertilisers – but in all other respects, his statistical state of the nation is remarkably full and informative. As a result of such changes in thinking, by 1700 the government has a budget. Politicians are aiming to improve the balance of trade. They are more professional than they have ever been before.

Just as the seventeenth century sees us switch from a faith in God to medical practitioners to save us from ill health, so we switch from faith in God to fire insurance to save us from disaster. And we switch from God to a budget to save us from penury. There are several late-fifteenth- and early sixteenth-century events which might be said to mark the start of the modern world – the ascendancy of guns on the battlefield, for example, or the publication of the Bible in the vernacular, or the discovery of the New World. However, to my mind, this shift from natural philosophy to scientific calculation in the late seventeenth century has the best claim of all. You can reason with someone in 1700 and prove that one or the other of you is right. Before that, the very concept of proof is much more nebulous. It is your word against someone else's. And judgement is left to God.

R IS FOR RACING

The Puritans in the 1640s are opposed to most things that might result in you having fun. They accordingly abolish activities like bear-baiting. Excellent news, you might think: no more cruelty to bears. Sadly, no. All the bears are shot. Puritans aren't interested in animal welfare, only preventing people from committing the sin of self-indulgence. They shoot all the racehorses too. So when Charles II returns to England in 1660, horse racing, the sport of kings, needs restoration – just like the monarchy itself.

The Merry Monarch is as much in favour of anything that constitutes fun as the Puritans are against it. He loves gambling and, most of all, betting on horse races. He therefore starts the race meetings at Newmarket again in 1664. Two years later he establishes a race there called the Town Plate. It is run on the old Round Course according to a set of rules devised by the king himself. Charles II takes part and wins one year – thereby becoming the only reigning monarch to ride a winner in any horse race. The Town Plate, in accordance with Charles's instructions, is still run every year to this day.

My reason for highlighting horse racing as worthy of your attention is because of Charles II's rules. As far as I can see, they are the earliest written rules for the conduct of any sport. Before 1666 we have descriptions of sports and how they are played but no formal codification. In the eighteenth century we have rules for cricket and, in the nineteenth, for football, rugby and tennis and so on. But the first set of rules laid down for any sport are those devised by Charles II for racing horses. We may well think of him as fun-loving – and he most certainly is – but he also is a king who uses his position to build things of permanent value. The monarchy is the most important of them. The playhouses are another example. Gentlemanly conduct in sporting affairs is arguably a third.

S IS FOR SUPERSTITION

Whenever I begin to write about a historical period, I buy a handful of low-value coins minted at the time. To me, these things are inspirational. They are miniature artworks in silver and copper. They have been rubbed and worn as they have passed from hand to hand. Each one has threaded its way from pocket to purse and in and out of our lives, sewing us all together, as it were, with an invisible cord. They have purchased everything money can buy, literally, from bread and milk to sex, drugs and chamber music. They have been spent in hope and in despair. Some have been lost and found; some have been stolen. I love the poetic mystique implicit in the fact that, although they each have a real past, we will never know what it is, for we will never be able to find out where they have all been. And I love the fact that while I was writing *The Time Traveller's Guide to Restoration Britain*, I read that in the London markets, the traders would always take the first coin they received in the morning, spit on it, and put it aside in a pocket for good luck throughout the day. How many hundreds of times have my treasured coins been spat on over the years!

Society is riddled with little superstitions like this. As Robert Burton notes in his book *The Anatomy of Melancholy*, first published in 1621 but reprinted many times, 'sorcerers are too common; cunning men, wizards and white witches as they call them, in every village, which, if they be sought unto, will help almost all infirmities of body and mind'. Valentine Greatrakes, an Irish faith healer, comes to England to practise in 1666 and impresses many people with his ability to alleviate their suffering by 'stroking' them with his hands. You've already heard about the king's supposed power to cure scrofula by touching those affected. Ceremonies are accordingly held in which the king touches a coin and hands it to each sufferer who has obtained a place in the queue. On a similar note, it is widely believed that when somebody is desperately ill and going to die, and every medical procedure has been tried and failed,

the very last resort is that of applying freshly killed pigeons to the feet. This happens to Charles II's queen, Catherine – and, Lo! The pigeons work their magic and she recovers.

Such superstitions as putting a coin in your pocket and touching for scrofula are positive ones. No one is harmed. No one is put to any expense except the king in handing out hundreds of coins, and he wouldn't do it if he also didn't have something to gain. Indeed, the cost-effective nature of superstitions is one of the reasons why they last so long. But there are some negative superstitions in society too, and none of these is more notorious or more damaging than witchcraft.

Contrary to most people's assumptions, witchcraft is not a medieval crime. It is simply an aspect of everyday life. It only becomes a felony when Henry VIII introduces the first Witchcraft Act in 1542. This is repealed on his death five years later but another Witchcraft Act is introduced by Elizabeth I's government in 1563. This makes it illegal to kill people through witchcraft. You may think this harmless. The trouble is that the practice of witchcraft is officially recognised, so if someone accuses you of killing their child through malefice, how are you going to defend yourself? It isn't a valid defence to say witchcraft is just bunkum. Besides, it turns out to be more complicated than that. Sometimes, in situations where people really do believe in witchcraft, the very shock of being cursed by someone they believe to be a witch can cause them to die. The phenomenon has been described as 'Voodoo Death'. The superstition of witchcraft is thus doubly pernicious as it creates the grounds for its own murderous success.

The third Witchcraft Act is passed by James I in 1604. This is the nasty one, which makes it punishable by death even to invoke magical spirits or be a witch. All those sorcerers, wizards and white witches that Robert Burton noted are under threat. People are regularly hanged for witchcraft in England. The last death sentences are delivered in Exeter: to the three Bideford Witches in 1682 and to Alice Molland in 1685. The judge who sentences them to die for witchcraft is no hick from the sticks; he is a fully qualified London assize judge. It is a salutary thought that Isaac Newton's *Principia*

Mathematica – the fundamental work of modern science – is published just two years later, in 1687.

T IS FOR TOBACCO

There are some Restoration people who think that smoking tobacco is bad for you. However, they are in the minority. Most people think it nourishing. Boys at some schools in the west of England are given tobacco and taught in their first lesson of the day how to breathe in all that wonderful smoke. At Eton College, boys can be beaten if they refuse to smoke because it is considered a preventative against the plague. One summer day, Thomas Baskerville is riding through a town in Wiltshire at 4 a.m. He notes how all the old women are sitting in their doorways knitting and smoking pipes. Pipers at the gates of dawn.

How much do people smoke? As much as they can, in many cases. And it is not that expensive. You can buy nine clay pipes for 1d and the cheapest tobacco from Virginia only costs about 3s 4d per lb. In addition, it is important to remember that a little can go a long way: all tobacco is consumed unfiltered. As for specific quantities, some evidence is afforded by the personal accounts of the duke of Bedford. His sons have their own allowances, so we can be fairly sure that his personal supply is for him alone. On average, he gets through 30lbs per year. That is the equivalent of more than an ounce and a quarter every day. If he were to roll that much in the form of modern cigarettes, his consumption would be at least fifty fags a day. The consequent damage to his lungs probably contributes to his early death – at the age of eighty-four.

U IS FOR UNHAPPINESS

As you can see, there are many reasons to be unhappy if you find yourself in Restoration England. It's very cold yet there's a good chance that your town will burn down, taking your house with it. Justice is so questionable that you can be locked up if you're on the *jury*, never mind being in the dock. You might find yourself hanged for witchcraft and it is not likely that a rotten tooth will kill you. Yet the suicide rate is surprisingly low. As we saw in 'H is for Health', the number of people hanging themselves in London only accounts for one death in 500 of those aged over ten. The overall suicide rate – deaths in relation to population – is just 56 per million in 1700. Today it is about twice that – 105 per million.

That contrast might surprise you. But it prompts the question: when are the highest suicide rates in English history? The answer: the period generally supposed to be the most halcyon in English history – the first decade of the twentieth century. The peak is 305 per million in 1905. I would suggest the social expectations of Edwardian Britain and the pressure to succeed – in business, in a career, in marriage, in society, in politics – are the root causes of the raised rate. During both World Wars, it falls back to 120 per million. I suppose that is when the pressure is off. Life is relatively simple: fight, survive, look after each other, win, and have a cup of tea. High and low statistics from other countries suggest that high-pressure situations and an ageing population are reasons why greater numbers of people kill themselves.

Reading across from this is, of course, a very uncertain way to gauge unhappiness. But we have to note that, despite all the negative aspects of life in the late seventeenth century, the low suicide rate suggests that people were not subject to the pressure to succeed in marriage or their career, and they weren't abandoned in their old age but looked after. In all, it is not an unhappy time. But that is in 1700, forty years after the Restoration. Whether we can say the same for England in 1660, after twenty years of civil wars and puritanism, I am not so sure.

V IS FOR VIOLENCE

Is Restoration society violent? A bit, yes, but it is not that bad – it is not like the Middle Ages. As a result of improvements in the system of law and order, the homicide rate in England has dropped from

23 per 100,000 people per year in the fourteenth century to just 4 per 100,000. That is four times the modern level but lower than that of the present-day USA. So, if you regard the USA as a safe place to visit, you should be quite happy with the level of violence you encounter in Restoration England.

Having said that, I need to mention one big caveat to any gentlemen. Duelling.

If you are a man of substantial wealth and dignity – especially if you have a commission in the army – you may be expected to fight a duel to defend your honour if someone insults you or you insult them. Note that you will fight with swords – duelling with pistols doesn't start until 1711. Also note that swords are the more dangerous weapon in a duel. When shooting a pistol, you can miss or deliberately shoot wide and say honour has been assuaged. You can't do that with a sword. And when fighting with swords, there is a very good chance you will get blood poisoning, even if you do not die from the loss of blood. Hot lead is not as infectious as cold steel.

Why would you even think of fighting a duel? Perhaps the most common cause is to defend a woman's virtue. But such encounters don't always go that well. In 1668 the earl of Shrewsbury challenges the duke of Buckingham to a duel because the duke has been having an affair with the countess of Shrewsbury, his wife. It is all very romantic – except for the fact that the duke kills the husband. After that, the countess finds herself a kept woman under the same roof as the duke's wife until the duke tires of her and packs her off to a French convent.

Most other causes for fighting duels are rather ignoble. Lord Chesterfield fights a duel over the price of a mare. Conyers Seymour is killed after being challenged by someone who doesn't like the way he dresses. The honourable William Wharton is killed in a duel over one of his poems. That last one leaves me conflicted. While I can't imagine challenging anyone who didn't like one of my poems, you have to have some respect for a man who is prepared to defend his artistry with his life.

W IS FOR WOMEN

Is life getting any better for women in these years? On the basis of some of the points made above, the temptation is to say yes, it is. For a start, the Adultery Act no longer threatens women with the gallows if they become pregnant as the result of an affair. Women can now earn a living on the stage, should they wish to do so. Some women find this is the best way to attract a gentleman who will keep her as his mistress for a while. Although this is not a career path that all would wish to follow it does allow girls like Nell Gwyn to catch the eye of a handsome 'protector'. Some actresses, like Mrs Elizabeth Barry, fight through the shame and the stigma to become honoured actresses in their own right. A few like Anne Bracegirdle gain fame on the stage without having to sleep with a rich man. Nor is the theatre the only way of making a living as an independent creative woman. Aphra Behn shows it can be done through writing novels and plays. Mary Beale demonstrates it can be done through painting portraits of the wealthy.

To be honest, though, this is a superficial view of how female fortunes are changing. Most ordinary women are not able to make a living from their acting or writing. Most cannot write. As society becomes more professional, so medical skills are associated with qualifications, which are only available to men. Whereas Elizabethan women could put their experience looking after the sick to good use, medically minded women in the Restoration are limited to being nurses and unable to charge the fees that men are paid.

On top of this, the old manorial system is breaking down. The consequences for ordinary women are serious. Instead of a husband and wife being co-tenants of a parcel of manorial land, which they farm in common, the land is owned by the husband alone. Worse, for those who are forced into towns by the enclosure of common land, a division of labour takes place. The husband goes out to work – because men are paid at least twice as much as women – and the wife tends the house, looking after the children and performing the domestic functions. Thus we see a shift from the couple being equal partners to the husband being the breadwinner and the owner of the income and the wife being little more than the chief servant. The disadvantages to the women are obvious: the man holds all the money. This only strengthens the imbalance of a married couple being legally a single entity represented solely by the man.

X IS FOR XENOPHOBIA

There aren't many black people in Restoration Britain – perhaps 5,000 in all – and their lot is generally not a fortunate one. On the positive side, English law does not permit the existence of slavery. As the lawyer Sir John Holt declares, 'as soon as a [black person] comes into England, he becomes free; one may be a villein in England but not a slave'. However, the very fact that black servants have to wear a collar with the name and coat of arms of their owner gives the game away. They are bought and sold. Black women and girls are often used by their masters for sex or lent out to their friends, just as they are in Elizabethan England. They are slaves in all but name.

Sometimes courts will side with a black servant in a disagreement with his or her master or owner. Dinah Black is brought to England by her owner but refuses to return to the Plantations when instructed to do so. The case goes to court and the judge in Bristol declares her mistress has no power to force her on to the boat. But even when black men and women win the right to remain in England as independent people, the question arises of how they can support themselves. Most have to work as a servant for a wealthy household. As there is some prestige in having a black servant, it is not difficult for them to obtain such a position. But the presumption is that the servant in question is owned – and that is entirely due to the colour of his or her skin.

Y IS FOR YOUR ANCESTORS

I reckon that about 1,560 of my ancestors are alive at some point during the four decades of the Restoration. And that is just direct ancestors – it doesn't include distant uncles or cousins. I was born in 1967, so if you are younger than I am, the chances are that you have more Restoration ancestors even than that. In contrast, how many relatives do you have alive today? Perhaps thirty or forty, including all the cousins, nephews and nieces, uncles and aunts you may know. It follows that, in some senses, this society I have been talking about represents your family even more than your current crop of relations do. Your Restoration family is perhaps forty times larger than your current family. But then, England's population is one-twelfth of the size. So your Restoration family represents almost 500 times as much of the population as your present-day family.

The implication of this is that we are all the beneficiaries and the survivors of everything that happened in these years. Even if we are not descended from a particular individual, we are the descendants of those who knew him or her. The seventeenth century is not that distant – we are only talking about your seven-greats, eight-greats and nine-greats grandparents here – perhaps a few six-greats, if you're older than me. Moreover, the majority of those Restoration men and women who have descendants alive today have thousands of them – many more than we have ancestors. The Restoration is thus the progenitor of an enormous family with which we should feel intimately connected.

Z IS FOR ZENITH

What is the zenith of this age? What aspect of English culture reaches its pinnacle in these years? Perhaps individualism – as exemplified in the diary of Samuel Pepys and the panache of the rakes. But does this really compare with the cathedrals – the zenith of the Middle Ages – and the works of Shakespeare? What else might count? Coffee and tea? Champagne? Royal immorality? None of these things. The zenith of the age has to reflect the great shifts I have mentioned: from believing that God alone will cure you to trusting a medical professional to do so. From praying that your house will not burn down to paying an insurance premium. From natural philosophy to science.

You might remember from my medieval A–Z that natural philosophy is 'the exploration of the physical state of God's creation' and 'science without the mathematics'. In the Restoration, the understanding that natural philosophers are exploring God's creation remains relevant. The greatest natural philosophers are all deeply religious men who believe that exploring nature and discovering God are part and parcel of the same activity. Robert Boyle, the chemist after whom Boyle's Law is named, has Bibles printed for the poor at his own expense. Sir Isaac Newton sees his research as less important than his commentaries on the Bible. But these men push the boundaries of natural philosophy so far that the other defining characteristic of natural philosophy – that it lacks mathematics – ceases to be true.

The story begins, like so many Restoration developments, with Charles II. The man is genuinely interested in natural philosophy, especially biology and chemistry. In 1662, on being informed that a group of like-minded natural philosophers are meeting at Gresham College in London, he grants them a charter of incorporation as the Royal Society. Their motto from the outset is *nullius in verba*, which means 'take nobody's word for it'. Accordingly, they set about experimenting. Robert Hooke is employed as their chief researcher. The *Transactions of the Royal Society* are printed and circulated from 1665, allowing the accurate transmission of knowledge around the whole of Europe. The same year, Hooke publishes his *Micrographia*, an extraordinary work containing engravings of miniscule objects and creatures as seen through a microscope. Being the adaptive genius he is, Hooke not only can make the lenses for such instruments, he can also use them effectively and engrave what he sees.

Micrographia contains one of the most famous images of the age: a flea, magnified and accurately engraved so that the image is 18 inches across. The reading public are stunned. Their eyes are suddenly open to things they have never previously imagined. Hooke's work has an effect similar to that of Columbus crossing the Atlantic 170 years earlier. Just as Columbus shows people how the revered writers of the ancient world did not know everything, and that there are wider horizons to explore, so Hooke broadens the horizons of his contemporaries. After they see Hooke's flea, everyone knows there is much more to the natural world than meets the eye.

Charles II also has a hand in the establishment of the Royal Observatory in 1675, appointing the first astronomer royal, John Flamsteed,

> to apply himself with the most exact care and diligence to rectifying the tables of the motions of the heavens, and the places of the fixed stars, so as to find out the so much-desired longitude of places for the perfecting the art of navigation.

This leads to the finest clockmaker of the century, Thomas Tompion, being commissioned to make a pair of accurate clocks for the observatory. Each of these has a pendulum 13ft long and can run for a whole year on a single winding. They are accurate to 2 seconds per day – by modern calculation – which is extraordinary, considering the pendulum clock has only been around for twenty years when Tompion makes them.

Without doubt the greatest natural scientist of them all is Isaac Newton. He is 'the Shakespeare of Science', the man who sets about applying mathematics to real life. Indeed, his *Principia Mathematica*, published in 1687, is often likened to Shakespeare's First Folio. You have already heard how some of the most agile minds of the age are applying quantitative methods to the economy, insurance, and life expectancy, among other things. In *Principia Mathematica*, Newton does the same – but with the whole of existence in mind. Celestial objects, Earth-bound forces, gravity – you name it. In his work on optics he explores the nature of light, showing how white light is composed of colours, allowing the scientific study of light wavelengths. He devises and builds the first reflecting telescope. He even reorganises the nation's money supply. And yet, as mentioned a moment ago, he considers his commentaries on the Bible to be the culmination of his life's work. That says a great deal for the man.

He achieves so much because he has an extremely well-informed critical audience, namely God.

And that is why the shift from natural philosophy to science is the zenith of the late seventeenth century. It is a scientific approach that springs from deep faith and touches almost every walk of life. It causes explorers to discover the flora and fauna of the world. It inspires astronomers to map the stars to facilitate the explorers' endeavours, and clockmakers to make extremely refined timepieces to improve the work of the astronomers. Apothecaries and botanists test the new-found plants for medicinal and nutritional value. Mathematicians like Newton work out how bodies move and how light works. The divine touches daily life and vice versa. Physicians answer prayers for improved health; insurance companies answer prayers for safety and security. And practical inventors pick up on the spirit of enquiry and run with it – not out of any great desire to understand creation in a religious sense but rather to discover the potential of the physical world.

One such man, Thomas Savery from Devon, is keen to experiment with pumps. In 1698 he obtains a patent for a new machine that can pump water from mineshafts. He is not the man who eventually makes it work on a cost-effective basis – that falls to another Devonian, Thomas Newcomen – but Savery is the one who has the idea. And, in Newcomen's hands, it changes the world.

Today, we call it the steam engine.

PART FOUR

A TO Z

OF REGENCY ENGLAND

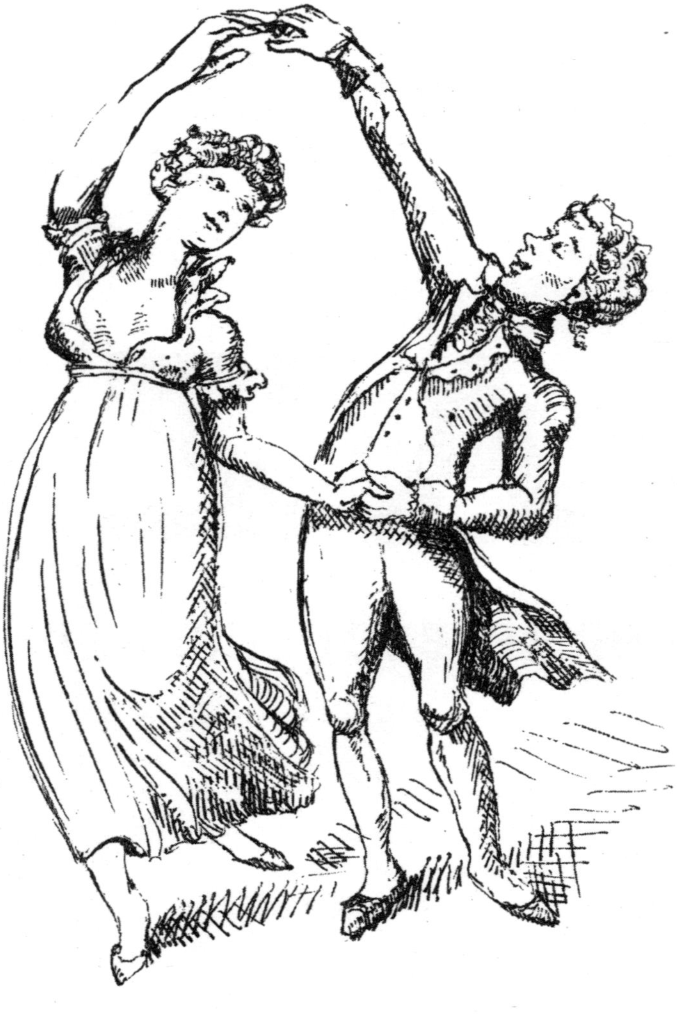

REGENCY ENGLAND

1789–1830

The Regency is the period during which the Prince Regent, the future George IV, exercises the offices of the head of state. His father, George III, has prolonged bouts of madness in his final years, preventing him from ruling. Thus the Regency *officially* lasts from 1811 (when Prince George becomes the Prince Regent) to 1820 (when the old king finally dies). However, there is a cultural continuity over the years from 1789 to 1830, so we often refer to the whole period as 'The Regency'. It is this 'long Regency' that is the subject of this A–Z.

The Regency is one of the most popular periods of English history. I have no doubt this is partly due to its grand name – the *Regency*. It sounds like drinking champagne on a deep blue velvet sofa while having your feet massaged. But another important reason is the far-reaching influence of Jane Austen's novels and the Regency romantic stories that have been written in their wake. On top of these, we have to consider the glamour of the period, exemplified perhaps by the romance of Nelson and Lady Hamilton. The Napoleonic Wars add a dash of heroism: these too have spawned a number of novels. Another reason for the popularity of the period is that it sees some of England's finest poets at work – including Lord Byron, Percy Shelley, John Keats, William Wordsworth and William Blake. Consider too all the industrial breakthroughs, from suspension bridges to steamships and railways. But mostly we love the Regency because of the elegance of its architecture and design, which many people feel has never been bettered. This brilliant array of achievements, coupled with the fact that this is the last generation that experiences England's 'green and pleasant land' before it is aesthetically marred by the 'dark, satanic mills' of the Industrial Revolution, means that many people look back on the Regency period with bundles of muslin-and-lace-wrapped nostalgia.

Therefore, without more ado, let me reveal my A–Z, which begins with the most predictable 'A' of them all:

A IS FOR AUSTEN, JANE

Born in Hampshire in December 1775, Jane Austen starts to write at a young age. She completes the first draft of *Pride & Prejudice*, which is originally called 'First Impressions', at the age of twenty-two. This ostensibly tells the story of how Elizabeth Bennet meets and eventually marries Mr Darcy, a gentleman with a substantial estate. But the author's main concern is an exploration of the nature of people's characters and judgement. Her book also critiques the manners and mores of the English landed gentry and the upper middle classes, with much wry humour. It isn't published for fifteen years, however, only appearing in 1813, two years after her next work, *Sense & Sensibility*. Two more novels follow in her lifetime, *Mansfield Park* in 1814 and *Emma* at the end of 1815. Then Jane tragically dies in July 1817, aged just forty-one. Her other two completed novels, *Northanger Abbey* and *Persuasion*, are published posthumously.

Jane Austen's works have such charm and intelligence that they win over more admirers with every passing generation. They contain extraordinarily perceptive views on personality and show Regency people to be just as sophisticated and intelligent as we are. Indeed, one of Jane Austen's great achievements is to combine a sense of the universality of human nature with a unique point in time, namely the years around 1800. Thus she allows us to imagine what it would be like for us to live in England during this period. She is definitely the poster girl for the bright side of Regency life.

    Let me emphasise the 'she' – the feminine element – in that statement. Although men enjoy Jane Austen's works just as much as women (the Prince Regent and Sir Walter Scott are both big fans), events in her novels are presented from the female point of view. Yes, the men are predominantly still the landowners and the bigwigs in society but in social situations, they often haven't got a clue. It is the women who are most aware and in control. No one has really done this in literature before. Jane Austen prioritises a female perspective on the world in which women aren't being taken advantage of or treated as less-significant, even if society does regard them as less important. You have to add into the mix the fact that her heroines are all from privileged backgrounds and all young. Their lives are before them. Not only do her readers have the chance to escape into a world of taste and elegance but also we can share in the enormous optimism of youth.

Jane Austen's legacy is tremendous. Her works are the reason why so many historical romances are set in the Regency period. Inspired by her, the twentieth-century writer Georgette Heyer creates a series of novels that echo this wonderful escapist, optimistic and female-centred view of the world. These works are successful because they are believable, located in the world of Jane Austen – which Jane herself has shown us is real. So it's easy for us to dream about meeting our own Mr Darcy or Mr Knightley. Or, if you are an old-fashioned chap like me, having Miss Bennet or Miss Woodhouse suddenly realise she loves you after all. And from Georgette Heyer on, the legacy has only grown greater. Jane Austen is still giving us Regency romance stories, albeit indirectly.

Having said that, her focus is very much on the landed gentry and the upper middle classes. She almost entirely ignores the aristocracy and the politics of the age, and only mentions the lower middle classes in relation to their social superiors. The heroine of *Emma*, Emma Woodhouse, declares at one point 'the yeomanry are precisely the order of people with whom I feel I can have nothing to do'. And you suspect that many of Jane Austen's characters would think likewise. As for the working classes, who make up over 70 per cent of the population, she ignores them altogether. They only appear as functionaries in her books.

This A–Z is therefore not about *Jane Austen's* England so much as the England that lies outside the scope of her novels. Brilliant and influential though she is, her well-drawn characters represent a tiny segment of society. As one review of my book, *The Time Traveller's Guide to Regency Britain* puts it, 'Jane Austen… would have found in its pages not only her own world, but other Regency worlds she probably never knew existed.'

B IS FOR BEAU BRUMMELL

According to Lord Byron, the three most important men in Europe are Napoleon, Beau Brummell and Lord Byron himself. As you might have guessed, Lord Byron is wont to say such things. But why does he give such prominence to Beau Brummell? Who is this man and why does Lord Byron think he is important?

Let's start with the 'importance' bit. For centuries powerful men have demonstrated their social superiority through their extravagant clothing. This is still the case in 1789, on the outbreak of the French Revolution. If you look at the accounts of royal events in *The Times*, you will read that the prince of Wales – the future George IV – wears waistcoats bedecked with jewels and embroidered with silver or gold thread, silk stockings with high-heeled shoes with solid gold buckles and coats with solid gold buttons and solid gold epaulettes. He revels in being described as the best-dressed man at every function he attends. He even wears pink high-heeled shoes when he takes his seat in the House of Lords.

But then Beau Brummell enters the picture and centuries of ostentatious behaviour come to an end.

Beau Brummell – George Brummell – is initially a friend of the prince of Wales. He is supposedly very witty although I doubt you'll laugh at any of his jokes. 'Bedford, do you call this thing a coat?' he says – to the duke of Bedford, feeling the cloth of the duke's lapel. When Prince George himself greets Lord Alvanley and ignores Brummell, Brummell quips, 'Alvanley, who is your fat friend?' He also claims to have called off his engagement to a woman on discovering she eats cabbage. But he is in the right place at the right time.

In 1789, he is fifteen years old. During the Terror, when the French start guillotining their aristocracy, he is nineteen. In Paris – the fashion capital of Europe – men and women of high status eschew lavish clothing for the good reason that it is likely to cost them their heads. The men accordingly adopt a form of military fashion. They avoid flashy waistcoats and wear plain ones with practical brass buttons. They take to wearing trousers like soldiers, not stockings and breeches like gentlemen. They present themselves as serious men of action.

Brummell sees all this and realises that what is happening in Paris has a lot in common with some basic English virtues. Gentlemen should demonstrate their nobility of character through what they say and do, not by how they dress. They should aim to impress with the quality of the cut of their clothing, not the quantity of bling they wear. In Brummell's opinion, everything a gentleman does should appear effortless. Understatement is both a virtue and an art. For this reason, when you hear the word 'dandy' – and Brummell is the *arch* dandy – you should imagine an English gentleman whose clothing is not flashy or foppish but sober, refined and perfectly tailored. Trousers, not stockings. Brass buttons, not gold. Plain waistcoats, not embroidered ones. As a group, the 'dandies' are an irritating bunch of privileged young gentlemen who are quick to criticise anything that does not pass their pompous, monocled inspection. But to be fair, they are show-offs in what they *do* and *say*, not the ostentation of their clothing or their social status.

Beau Brummell's standards eventually seep through the ranks of society to affect the way we all dress and behave. If you see a group of English gentlemen in the first decade of the nineteenth century, the chances are that the senior generation will still be wearing formal breeches and stockings while the younger men will be in buff trousers and boots. Twenty years on, and only very old men and servants will still be wearing breeches; almost all the gentlemen will be in trousers. Today, we are still wearing trousers. No one wears breeches. Suits are still judged by the quality of the cut, not the lavishness of the decoration.

This is why Brummell is important, even more so than Lord Byron. After centuries in which expensive cloth, gold and jewels are enough to guarantee admiration, now you have to do or say something to command attention. Status alone is not enough. And style is no longer just a matter of what you wear: it acquires an extra dimension. It requires character.

C IS FOR CLEANLINESS

For anyone planning to travel to the past, I have to break it to you that some of your ancestors are not quite as clean as you are. To put it bluntly, they might whiff a bit. However, I'm glad to be able to say that things are changing. Beau Brummell, in fact, contributes to this cause. He insists that gentlemen should be fastidiously clean. And he practises what he preaches. Every morning, he spends three hours getting ready to face the day. This includes having his body scrubbed with a pig-bristle brush – to get rid of any loose skin.

You could be forgiven for thinking there is something of a craze about personal cleanliness in this period. Gentlemen and ladies all over the country are having bathrooms installed. Whereas in the 1770s and 1780s you'll be hard-pressed to find a bathroom even in a high-status house – and you'll have to wait for the servants to get out a copper bathtub if you want to immerse yourself in warm water – from the 1790s, bathrooms become popular. Cold plunge baths are all the rage too – in cellars or in outdoor buildings. Cold water bathing is deemed particularly good for you.

Lower down the social ranks, a similar revolution is taking place. Public bathhouses are springing up in the major towns. You can have a hot bath in most places for sixpence or a Turkish bath for a shilling. That's still quite a lot of money for a family that is having difficulty making ends meet. But even among the working classes, people are beginning to take cleanliness far more seriously.

One of the prime reasons for this change is a book, *Domestic Medicine*, by Dr William Buchan. It first appears in 1769 but stays in print for decades, going through dozens of editions. Dr Buchan persuades people they need to be clean to avoid illness. Moreover, that obligation isn't just about self-improvement, it's also about benefitting their neighbours and, in turn, their neighbours' cleanliness benefitting them. Dr Buchan explains in short, clipped sentences that, if working people do not wash themselves regularly, they are liable to catch diseases. If that happens, they will be unable to work, will not get paid and will be unable to feed their families. So he makes cleanliness a matter of social importance. As he puts it, 'anybody who can get hold of clean water has an obligation to be clean'.

I can't guarantee you that your Regency ancestors won't smell when you meet them but, if you do drop by for tea, you can be sure that they are less likely to offend your nostrils *after* they have read Dr Buchan's book than before.

D IS FOR DUELLING

You might recall me mentioning in the previous A–Z that England isn't that dangerous in the late seventeenth century – you are less likely to be murdered than you are in twenty-first-century America. So you will be delighted to learn that Regency England is even safer. The homicide rate is down to 2 per 100,000 people per year (roughly twice the level in modern Britain). But once again, I have to warn any hot-headed upper-class men that you are risking your life by visiting this period. If working-class chaps have a serious disagreement, they take their quarrel outside and punch each other. If middle-class fellows cannot see eye-to-eye, they engage lawyers and go to court. But if gentlemen fall out, it's pistols at dawn. And I do mean *dawn*. Duelling is illegal, so you have to get up early to avoid arrest. You won't even get a lie-in on the day you get shot.

It might seem the very height of ridiculousness that the way to solve an argument is to let your angry adversary load a gun, aim at you and pull the trigger. But that is what the honour code dictates. A man of consequence – a public figure or a man with responsibilities – cannot live publicly unless he is prepared to uphold his honour. Therefore the higher your status in Regency Britain, the more likely it is you will be challenged to a duel. The prime minister, William Pitt, fights a duel over his military policy. Another prime minister, the duke of Wellington, fights a duel over his Catholic policy. Even the second-in-line to the throne, the duke of York, fights a duel with another aristocrat over his methods of military command. Every gentleman of rank is liable to have to defend his honour with his life. Only the king and the next in line to the throne are exempt (because, according to Edward III's law of treason, it is illegal even to imagine killing them).

If you are challenged to a duel, your adversary's second – that is to say, his accomplice – will deliver a letter informing you of the fact. If you accept, you will appoint your own second to take a written notice to your adversary, stating the time and place where you will meet. You will choose somewhere remote, very early in the morning, to escape detection. This is not least because, if you kill your challenger, you will probably have to flee the country to avoid being arrested for murder. When you arrive at the place, your seconds will agree how many paces apart you will stand and whether you will fire simultaneously or whether the challenger will shoot first. You may not spend much time taking aim: that is considered bad form. When it is your turn to shoot – presuming your challenger has missed – you will raise your pistol arm, take aim and fire straight away. If you fail to kill your challenger, you will normally have one more shot each. After that, the seconds may well agree that honour has been maintained. However, occasionally the seconds join in and there is a bloodbath. Overall, the risks of dying in a duel are about 21 per cent. In addition, you have a 28 per cent of being seriously wounded. This means half of all duellists walk away unscathed. But only half. If you fight many duels, your chances of surviving into old age will diminish.

In 1809 the war secretary, Lord Castlereagh, challenges the foreign secretary, George Canning, to a duel. These two men are members of the same political party and serving in the same cabinet. Can you imagine it today? Two members of the current cabinet challenging each other. What's more, they don't take it in turns to shoot, like gentlemen, but both fire at the same time, which normally means they are determined to kill each other. As it happens, both ministers miss with their first shot. But then Castlereagh hits Canning in the leg with his second bullet, forcing him to seek medical help. Canning survives – and, eighteen years later, becomes prime minster.

E IS FOR EXPECTATION OF LIFE AT BIRTH

As you have already heard, life expectancy at birth fluctuates over the centuries. Just to remind you, today in the 2020s it is about eighty. In the Middle Ages, it varies between twenty-five and thirty-five. In Elizabethan England, it fluctuates between thirty-five and forty. It drops back a bit and hovers around the mid-thirties during the Restoration period but is approaching forty again in the Regency.

These figures are all national averages. They don't reflect the expectation of life at birth for the poorest of the poor.

If you live in Regency London and are wealthy, life expectancy at birth is forty-four. If you are a tradesman in the city, you can expect your children to live to about twenty-five. But if you're working class, newborn members of your family are unlikely to live beyond twenty-two. Half as long as the wealthy.

That sounds shocking enough. But London is not an industrial town compared to some of the powerhouses in the north. In Manchester, across the whole city, life expectancy at birth is nineteen. In the working-class areas of Liverpool, it is sixteen. But if you go to some industrial towns and investigate those streets where there are no drains – the slums – life expectancy at birth is less than fourteen. In parts of Bury and Ashton under Lyne it is thirteen and three-quarters in the 1830s. In all the centuries I've looked at, I've never seen such a dismal situation. Life expectancy among slaves in Trinidad is better than that. They can expect to live to seventeen.

F IS FOR FRANKENSTEIN

From one cheery subject to another – I did warn you Regency England isn't all one big Jane Austen novel.

The author of *Frankenstein*, Mary Shelley, is just eighteen when she produces her great work. She starts it one day in 1816, when she has a competition with her future husband, Percy Shelley, her stepsister, Claire Clairmont, and Claire's lover, Lord Byron, to see who can write the best ghost story. Mary's creation knocks everyone else's into a cocked hat.

In my view, *Frankenstein* represents the spirit of the age. If you were to ask Regency people what *they* think 'the spirit of the age' is, the word you are most likely to hear is 'evil'. You find this over and over again in people commenting on the state of affairs. Those who have property feel threatened by the French Revolution: they talk of the 'evils' of the time. People who are aware of the widespread calls by middle-class and working-class radicals for political reform similarly speak about these things as 'evils'. People talk about the idea of a police force as an 'evil' – they fear the police will persecute them. They regard science as an 'evil' because it results in all sorts of inventions and concepts that they don't understand. Mary Shelley has her finger on the pulse. She understands the worries running through society. She taps into all the 'evils' of the age.

In *Frankenstein*, the fears she addresses are new and thus all the more frightening. In the late eighteenth century, Luigi Galvani conducts a famous experiment. He puts electric currents through frogs' legs, making them twitch, which makes people think that electricity has something to do with the creation of life. And as we all know from *Frankenstein* itself, the idea is circulating that maybe we can create new life forms. What will be the consequences of mankind being able to control life? What are the implications and responsibilities of all this knowledge?

If you've read the book, you'll be aware that Doctor Frankenstein, having created his monster, realises he's responsible for the monster's happiness. So he thinks, perhaps he should make the monster a mate. But what happens if they have children? What if they multiply and destroy mankind? He can't allow that. All these questions about responsibility and science are wrapped up in the novel, and it's a wonderful metaphor for the age. And for the whole of modernity. Because ever since it was published, in 1818, we have created more ways to destroy ourselves – through making more proverbial 'monsters'.

G IS FOR GAS

If you sail along the south coast of England every year at night from 1789 to 1830, you will see something remarkable happen. Gradually, the whole coast becomes brighter and brighter. If you look towards the shore in 1789, you might see a few pinpricks of light here and there between the big coal-burning lighthouses off the coast of Cornwall, Devon and Dorset, but that will be about all. There are relatively few houses facing the coast, so not many glimpses of candles, chandeliers or carriage lamps will reach you out at sea. But as the 1700s become the 1800s, more and more people choose to live on the coast. That means a few more chandeliers and lanterns and a line of oil-fuelled streetlights here and there. But after 1815, when the end of the Napoleonic War means there is no more risk from the sea, suddenly people want to live facing the water. The most prestigious houses in fashionable Brighton face the beach and this sets a pattern for many more south-coast towns. This in turn means more chandeliers, lanterns, lamps and streetlights on the coast. And then, in the 1820s, gas lamps start to light up the night sky. As the lights grow in number, so they also grow in brightness. Over these years, you will see the south coast increasingly lit up.

Of course, it's not just the coast that is lit by gas. Most major towns receive their first gas streetlights in this era. Only a few – such as Plymouth and Newcastle – are still reliant on oil lamps in 1830. Everywhere else there is 'enlightenment'. Because if it's light outside, people no longer have to be so worried of the dark. It's not a place where you expect to be murdered or mugged. You go out knowing that other good, honest people are around. You can start to enjoy yourself after nightfall. The centuries during which the night is a frightening, subversive, mysterious time are coming to an end. Gas obviously has many other positive benefits – from domestic lighting with indoor gas lamps to theatre lighting and other night-time entertainments, such as being able to buy late-night street food. It thus transforms people's lives.

H IS FOR HOTELS

Hotels start to take the place of inns in this period. The very first one is the German Hotel in Suffolk Street in London. This caters specifically for German-speakers and is in business by the end of 1709. In remains the only hotel in the country until 1768, when The Hotel in Exeter is established. And that starts a trend. The following year, the Polygon Hotel in Southampton becomes the third to open. London acquires a French hotel and an Italian hotel about the same time. It also gains several hotels catering to English visitors, including the Royal Hotel in Pall Mall and several in Covent

Garden. The first seaside hotel, the Margate Hotel, starts up in 1774. By 1800 there are about 200 hotels in London and probably as many again dotted around the country. Hotels, it is fair to say, are a late-eighteenth-century phenomenon.

What makes a hotel different from an old English inn? Inns are wonderful establishments and many of them provide high-quality accommodation. The best ones are as good as almost any hotel. But inns are, on the whole, socially inclusive. Most of the biggest establishments are stopping places for stagecoaches and carriers. They may be luxurious but they are also practical. They are *public* houses. And for foreign visitors of high rank, that is a problem. German and French lords visiting London don't want to have to rub shoulders with carters in smocks and workers with straw sticking out from under their hats. Having arrived by coach with few or no servants, they want to be given good accommodation and to be able to speak to the hotel staff in German and French. If they need a haircut or their shoes shined, they want to be provided with these things in the hotel. They don't require stables or carriage houses but they do demand comfortable bed chambers, good service, warm parlours with the newspapers from back home and their native cuisine in the hotel dining room.

The finest hotels in the West End of London in the early nineteenth century are definitely a cut above the rest. In 1814 the king of France, Louis XVIII, stays at Grillon's Hotel in Mayfair. The same year, the tsar of Russia, Alexander I, declines the Prince Regent's invitation to stay at St James's Palace and goes to the Pulteney Hotel in Piccadilly. Another up-market hotel is Milvart's, which stands on the site of what is now Claridge's.

A German prince, Prince Hermann Pückler-Muskau, stays at the Clarendon Hotel in New Bond Street in October 1826. The editor of his letters describes him as 'Rogue, rover and rake... markedly eccentric, handsome, dashing and brave, a great traveller, a gifted writer and a wonderful landscape-gardener'. His wife Lucie is just as passionate about landscape gardening as he is. In the course of their engagement, he plants more than a million trees. Unfortunately, they bankrupt themselves through all their landscaping projects.

Lucie then has an idea. If they get divorced, the prince can come to England and find a wealthy eligible heiress. He can then marry this other woman, restore the family fortunes and they can all do landscape gardening together. It's a bizarre and bewildering situation. Prince Hermann clearly loves Lucie because, after their divorce and his voyage to England, he writes back to her regularly – sometimes three or four times a week – in great detail about everything he's been getting up to and all the women he's been seeing. And *not* marrying. In fact, he never does find a wealthy bride. But the letters he writes to Lucie are published in 1830 and become an international bestseller. The couple remain close until Lucie's death in 1854.

This is what Prince Hermann tells Lucie about the Clarendon:

> Everything is far better and more abundant than on the Continent. The bed, for instance, which consists of several mattresses laid one upon another, is large enough to contain two or three persons. On your washing table you find not one miserable water bottle with a single earthenware or silver jug and basin and a long strip of towel, such as are given you in all the hotels and many private houses in France and Germany, but positive tubs of handsome porcelain in which you may plunge half your body; taps which instantly supply you with streams of water at pleasure; half a dozen wide towels; a multitude of fine glass bottles; and glasses, great and small; a large standing looking glass; footbaths, etcetera… As soon as you awake, you are allured by all the charms of the bath… Good carpets cover the floors of all the chambers and in the brightly polished steel grate burns a cheerful fire.

Clearly Prince Hermann enjoys his stay at the Clarendon. But Mayfair hotels suitable for a prince don't come cheap. Tsar Alexander racks up a bill for 210 guineas (£220 10s) for a week's stay at the Pulteney Hotel. One meal at the Clarendon will cost you

£3 a head, not including wine, for which you'll pay an extra £1 per bottle. When you think that a working man earns no more than 10 shillings a week, you can see that a top London hotel is unaffordable for most people.

I IS FOR INEQUALITY ON AN INDUSTRIAL SCALE

The Industrial Revolution starts in the second half of the eighteenth century and sees the manufacturing output of the United Kingdom grow massively throughout the Regency period. English goods are exported across the globe, with the result that huge amounts of money flood into the country. England is wealthier than ever before. But does this huge wealth make us more equal? No, it has just the opposite effect. The Industrial Revolution teaches us that huge influxes of wealth can accompany dire poverty – and even contribute to people's worsening standards of living. It explains why some of the greatest levels of inequality are to be found in the richest nations.

Let me begin to explain this with a question: why did the Industrial Revolution start in England?

Cast your mind back to the late seventeenth century and in particular the years 1690–1710. This is when a series of harvest failures wipes out about a tenth of the population of Europe. A tenth of France starves to death (2 million people). A tenth of Scandinavia likewise starves. A tenth of the Scottish population emigrates to England or Poland. These years see real hardship. But in England there are very few casualties. Why does it affect everywhere else in Europe and not us?

When you look at the inventories that survive for English yeomen farmers in this period, you get an inkling. A list of all the possessions of a yeoman with, say, £250 in chattels and goods, will contain perhaps as much as £180 of grain, cattle and cheeses. Prosperous farmers keep much of their wealth in the form of food.

The highly developed market system means that much of this food can be moved fairly efficiently to places of great need, where prices are high. In addition, the system of poor relief allows parishes to buy food for the poor even when it is expensive. This is the situation when the Agricultural Revolution starts in the early eighteenth century. People look at new ways of tending and improving their land, researching forms of fertiliser and crop rotation, and breeding ever larger animals. They want to make sure they will always have an abundance of food for themselves and surpluses to sell.

The result is that, over the course of the eighteenth century, England's food supply significantly improves. In addition, we start to import more wheat. The population increases as a consequence. It has never been much more than 5.25 million: the prohibitive cost of basic grain and protein has always restricted family growth, with the poorest suffering the greatest hardships and the highest levels of infant mortality. But in the eighteenth century the population grows dramatically – from 5.1 million to 8.2 million. That means there are many more poor people. They have nothing to sell but their labour. They do not even have anywhere to live. And that explains the *industrial* element of the Industrial Revolution. Huge numbers of people are looking for work – which means they have to compete for lower and lower wages to make sure they get jobs. And, if you are an entrepreneur, you have a desperate and cheap workforce ready to do whatever you want.

Employment opportunities are not evenly spread across the country. They are concentrated in the Midlands and the north. People accordingly flock to towns such as Manchester, Liverpool, Birmingham and Preston looking for work and houses. They have to accept lower wages, undercutting each other. Irish immigrant workers compound the problem, sometimes offering to work for half of what employers pay the English. At the same time – and this is the really nasty twist – these workers have to outbid each other to get somewhere to live. Thus the working classes are caught in a double trap – having to work for lower wages while paying more and more in rent.

At the other end of the wealth spectrum, the landowners and middlemen are making greater profits than ever before. The rents they receive are going up. Their land is being developed for new housing and factories. Employers too are earning more than ever, benefitting from the cheap wages. Many entrepreneurs make fortunes of hundreds of thousands of pounds – even millions. The brewer Samuel Whitbread is said to be worth £1 million when he dies in 1796. Richard Crawshay, an iron merchant, is worth £1.5 million when he dies in 1810. John Marshall, a flax-spinner from Leeds, is worth £2 million in 1830. These sums put them ahead of all but the richest earls and dukes. Some landowners – especially those who invest in mining – become rich because of industry as well as their vast estates. John Lambton has coalfields in County Durham paying him an annual income of £80,000. Meanwhile many working-class households struggle to make £25 over the course of a year. And all of that goes on food and rent.

There is another way in which the Industrial Revolution leads to greater inequality. At the outset, entrepreneurs pay workers to produce goods by hand. But as their businesses compete with each other, they increasingly move to mechanisation. Now, rather than paying workers piecemeal to weave cloth on looms, they pay factory operatives to tend to machines. When steam power is introduced to factories in the early nineteenth century, mechanisation takes over. Many weavers are laid off and forced to seek work as unskilled labourers. Those who are still employed are no longer weavers but machine operators. Their old skill, which set them above unskilled workers, is no longer valued. This means they sink even lower in the social hierarchy. In this way, the Industrial Revolution shows us that massive economic growth can lead to increased inequality, not a 'levelling up'.

J IS FOR JUSTICE

I've said this before but it bears repetition: 'Justice is a relative concept in all ages and the Regency period is no exception.' The eighteenth century sees the growth of the Bloody Code, so that, by 1800, there are about 200 crimes that merit the death penalty. Lord Halifax's principle of deterrence – that men are not hanged for stealing horses but that horses may not be stolen – is widely believed, especially by people who own horses. You can be hanged for breaking a pond, digging a hole in the highway, going out at night with a blacked-up face or consorting with gypsies. On top of this, judges still have no power to impose lesser sentences. If you are found guilty of doing any of these things, you will be hanged. If someone catches you shoplifting or pickpocketing, it could well be the gallows for you. Even if you are just nine years of age.

Into this bloody arena steps Sir Samuel Romilly. He has one great mission: to eradicate the death penalty. In 1810 he persuades Parliament to repeal the Act that makes pickpocketing punishable by death. Five times between 1810 and 1818 he puts forward Bills to stop people being hanged for shoplifting. Every attempt fails but each Bill gets closer to being successful. The reactionary MPs who are in favour of keeping the Bloody Code realise that they're winning battles but losing the war. After Romilly's death in 1818, his friends carry on his good work. One of those friends is the home secretary, Robert Peel. In 1823 Peel succeeds in passing an Act that abolishes the death penalty for more than fifty crimes. Even better, it gets rid of the rule that judges *must* deliver the death sentence. If you are found guilty of a capital offence after 1823, the judge can give you a lesser punishment for any crime except murder and treason.

These changes really do advance the cause of justice. The extreme severity of the law prior to 1823 means that juries are often reluctant to deliver a guilty verdict because they know the accused person will hang if they do. But when they know that their decision will not automatically lead to someone dying but a more appropriate sentence, they are more willing to convict. And this knowledge proves just as much of a deterrent. Indeed, the 1823 Act might be said to be the first step towards the modern understanding of crime prevention – that it is the likelihood of being caught and convicted that is the main deterrent, not the severity of the eventual punishment.

K IS FOR KINGS

George III. A moral, conscientious, intelligent, enlightened man, who cared about his people but who was plagued by mental illness. Unfortunately for his kingdom, few of his fine qualities were inherited by his seven sons.

What is George III really like? Americans often refer to him as a tyrant. However, American rebels calling his reign a 'tyranny' is nothing more than a rallying call when they are trying to obtain their independence from Great Britain. That's a bit like one football team calling the manager of another a 'tyrant' simply because he is on the other side. Once you get to know him, you realise George is about as far from a tyrant as you can get. His greatest cultural contribution is amassing the biggest private library the country has ever seen. (Today, it forms one of the core collections of the British Library.) His passions are spending time with his daughters and going for walks in the countryside. He'll wander off around the estates near Windsor Castle and chat to the farmers he meets, earning himself the nickname 'Farmer George'.

So a tyrant he is not. But a mentally ill man, yes, that is what he becomes. From the early 1780s he starts to suffer bouts of mental sickness and, by 1788, it has become apparent that he is no longer fit to govern the realm. The following year a Bill is put forward to Parliament, proposing that the powers of the monarch are transferred to his eldest son, Prince George (the future George IV). Fortunately, George III recovers his senses in the nick of time, before the Bill is passed. Consequently it isn't until 1811, when George III finally loses control of his mind, that Prince George becomes the Prince Regent. He holds this position until 1820, when George III dies. After that, he becomes king in his own right.

George IV is a very different person from his father. He is selfish, obese, self-indulgent and uncaring. Prince Hermann Pückler-Muskau describes him as 'the chief actor in a pantomime who deems everybody in the audience infinitely beneath him'. But this 'pantomime' is no laughing matter. George IV is a ridiculous character, and he makes a mockery of the widespread support for the English royal family. Charles Greville, clerk to the privy council, describes him in his diary in the following words: 'a more contemptible, cowardly, selfish, unfeeling dog does not exist. There have been good and wise kings, but not many of them. And this I believe to be one of the worst.' Sir Robert Herron sums him up in just three words. 'Faithless. Worthless. Heartless.'

You'd expect the leading newspaper of the day, *The Times*, to be more respectful in its obituary. However, with George IV there is no point being respectful. He has scant respect for anyone else. This is what the paper says about him on the day after his funeral:

> An inveterate voluptuary: of all known beings the most selfish. There never was an individual less regretted by his fellow creatures than the deceased king. If George IV ever had a friend, a devoted friend, in any rank of life, we protest that the name of him or her has not yet reached us.

L IS FOR LONDON

George IV does have one significant redeeming feature: he is one of the greatest royal patrons of architecture and the arts. This does not outweigh all the negative things his contemporaries say about him but at least it permits one positive factor in an appraisal of his reputation.

You may be familiar with his creation of Brighton Pavilion, a bizarre and higgledy-piggledy yet somehow wonderful cornucopia of a palace, replete with Mughal-inspired domes, French doors and Islamic minarets. Not everyone loves it – Prince Hermann Pückler-Muskau thinks it would be no great loss if it were demolished – but it definitely broadens English architectural horizons.

George IV's legacy in London is significantly greater. It begins with him being given Carlton House on Pall Mall for his residence as prince of Wales. Of course, the old building isn't good enough for George, so he has it modified in every way imaginable. He also makes it the centrepiece of his remodelling of the West End. Lower Regent Street leads north from Carlton House to Piccadilly Circus. Then the great Quadrant sweeps through 90 degrees at the bottom of Upper Regent Street before continuing along to Oxford Circus and then all the way up to Regent's Park. At the start of George's reign the park is just fields. By the end, the most magnificent mansions in London are laid out around it, designed by John Nash. Prince Hermann approves, saying the West End now 'has the air of a seat of government and not of an immeasurable metropolis of shopkeepers'. Writing about Regent Street, the Yorkshire gentlewoman Anne Lister declares: 'surely there is not so fine a street in Europe – so long, so spacious, so consisting entirely of beautiful buildings. Houses like palaces, noble shops...'

But this is George IV we are talking about. In 1825 he decides to move to Buckingham Palace and thus starts work there. Instead of leaving his architectural legacy intact, he orders Carlton House to be knocked down. The centrepiece of the whole arrangement of the West End is demolished. Despite the fact he has spent hundreds of thousands of pounds on it – and that its magnificent imperial staircase and reception rooms are widely admired – it is razed to the ground. It is somehow fitting that George IV ends up smashing up his greatest creation.

London, though, isn't just about royal patronage. It's a thriving and rapidly growing city. In 1789 it's home to about 800,000 people and by 1830 more than 1.4 million. What's more, it's not just the city itself that's growing, the suburbs are too. At the start of the period there are only three bridges over the Thames: London Bridge, Westminster Bridge and Blackfriars Bridge. In the early nineteenth century four more are added: Queen Street Bridge – later known as Southwark Bridge – Waterloo Bridge, Vauxhall Bridge and Hammersmith Bridge. These open up routes to new streets and squares south of the river, so people can ride into the city without having to dismount and pay a wherry or a ferryman. If you add in all the suburbs, the population of London is 1.9 million in 1831, which makes it the biggest city in the world.

You might recall Samuel Johnson's famous words: 'Why, Sir, you find no man, at all intellectual, who is willing to leave London. No, Sir, for when a man is tired of London, he is tired of life, for there is in London all that life can afford.' Never has that been truer of London than during the Regency period.

M IS FOR MONEY

There are several myths about preindustrial England that never seem to go away. One is that no one travels very far from home before the railways are constructed. The logic here is perhaps that there are limited means of travelling in comparison to our own day, so people *must* have travelled less. Or perhaps they know that, before the railways, people normally married someone from the same parish or the adjacent one and thus presume they never went very far. In reality, the reason for so many local marriages has more to do with people seeing a joint future with someone they already know well. It doesn't mean they don't travel beyond their own parish. You only need to look at the thousands of coaching inns up and down the country to know that lots of people are travelling regularly – and covering quite long distances. But such myths die hard.

Another common myth concerns money. Or, more specifically coins. Very often when watching a historical drama on TV or reading a historical novel, the heroine will turn up with a purse bulging with silver and gold. I suppose the assumption here is that – because no one has a credit card, and people today aren't generally familiar with Regency chequebooks and banknotes – everyone living in the early nineteenth century must use coins.

The truth is that you won't find many bulging purses in Regency England. Coins are scarce, for two reasons. The first is that we stop minting gold coins in 1797, when the war with France forces up the price of gold in a guinea to more than its £1 1s face value. People melt them down for the metal instead of spending them. The Royal Mint doesn't resume minting gold coins until after the war is over, in 1815. Much the same can be said for silver. Hardly any silver coins are minted between 1788 and 1815. As for copper, you may be familiar with the big old 1d and 2d 'cartwheel' coins produced in 1797. But they are huge and consequently very heavy, and no one wants to carry them about in any quantity.

The other reason why coins are scarce is counter-intuitive. We have *too much* money. The coins in circulation are just tokens of the nation's wealth. Regency people are spending that wealth so quickly that the supply of coins can't keep up.

What do they do instead? Some enterprising traders issue their own tokens – usually for very small amounts, such as 1d or ½d, to help with small, local purchases. The Royal Mint starts counter-stamping captured Spanish silver dollars, worth 4s 4d each, for use in the United Kingdom. Wealthy people who have bank accounts may be issued with chequebooks but these are generally only used for large sums. Banks start issuing banknotes in smaller denominations – usually £5, £10 or more – but these are of little use when buying a pint of milk. No Regency milkman is going to thank you for paying for a ½d pint of milk with a £5 note. Unless you tell him to keep the change.

People are enormously adaptive, however, and they already have the solution. They've been using it for centuries. It is called the shop book. When you go to buy something from a trader, he will not expect you to hand over cash but will write down what you owe in his shop book. Every month or so, you will settle up. *Then* you might use a £5 note to pay your butcher. Although many people presume credit is a modern invention, it is actually far older than the credit card – and older, even, than banknotes and cheques.

N IS FOR NAUGHTINESS

If you were to draw a graph of immorality as it affects people of various classes in Regency England, it would be shaped like an hourglass. Those at the top of society can get away with almost any moral indiscretion. If you are a wealthy gentleman and you have an adulterous affair, if it is made public knowledge you will still be a wealthy gentleman. Interestingly, this also applies to upper-class women. If you are the daughter of the duke of Devonshire, even if you have a string of lovers, afterwards you still be the daughter of the duke of Devonshire. If you are Lady Harley and you have so many children by different lovers that no one quite knows whose child belongs to which father, people may well refer to your progeny as The Harleian Miscellany, but no one will cross Lady Harley out of their address book in a fit of moral indignation.

This is not true if you are a middle-class woman. The pressure on the middle classes to conform to high standards of moral behaviour is very great indeed, and women who have affairs are likely to find themselves shunned. Their husbands will feel humiliated and lessened in status if their wives cuckold them. Middle-class men use prostitutes in great numbers but it is done furtively and normally with women of a lower class. Those who write about the subject often express their shame. If they are discovered, the shame is greatly increased.

At the bottom of society, the naughtiness begins to expand again. Women are less worried about their reputations – they have more urgent things to think about, such as where the next meal is coming from. Thousands turn to prostitution. Others do not become prostitutes as such but informally share their sexual favours with men they know. Inspectors who investigate slum conditions in the industrial towns often note that men are sharing beds with multiple women. Immorality is rife. Many women have nowhere else to go but to seek someone's protection – whether that be a local gang leader or a married sister's husband.

Given the degree of naughtiness in the Regency period, it seems an appropriate moment to look into the matter with another mini A–Z.

THE A–Z OF REGENCY NAUGHTINESS

A *is for Adultery*

The hourglass of immorality particularly applies to adultery. The wealthy are intoxicated with the idea of the freedom of the individual. This includes high-status women. As one of James Boswell's female friends says to him, 'I do not see why I should not indulge myself in gallantries with equal freedom as my husband does, provided I take care not to introduce a spurious issue into his family.' Occasionally that happens, though. The second Viscount Melbourne, the future prime minister, is supposedly the second son of the first Viscount Melbourne. It is more likely that he is the result of the countess's alleged affair with Lord Egremont, who keeps fifteen mistresses and sires more than forty illegitimate children at his country house, Petworth, in West Sussex.

B *is for Betting*
Regency gentlemen are besotted with betting. They will undertake almost anything for a wager. One magazine in 1790 carries a report of a man in Windsor eating a live cat for a bet. The man suffers considerable loss of blood as the poor animal puts up a spirited defence but eventually only its bones remain. Perhaps the most entertaining bets are those recorded in the betting book at Brooks's Club in St James. My favourite is Lord Cholmondley's bet of 500 guineas, payable – in the words of the betting book – 'whenever [Lord Derby] fucks a woman in a balloon a thousand yards from the Earth'.

C *is for Cross-dressing*
Society is tolerant – even encouraging – of women who dress as men. The same cannot be said for men who dress as women. However, one of the most famous male transvestites in English history lives in London in this period. His name is the Chevalier Charles d'Éon. He has in his keeping letters that incriminate the French king, Louis XV, in some secret business. After Louis XV's death, Louis XVI pays the chevalier a royal pension in order to buy his discretion but insists that he should wear female attire for the rest of his life. Charles accepts on the condition that he can continue to wear his military medals. Thus he dresses as a woman every day for the next three decades, even demonstrating his fencing skills in a dress.

D *is for Dice*
Of all the forms of betting that gentlemen and ladies pursue, the most common must be cards and dice. Vast fortunes are won and lost on the throw of a dice in games of Hazard. As Lord Byron says, 'I have a notion that gamblers are as happy as most people – being always *excited*. Women – wine – fame – the table – even ambition – sate now & then, but every turn of the card & cast of the dice keeps the gambler alive… [I love] the glorious uncertainty not only

of good or bad luck – but of any luck at all.'

E *is for Erotica*
Admirers of the political cartoonist Thomas Rowlandson sometimes are shocked to discover he is also the artist responsible for outrageously coarse depictions of couples fornicating, women being seduced or masturbating, or hitching up their skirts to urinate. In truth, there is quite a lot of erotica circulating. Not all of it is as coarse as Rowlandson's drawings; some of it is relatively tame, such as 'The Merry Accident' – a print showing the celebrity courtesan Kitty Fisher's uncovered legs after she tumbles out of a carriage. A great deal of it is simply voyeurism. But some of it is so outrageous it would even put Rowlandson to shame.

F *is for Free love*
The idea of individual liberty fires up some people to advocate a radical new idea, namely free love. The feminist Frances Wright opposes marriage and espouses free love as part of her vision of equality between the sexes. She is supported in this by Richard Carlile, the editor of *The Radical*, who states 'a true moralist sees no crime in what is natural and will never denounce an intercourse between the sexes where no violence nor any kind of injury is inflicted'. Their views remain in the minority, however. Those who believe in free love tend not to preach but practise it – at every opportunity.

G *is for Gluttony*
Some people are addicted to food. The prince of Wales is the most obvious example. His household consumes 22oz of meat per person every day in 1816 – but you can bet your last farthing that the prince himself eats considerably more than his 119 servants. He is not alone in stuffing his face. The duke of Norfolk has been known to consume fifteen steaks in one meal. Fortunately there is a society to help people like this. It is called The Sublime Society of Beef-Steaks.

H *is for Harris's List of Covent Garden Ladies*
If you are a gentleman in London on the lookout for

sexual entertainment, you might wish to peruse this guide to the high-class prostitutes to be found in the West End. It is published annually from 1757 to 1795. Most of the women listed are in their early twenties and charge between 10s and 5 guineas for an amorous encounter. The anonymous author's descriptions are not without wit. For example, the 1793 edition tells you that at no. 16 Edward Street, Cavendish Square, you will find Miss Jones. She 'was born in the country but the circumstances of her parents, when she was sufficiently grown up, obliged them to send her into London to get a livelihood. It was not long before she got a place in St James Market where, whether by being accustomed to see the poor lambs bleed or rather a desire of becoming a sacrifice to the goddess of love is left for the reader to judge, but she was shortly found stabbed to the heart in the most tender and susceptible part of her body; in short, she was unable to withstand the powerful impulse of nature any longer, so was ravished with her own consent at the age of sixteen. Her mistress on the discovery thought proper to send her going for fear her good man should take it in his head to kill the lamb over again. She enlisted under the banners of Cupid and marched at the head, being of a courageous disposition, and always ready to obey standing orders; she had great success and often made the enemy to yield, by which means she gained no inconsiderable share of spoil, but her charitable disposition (being always ready to relieve the naked and needy) soon reduced her. She is now about twenty-six and though she has been many times besieged and innumerable times bombarded, she looks well and is remarkable for her gentleness and affability.'

I *is for Incest*
You might be surprised to hear that there is no law against incest in Regency England. However, some immoral acts are not just naughty but break fundamental taboos. Lord Byron is forced to leave the country in 1816 as a result of being pilloried in the press –

part of the reason being the scandal of his alleged affair with his married half-sister, Augusta Leigh.

J *is for Joking*
Regency England is full of jokers and teasers. One of the most notable is the heavy-drinking playwright, impresario and politician Richard Brinsley Sheridan, the author of *The Rivals* and *The School for Scandal*. One day he is found by a constable lying inebriated in the street. The constable demands to know his name. 'A Member of Parliament,' replies Sheridan, not getting up. The constable is unimpressed and asks him again for his name. Sheridan says he will only tell him on the condition of the utmost secrecy. When the constable agrees, Sheridan gets up and whispers the name in his ear: 'William Wilberforce'.

K *is for Kissing under the mistletoe*
If someone catches your eye, one of the easiest ways to make your feelings apparent to him or her is to seize the opportunity to kiss them when standing underneath some mistletoe. As the author of *Popular Pastimes*, published in 1816, puts it: mistletoe 'is still beheld with emotions of pleasurable interest, when hung up in our kitchens at Christmas; it gives licence to seize "the soft kiss" from the ruby lips of whatever female can be enticed or caught beneath. So custom authorizes, and it enjoins also, that one of the berries of the mistletoe be plucked off after every salute. Though coy in appearance, the chariest maid at this season of festivity is seldom loth to submit to the established usage; especially when the swain who tempts her is one [of] whom she approves.'

L *is for Lesbianism*
Homosexual acts between men are taboo in this period. Love between women, however, is barely noticed. The Ladies of Llangollen are two Irish gentlewomen who live together as a couple for fifty years in a house in North Wales, dressing the same in both male and female clothes and signing their letters together. The

Yorkshire gentlewoman Anne Lister keeps a diary throughout her adult life describing the women with whom she has sexual affairs. She also goes into depth about her relationship with her sweetheart, Anne Walker, whom in later life she regarded as her wife.

M *is for Mistresses*
A mistress is normally exclusively the sexual partner of a man who keeps her and is not a prostitute, although some women blur the boundary between the two roles. Obviously a man has to be wealthy to maintain a mistress, so kept women tend to be associated with the upper and upper middle classes. Lower-middle-class and working-class men who wish to have extramarital sex use prostitutes instead. Some writers speculate that the taboos in England against middle-class married men having affairs is why there are so many more prostitutes in England than in France. In France, it is far more acceptable for men and women to take lovers.

N *is for Nelson and Lady Hamilton*
One of the most famous illicit dalliances of the period is the affair between the naval hero Admiral Horatio Nelson and Emma, the wife of Sir William Hamilton, the British ambassador in Naples. As both are married, the affair is seen by society as a lip-smacking scandal. This is even more so as the lovers' passion for each other is not only tolerated by Sir William but apparently encouraged. The three share a house in Surrey until Sir William dies in 1803. Emma gives birth to Nelson's daughter, Horatia, in 1801. Nelson's wife, Frances, writes to him begging him to break off the relationship with Emma but he returns her letters unopened. She is heartbroken.

O *is for Opium*
Opium is taken by all classes of society. It is either swallowed in tablets or dissolved in alcohol to make laudanum. It is as laudanum that Thomas de Quincey becomes addicted to it, resulting in his great work, *Confessions of an English*

Opium-Eater, first published in 1821. Samuel Taylor Coleridge is high on opium when he pens his great poem 'Kubla Khan'. But it is also given to children to quieten them down and to sooth pain, to help sleep and to alleviate menstrual discomfort. Laudanum will set you back 4d for 100 drops; tablets cost between 10s and £1 per lb.

P *is for Prophylactics*
If you consort with prostitutes, you are almost certainly going to catch a sexually transmitted disease such as syphilis or gonorrhoea unless you plan to put on 'armour' (to use James Boswell's word for condoms). These are made from pigs' bladders and fastened with a ribbon around the opening. Unfortunately they are quite expensive. As a result, prostitutes generally are unable to provide them for their clients. However, in some up-market brothels, uniformed footmen offer condoms to clients on arrival, to minimise the spread of disease and the damage to the valuable younger women. It isn't good for business if they catch syphilis and their teeth fall out.

Q *is for a Quickie*
Many young men on arriving in London avail themselves of the first woman they pick up in the streets and have sex with her in a court, garden, alleyway, down on the riverbank – anyway they can find. The majority of women in London selling sex operate this way, walking up and down the streets, making themselves available for a brief assignation for 1s or 6d. Magistrates put the numbers of women selling sex in London at 50,000 in 1796 and 70,000 in 1807. That is roughly one-fifth of all females in the city between the ages of fifteen and sixty-five.

R *is for Royalty*
You might think that, with regard to morality, responsible members of the royal family would set a good example. George III certainly does. The sexual shenanigans of his seven sons, however, undo his good work. They all keep mistresses. They don't treat them well, either. William, duke of Clarence, takes the famous ac-

tress, Dorothea Jordan, as his mistress in 1797. She bears him ten illegitimate children (in addition to the four others she has already had with other men). When William leaves her after fourteen years, he keeps custody of their sons and insists that she give up her acting career. Shortly afterwards, she is forced to break her promise not to act in public so that she can pay off her son-in-law's debts. William then cancels her allowance and takes away her daughters too.

S *is for Sodomy*
While lesbianism is hardly acknowledged to exist, homosexual acts between men are considered worthy of the death penalty. At least forty-five men are hanged for sodomy between 1805 and 1830. Nor is there any allowance made in the case of youth. Thomas White is just sixteen when in 1810 he is accused of having sex with the forty-two-year-old John Hepburn. Both the boy and the man are hanged.

T *is for Titillation*
In a world in which clothing plays a major part in assessing someone's status and propriety, even the slightest disorder in the dress can be a turn-on. Women who wish to advertise their charms wear dresses that display as much cleavage as they dare. The requirement for the skirts of dresses to be long means that the very thought of reading the mottoes that some young women wear on their garters holding up their stockings is an incitement to lust. But perhaps the biggest titillation is the 'breeches roles' played by women on the London stage. Actresses with shapely legs wear tight-fitting breeches to show off their figures. One woman, Madame Vestris, has such an attractive figure that if she plays a breeches role, the box office receipts can be guaranteed to go up by £300.

U *is for Underwear*
Men wear both short and long forms of drawers, made of linen. The long form are rather like long johns. Alternatively they might simply fold their long shirt tails under their backsides. Women don't wear drawers unless they mean to

encourage the male gaze by exposing their legs. This is not done in public until 1796 when a fashionable lady appears at a ball wearing 'flesh-coloured pantaloons, over which [is] a gauze petticoat, tucked up at each side in drapery, so that both thighs [can] be seen'. After that, pantalettes (as they come to be called) are an undergarment that even a respectable married woman might wear. Normally it is considered enough just to reveal the frills around the bottom of the ankle, not the whole leg.

V *is for Venereal diseases*
Georgian people believe that the clap and the pox are variations on the same venereal disease, with the clap being the less severe version. By 'the clap' they meant gonorrhoea; 'the pox' is syphilis. When Boswell arrives in London, he writes in his journal, 'I had now been sometime in town without female sport. I determined to have nothing to do with whores as my health was of great consequence to me... [But] I was really unhappy for want of women. I thought it hard to be in such a place without them. I picked up a girl in the Strand and went into a court with intention to enjoy her in armour. But she had none. I toyed with her. She wondered at my size, and said If I ever took a Girl's Maidenhead, I would make her squeak. I gave her a shilling; and had command enough of myself to go without touching her. I afterwards trembled at the danger I had escaped. I resolved to wait cheerfully till I got some safe girl or was liked by some woman of fashion.' Boswell's caution is sensible (although he does not manage to maintain it in the long run). One in five men in London contracts syphilis by the age of thirty-five. Which means almost all prostitutes have it too. Other towns and cities are infected to a lesser degree – about one in ten men – but there is still no room for complacency for those who 'joust without armour'.

W *is for Wilson, Harriette*
Harriette is probably the best-known courtesan in Regency England. At the age of fifteen,

she sets off for fashionable Brighton to find herself a rich lover. She succeeds – in fact, she finds dozens. First she attracts the attention of Lord Craven. Then the Hon. Frederick Lamb (the son of Viscount Melbourne) pays court to her. These men are followed by Lord Frederick Cavendish-Bentinck (the son of the duke of Portland, the prime minister), Lord Lorne (the son of the duke of Argyll), Lord Ponsonby, Lord Hertford, Lord Brougham, Lord Worcester (the son of the duke of Beaufort), Lord Deerhurst, the duke of Devonshire, the duke of Leinster and even the duke of Wellington. She retires in her late thirties and publicly announces her intention to write her memoirs, adding that any gentleman willing to pay £200 will not be named therein. This allegedly elicits the duke of Wellington's famous response: 'Publish and be damned!'

X is for eXotica

Steatopygia is the accumulation of considerable amounts of fat on the buttocks and thighs, creating a significantly enlarged and rounded posterior. It is particularly associated with the Khoisan people, known in the nineteenth century as the Hottentots. One woman from south Africa is brought to London in 1810 and put on display as Sara 'the Hottentot Venus'. She is shown naked at public exhibitions so that people can view her enormous behind and inspect her hugely enlarged labia, which many believe to be a separate organ unique to the Hottentots. Cartoonists cruelly satirise her features and express the strong feelings of lust or disgust that she inspires in viewers.

Y is for Youth

In previous centuries, when members of the upper classes were betrothed to one another, the expectation was that they would cohabit from about the age of fourteen. Harriette Wilson is therefore not behaving that outrageously by becoming the mistress of a lord at the age of fifteen. Besides, she is certainly not the youngest mistress in Brighton. Madame Mary Mathews keeps a brothel in the same town where she specialises in offering sex with girls of fourteen and under; one of whom is only eleven.

Z *is for Zounds!*
The word 'zounds' is a shortened form of 'God's Wounds!' It is a blasphemous exclamation. Elizabethan playwrights use it, as do many of their contemporaries. But by Commonwealth times, blasphemy can incur the death penalty. It is common again in Regency England, although the pronunciation has shifted from 'zoonds' to 'zownds'. Some Regency people might raise an eyebrow but using such a word hardly even counts as naughty.

It just goes to show how rapidly and how completely understandings of immorality changes. And that applies to many of the above points. We no longer hang men for homosexual acts; we don't frown so much on cross-dressing or lesbianism, and we are far more accepting of the principle of free love. On the other hand, we are far less tolerant of opium use, much less sympathetic to men who use prostitutes, and deeply hostile to those who sleep with young girls. Morality shifts and changes more rapidly perhaps than any other social attitude but, as these examples show, such shifts are not always in a more-liberal or less-liberal direction.

And now back to our main A–Z of Regency England.

O IS FOR OCCUPATIONAL HEALTH

You could be forgiven for thinking that there is no such thing as occupational health, only occupational illness. Employers have a 'disposable-pack' attitude to employees: the numbers of people available to work in factories are so great that anyone who is killed or maimed is easily replaced. But the Regency period is full of philanthropic heroes and heroines. You've already heard about Sir Samuel Romilly and his determination to abolish the death penalty, and no doubt you know about William Wilberforce and his quest to abolish slavery. Perhaps you also have heard about Elizabeth Fry and her campaign for prison reform. Now let me introduce you to another social hero, Charles Thackrah, the founding father of modern occupational health.

Charles Thackrah is a young doctor from Leeds, born in 1795. When he is conducting his studies in the 1820s, he happens to notice that in his hometown, many men and women are suffering unnecessarily from the work they do. He calculates that about 350 inhabitants die every year, just from earning a living. Many hundreds more are invalided and left destitute. Very few doctors have ever taken a serious interest in workers' ailments before – the only substantial book on the subject is one published in Latin in 1700 by an Italian called Bernardino Ramazzini. In addition, there have been a few pamphlets and journal articles on individual occupations, but they have led nowhere. Thackrah decides to do something about it.

Thackrah systematically investigates the occupational practices of more than one hundred trades and industries, from the obviously dangerous activities – such as mining and working with molten steel – to seemingly innocuous ones, such as tailoring. Who would have thought that cutting cloth could be so bad for your health? But Thackrah measures a representative sample of tailors and discovers that, on average, a tailor's chest is 3 inches less than that of an ordinary man in the street. The cause, he surmises, is their working posture, for tailors in the 1820s are still sitting cross-legged on their workbenches, as men of their craft have done for centuries. Thackrah says that this is why so many of them have stomach problems and lung defects. He publishes the results of his investigations, *The Effects of Arts, Trades and Professions and of Civic States and Habits of Living on Health and Longevity*, in 1831.

Thackrah's book makes an impact almost straightaway. Michael Sadler MP puts a Bill before Parliament in 1833 proposing limitations on the employment of children in factories, and it is passed as the Factory Act. During the debate in the House of Commons, he holds up Thackrah's book as he speaks in favour of the reforms. And, although Thackrah himself dies that same year, doctors continue to cite his work for the rest of the century. He is not just a philanthropic man himself – he inspires other people to be more thoughtful and caring. And what more could one look for in a hero than that?

P IS FOR PORT

If you have ever wondered why historical novels set in the Regency period describe all the gentlemen drinking port rather than any other wine, the prime reason is simple: war. We fight the French almost continually from 1793 to 1815. This forces us to source our wine from elsewhere – mostly from the Iberian Peninsula. More than half of all our wine comes from Portugal. There is a good reason why Portugal is our oldest ally – and remains so to this day.

Fortunately, we have an excellent man to steer us through this crisis, namely William Pitt the younger, perhaps the finest prime minister we've ever had. And when it comes to winning this war, he has a vested interest. At the age of fourteen, a physician tells him, 'William, my boy, you're going to have to drink a bottle of port every day for the sake of your health.' William dutifully leaves nothing to chance and, when he is prime minister, is alleged to drink *seven* bottles a day. Occasionally he is found asleep in the House of Commons. The man does nothing but drink heavily and run the country. I suspect that the two things go together.

So how does his consumption of port compare with modern standards? A bottle in the 1790s (before the Weights and Measures Act of 1825) is an old pint of 473ml. However, according to hydrometer readings from the early nineteenth century, port is about 23.5 per cent alcohol. So Pitt's alleged intake adds up to more than seventy units of alcohol *per day*. He can't possibly have done that on a regular basis, so perhaps seven bottles is the mark of a special occasion. But William is not the only person drinking on this scale. Richard Brinsley Sheridan is also said to consume seven bottles of port in a day. The duke of York supposedly drinks six bottles of claret every day. Obviously we have to allow for a bit of exaggeration but, all the same, there are Regency men who will drink you under the table – and write brilliant plays and defeat the French while they're at it.

These fellows are all wealthy gentlemen. What about the rest of society?

If you work out how much alcohol is being consumed from the customs duty paid on all the wine, gin and beer produced in England, and add the total of all the wine imported from other countries, and then if you average the whole nation's alcohol consumption across all the people over the age of fifteen, it works out at about twenty units of alcohol per person per week, which is only a little higher than the modern-day average of eighteen. Having said that, today we pay duty on almost all our booze. Regency people don't. A lot of wine and brandy comes across the Channel illegally, courtesy of smugglers. A huge amount is homebrewed – even Jane Austen's household has recipes for gooseberry, cowslip and elderberry wine – and the alcoholic content of these can be well in excess of 20 per cent. And it has to be said there is a fair amount of moonshine (homemade gin) distilled too. I think you can rest assured that, if you visit Regency England and are in desperate need of a drink, you won't have to worry too much about the French blockade on the supply of wine.

Q IS FOR QUACKS

'Quack' is short for quacksalver or 'quack doctor' – an unqualified charlatan practitioner of medicine. And such unscrupulous men are numerous at the start of this period. Indeed, in 1800 you will have difficulty finding a doctor who is *not* a quack. By 1830 there are many fewer: the medical profession has upped its game. But the story is very far from a straightforward one of progress.

The quack doctor develops out of a desire to shortcut the lengthy and expensive process of obtaining medical help. To understand this, you need to know how the medical system works. There are three categories of medical practitioner. The first is physicians, who deal with internal ailments. The second is surgeons, who deal with cutting the skin and external afflictions. The third is apothecaries, who supply medicines in line with the directions of the physicians and surgeons. As people consume more and more medical remedies, so physicians and surgeons charge increasing amounts for their services. Patients start to wonder whether they can save money by cutting out the middle man – the physician or surgeon – and just going straight to the apothecary. And that is what they start to do. But then some suppliers on the periphery of the apothecarial profession think, 'If so many people want to buy these popular medicines, why bother having a shop and waiting for them to come in? Why not just hawk the medicines around?' And that is what many medicine vendors do. Except that then some even more unscrupulous snake-oil salesmen think, 'If people are so gullible they'll buy named medicines from unlicensed vendors in the street, I can sell them any old rubbish at half the price and make a killing.' Unfortunately they often make a literal killing – people die from buying ineffective and dangerous medicines. But that doesn't reduce the demand. People keep getting ill, and then they will try whatever remedies they can afford.

Really, they're buying hope. And being sold hopelessness.

Into this mess steps another medical hero: Edward Harrison, a doctor from Lincolnshire. In 1804 he decides to carry out a survey to see how many medical practitioners in the country have no qualifications at all. The answer is 90 per cent. Shocked, he starts to campaign for a standard, compulsory form of medical education and a suitable licensing system. He is stopped in his tracks by the Royal College of Physicians. They don't want a formal licensing system because they want to carry on controlling the top end of the business without interference from provincial physicians like Harrison.

Fortunately, Harrison is not alone. It takes years of fighting but finally, in 1815, the reformers persuade the House of Commons to pass the Apothecaries Act. It is revolutionary. It forces all would-be general practitioners of medicine to sit exams in anatomy, botany, chemistry, medicine and surgery, to practise in a hospital for at least six months and to be a licentiate of the Society of Apothecaries and a member of the Royal College of Surgeons. Soon afterwards, the legislation is amended so they have to study midwifery as well. After 1815 you may well still die from an infection or injury but, if you do, there's less of a risk it will be just because someone is taking advantage of your illness to enrich himself at your expense.

R IS FOR REFORM

It is possible to look at the political history of England since the Middle Ages as one long reckoning of how you hold authority to account. It begins with the struggle between King John and the barons, and the granting of Magna Carta in 1215. The next watershed is the holding of elections to Parliament in 1265 and the growth of parliamentary power over the sovereign in the fourteenth century. A signal moment comes in 1649 when Parliament executes Charles I. Arguably an even more important moment comes in 1689, when James II is deemed by Parliament to have abdicated by leaving the kingdom the previous year, and William and Mary are invited to take the throne but with significant limitations on their power. However, the truly earth-shattering moment in this story is the French Revolution of 1789–93. Despite all the developments over the years, the English system is still dominated by a land-owning aristocracy and gentry, who run the country in favour of land-owning interests. Much the same can be said for the rest of Europe. But then England and all Europe look on in horror as the French king and aristocracy are overthrown and killed on the guillotine. The *ancient régime* comes to a sudden and bloody end.

The whole Regency period is characterised by growing calls for reform. Many middle-class democrats and working-class radical politicians *want* a revolution in England on the lines of the French one. Members of the aristocracy obviously dominate the House of Lords. But they and the landowning gentry also control the House of Commons, because they own many of the boroughs that elect MPs. What's more, the MPs themselves are often the younger sons of aristocrats. The Cabinet is nearly always dominated by lords and the eldest sons of lords. And this comes at a time when the ordinary man or woman is suffering from want on a terrible scale. You have already heard about the low life expectancy in industrial towns like Liverpool and Manchester, the second and third largest towns in England. Those places don't have any representation in Parliament. This unites their tax-paying middle-class tradesmen and shopkeepers with the workers. Parliamentary representation of the people, not the landowners, is increasingly seen as a silver bullet.

Things get desperate in the years of the Regency proper, 1811–20. First, the Luddites' smash up new factories in the belief that machines are destroying ordinary people's livelihoods. Then there is the end of the war with France in 1815, which sees thousands of soldiers and sailors laid off without prospects. In 1817 there is an attempt to start a workers' revolution at Pentrich in Derbyshire. The same year 'the march of the Blanketeers' takes place. Large numbers of workers try to march on London to present a petition of their grievances. These protests are stamped on by the government, which employs spies to keep an eye on all the radical political organisations. But the calls for reform do not go away.

The most notorious event of these years is the killing of a dozen unarmed citizens at St Peter's Fields in Manchester. Local authorities are scared by the large numbers gathering to hear speeches by Henry 'Orator' Hunt so they call on the cavalry to disperse the crowd. Some 600 innocent people are seriously injured, including children. One of the dead is a veteran of the battle of Waterloo. One moment he is a hero fighting for king and country; the next, king and country kill him rather than give him the vote. It goes down in history as the Peterloo Massacre. George IV sends a message of thanks to the magistrates responsible.

Things cannot go on like this. But George IV will not allow any discussion of reform. Another crisis is narrowly averted after a widespread banking crash in 1825. Still George IV doesn't relent. In fact, he deliberately keeps Lord Grey – the leader of the reformers in Parliament – out of office. Not until George IV is dead can Lord Grey draft his proposals for reform. Two years later, in 1832, the Great Reform Act is passed. Don't celebrate just yet, however, because it doesn't even double the number of men who are able to vote. But it is still worth a modest cheer. It creates the precedent that the British parliamentary system will yield to pressure rather than risk facing a French-style revolution. It forces the upper classes to acknowledge a degree of responsibility.

S IS FOR STEAM

When giving public lectures I sometimes stop and ask the audience if anyone knows the name of the inventor of the steam engine. It amazes me how often I hear the answer, 'James Watt'. As you have already heard in my Restoration A–Z, Thomas Savery comes up with the idea and it is realised in practical form in about 1712 by his friend, Thomas Newcomen. Newcomen buys the patent from Savery and installs hundreds of steam engines to drain coal mines across Europe. More than a thousand have been constructed by the end of the eighteenth century. James Watt is simply the man who works out how to make Newcomen's engine four times more efficient – so that it is worth using even in places that don't have an abundance of coal. His firm, Boulton & Watt, continues producing steam engines until 1895. Hence, generations have grown up associating the name of James Watt with the steam engine.

If you go to Manchester in 1800 you won't find a single steam-powered cotton mill. There are no smoke-belching chimneys. No particles of soot get in your eyes as you walk down the road by the canal. All the cotton mills are powered by waterwheels. The first steam-powered mill in the town is built in 1806. But walk those same streets in 1818 and you'll see 2,000 steam engines, all belching smoke. Return twenty years after that and the number is 10,000. Steam engines transform the urban landscape over the course of a single generation.

Today we hear the words 'steam engines' and immediately think of steam locomotives. These make their first appearance during the Regency period. First, the Cornish inventor Richard Trevithick runs an experimental train in south Wales in 1804. This leads to the proprietors of Wylam Colliery in Northumberland commissioning steam engines to pull coal wagons to Newcastle. One of their early models, *Puffing Billy*, built in 1814, may be seen today in the Science Museum in London. George Stephenson, who is born in Wylam, goes on to design and build many more engines for collieries. Stephenson is also responsible for building *Locomotion*, the first train to run on the Stockton & Darlington Railway. On 27 September 1825 this pulls a carriage full of passengers – the first time that people have travelled between two places by train. Stephenson and his son Robert go on to build the world's first two regular passenger lines powered by steam, one between Canterbury and Whitstable in Kent, which opens in May 1830, and the other between Liverpool and Manchester in Lancashire, which opens four months later.

These early experiments in passenger railways only come right at the end of the period, so most Regency people are more familiar with the idea of travelling by steamship than train. Two such vessels are brought down from Scotland to London in 1815 to take up duties on the Thames Estuary. They are immediately popular. The ships are not dependent on the wind, so they can travel according to a reliable schedule. By 1825 more than 50,000 people are making the journey from London to Margate by steamship every year. In the late 1820s you can take a high-speed stagecoach from London down to Brighton, step on to the Chain Pier and, from that, catch a steam ship to Dieppe in France. All according to a timetable.

People's minds are opened to new possibilities. How far will things go? Lord Byron has an answer. As he puts it in his poem *Don Juan*, one day, steam power will take us to the moon. He says it as a joke, of course, but in a manner of speaking, he is not wrong.

T IS FOR TOENAILS

How do you cut your toenails in the Regency period? How do you cut them in any earlier age, for that matter? After all your toenails aren't like your fingernails: you can't just bite them. And if they grow too long, they can be very uncomfortable, whether you are wearing shoes or not.

The vicar of Branscombe in Devon writes the following entry in the parish burial register for January 1790:

> White, John, aged 77. This man lost his life by a very trifling accident, paring his toenail with a penknife a little too close, so as just to draw blood. It rankled and a mortification coming on, carried him off in a few days.

So there is your answer, a penknife. But the reason why John White's death is particularly worthy of notice is that it is avoidable. Nail clippers are available by 1790. They aren't cheap – they are likely to cost you 5s a pair – but, as you can see from John White's fate, it is a worthwhile investment. Several people die every year from cutting their nails with knives or scissors. We know about them from newspapers and medical reports. But it does make you wonder how many people down the centuries have died from sepsis after cutting themselves while shaving or trimming their nails. I don't know who invents nail clippers but I do know we should all be grateful for such small, life-saving innovations.

U IS FOR UNIVERSITIES

There are two ancient universities in England: Oxford and Cambridge. To say they are a little behind the times is an understatement. To give you an idea of how *far* behind the times Oxford is, in 1828 the vice-chancellor brings a working model of a steam engine into the university for the students to study – so it can be the subject for that year's prize for the best poem in Latin. Here you have a marvel of technology, and it's to be the subject of a poem in a 2,000-year-old language.

Cambridge is not much better. It does have a professor of mathematics but when it comes to appointing professors in new subjects, you've more chance of getting a chair if you're a lecturer in Hebrew or Aramaic than physics or chemistry. You have to swear a religious oath just to enter either of the old universities – to make sure no Catholics, Quakers or other nonconformists get in. It is no exaggeration to say Oxford and Cambridge are resting on their ancient laurels.

As a result of this backwardness, the philosopher Jeremy Bentham and his friends decide to set up a new university, London University, as they call it in 1826. These days we know it as University College London (UCL). The idea is that young men may go there to study ground-breaking subjects without having to swear an Anglican oath. Obviously the furrowed brows of the Church of England's dignitaries don't like this. In 1830 they respond by establishing King's College London, to be a religious rival to UCL.

That rivalry shows you what's really going on in higher education in this period. But I didn't realise this until one day when I was in the National Portrait Gallery in London. As I strolled between the sculptured busts of the great and the good, I noticed that the middle-class social reformers and industrialists – the 'new men' – are all shown in suits. The bishops and ecclesiastical dignitaries are all wearing religious robes and cassocks. And the upper-class statesmen and writers are in Roman togas with laurel wreaths. At that moment it dawned on me: the politicians see themselves as the heirs of Cicero, Caesar and the Roman senate. They believe they are the heirs of the greatest statesmen the world has ever known. That is why the Latin tradition continues to be so strong in the old universities. These men study Latin and Greek and write poems in Latin because the classics are the political antidote to the biblical teaching prevalent in universities. Young men are being taught to look to the great men of the past for inspiration and leadership. Perhaps that prize for Latin poetry, although antiquated, is not such a bad thing after all.

V IS FOR VERSE

Great poets are like buses: you wait for ages and then three come along at once. In this case, Byron, Shelley and Keats... but then you've got Wordsworth, Blake and Coleridge... There's a whole traffic jam of buses. If you really could walk into a Regency bookseller's shop, you would be well-advised to buy as many first editions as possible because the shelves are loaded with some of the most sought-after and most cherished books of verse ever published.

Having said this, it should be remembered that great poets are not always recognised by their contemporaries – and especially not in their youth. Take Lord Byron, for example. In 1808 he publishes his first slim volume, entitled *Hours of Idleness*, which consists of a number of poems he has recently composed since leaving Harrow School and going up to Cambridge with his pet bear, Bruin. Unfortunately the journalist who reviews the book for *The Edinburgh Review* seizes on this point to rip the young lord to shreds.

> So far from hearing, with any degree of surprise, that very poor verses were written by a youth from his leaving school to his leaving college, inclusive, we really believe this to be the most common of all occurrences; that it happens in the life of nine men in ten who are educated in England and that the tenth man writes better verse than Lord Byron.

It is unfair, really, because there are many parts of the book that are both good and original. I have a particular fondness for his 'Lines Inscribed on a Cup Formed from a Skull', the first four verses of which are as follows:

> Start not—nor deem my spirit fled:
> In me behold the only skull
> From which, unlike a living head,
> Whatever flows is never dull.
>
> I lived, I loved, I quaff'd, like thee:
> I died: let earth my bones resign;
> Fill up—thou canst not injure me;
> The worm hath fouler lips than thine.
>
> Better to hold the sparkling grape,
> Than nurse the earth-worm's slimy brood,
> And circle in the goblet's shape
> The drink of Gods, than reptiles' food.

Where once my wit, perchance, hath shone,
In aid of others' let me shine;
And when, alas! our brains are gone,
What nobler substitute than wine?

W IS FOR WOMEN

I have to ask the same question that I raised in connection with Restoration England: are things any better for women? Or are there as many new negatives as new positives?

You've already heard about some of the negatives. They stem from the fact that, when so many people in England have nothing to sell but their labour, the great wealth pouring into the country creates massive inequality. This affects women particularly badly. Not only do women earn half of the meagre wages of their male counterparts but also poor women are subjected to all sorts of sexual exploitation – from prostitution to the normalised rape of female servants by their employers. It is probably true to say that the miseries of women increase in inverse proportion to life expectancy: things are worst for women in places where lives are shortest. While the sexual exploitation of servant girls in the houses of the gentry may be considered horrific, the struggle of those same girls to survive in slums after they have been discharged from their employment on account of getting pregnant – with even greater vulnerability to sexual exploitation than before – might be considered even worse.

For the poor, marriage is the main protection against this everlasting downward spiral of wellbeing. But marrying an abusive husband might also prove to be a disaster. The medieval principle still applies: a married couple is a single legal entity represented solely by the husband. So people come up with a solution in the course of the eighteenth century, namely the wife sale.

It might seem ludicrous to suggest that it is a step in the right direction for a husband to be able to sell his wife in the marketplace to the highest bidder. It seems abhorrent to many middle-class

Regency people too. But the custom is on the rise. This is because it allows an unhappy working-class couple cheaply to divorce – not legally but in a way that their neighbours acknowledge as right.

Such a sale has to be with the woman's consent and has to be to a man she will accept as her common-law husband. Thus she can arrange to be 'bought' by her would-be lover and for responsibility for her maintenance to pass from her husband to a man more to her liking. Desperate situations call for extraordinary compromises and working-class Regency women are prepared to do anything, including undergoing the embarrassment of being 'sold', to rid themselves of an intolerable husband.

So much for the working classes. What about middle-class women? Although several of Jane Austen's characters are fearful of losing their status, there is also the sense that they can marry well and move *up* the status ladder. They do not come across as being unhappy simply on account of being female. Quite the opposite: having the chance to marry well gives them hope.

The age is full of creative, imaginative women living fulfilled lives despite facing deep prejudice. One reviewer dismisses Mary Shelley's *Frankenstein* on the basis that it is written by a woman but many other reviewers praise it. Much the same can be said for Catharine Macaulay, the author of an eight-volume *History of England*. She is advised by one reviewer to seek an occupation 'more befitting her sex' but ultimately is widely praised for her stance on liberty. It is true that Jane Austen advises educated females to 'conceal all your learning' but this is very much said tongue-in-cheek and done to mock conservatives who don't like young women being able to use their wit. And when it comes to performing on the stage, Mrs Siddons is the greatest star of the age – bar none. Similarly, the most famous singers of the time are the female opera singers. The freedoms of Elizabethan and Restoration women have grown and culminated in female stars being as highly thought of as their male counterparts.

What about the upper classes? You have already heard how many of them take advantage of the doctrine of personal liberty to have affairs and exploit their status to their advantage. For women in such a privileged position, their legal disadvantages in relation to their husbands are less important than those experienced by women lower in the social spectrum. But well-off women face another prejudice – that of being seen to be fortune-hunters in marriage.

Harriot Mellon is the illegitimate daughter of an Irish woman from a poor background who works with a theatre troupe. Eventually, having become a minor star of the stage, she becomes the second wife of Thomas Coutts, a banker. This incurs great envy from Thomas Coutts's three daughters by his first marriage.

Coutts is disappointed with their lack of grace. When he dies he leaves Harriott his 50 per cent share in his bank, making her one of the wealthiest people in England. She later marries the duke of St Albans and so becomes a duchess. At the same time, due to Thomas Coutts's careful provision for her, she does not have to surrender control of her fortune to her new husband. Indeed, she runs the bank very successfully. Her experience is perhaps the greatest rags-to-riches story of the century. By all accounts she is amiable, loving, good-looking, intelligent and much loved. Yet other wealthy women look down on her for rising so high from such humble origins. Her extraordinary tale perhaps reveals something else about living in an age of inequality. Even if a woman is fortunate enough to become a millionairess, and successfully runs a private bank, she will still face hostility on account of her sex – if only from other, less-independent, less-successful women.

X IS FOR XENOPHOBIA

We associate the Regency period with the last days of legal slavery so you might think me daft or, at least, insensitive, to suggest that xenophobia might be lessening. However, that very fact – that these are the *last* days of slavery – show that there are influential people in society who are no longer prepared to tolerate such abysmal treatment of their fellow human beings. Parliament legislates against the trans-Atlantic slave trade in 1807 and finally abolishes slavery as a legal condition in all British dominions in 1833. It is resisted to the last by those in favour of retaining their ownership of slaves, but their arguments are largely economic. The moral war has already been won: 1833 is just one of the final battles.

England itself has not recognised the legal existence of slavery on these shores since the sixteenth century – and then it did so only very briefly – and so there is a sense that England is a better place than America for black artists and writers to live and work. This is all the more the case after 1772, when the lord chief justice,

Lord Mansfield, declares authoritatively that slavery is so 'odious' it cannot exist except by the introduction of the law, and that no such law is in place in England to allow a slave owner forcibly to take another person – i.e. his supposed slave – out of the country. Although this ruling is intentionally narrow, it is widely seen as confirming that one cannot be a slave in England. As a result, black writers, actors and musicians come here in greater numbers, confident of being able to practise their art without being presumed to be a runaway slave or, worse, kidnapped and sold into slavery on account of their race. Miss Lambe, a leading character in Jane Austen's last, unfinished novel, *Sanditon*, is described as a half-black seventeen-year-old from the West Indies and of immense fortune. Perceptions of black people in England are definitely changing.

Having said these things, day-to-day racism is still common. You've already heard about 'The Hottentot Venus' being forced to stand naked to display her natural features to a curious and prurient public. Indian and Chinese sailors are accommodated in the ports but do not wander freely away from them. Antisemitic feelings are still common. On the one hand, Jewish financiers and prize-fighters demonstrate positive role models to Jews at both ends of the social spectrum; on the other, English Protestants look down on Jews. The German traveller Karl Moritz notes in his diary how people travelling in a coach from Knightsbridge do not see why a Jew should refuse to travel on the *outside* of the carriage along with the poor, because he is 'only a Jew'. Moritz adds that he has found antisemitic feelings are 'far stronger in England than in Germany'.

Y IS FOR YOUR ANCESTORS

If, like me, you were born in in the late 1960s, the chances are that you have about 200 direct ancestors alive between 1789 and 1830. In my case, that total includes more than half of my five-greats grandparents; all sixty-four members of the next generation;

all of their children – thirty-two of them – and three great-great-grandparents. You may well have spoken in your youth with people who, in *their* youth, had conversations with old men and women born in Regency England.

That is worth thinking about when you try to distance yourself from some of the adversities and moral crises covered in these pages. It's also thought-provoking when you consider what they achieved. You've probably met people who once talked with intermediaries who knew the men and women who abolished slavery, rode on the first steam trains and defeated Napoleon. This isn't distant history: this is history under the skin. And yet there's so much that divides us. They had no idea of germ theory, Marxism or evolution. They had no concept of the combustion engine, electric-powered gadgets or aeroplanes. Sometimes you just want to reach across the 200 years that separate us and give them each a hug and say, 'This is what will come to pass' – and acknowledge all the glories and horrors – and let them say to you: 'This is how we got by.'

Z IS FOR ZENITH

I cannot help but feel there is one outstanding candidate for the title of the zenith of the Regency period – classical music.

I know what you're thinking. This may well be the greatest period in the history of classical music internationally, but the greatest composers are all foreign. Haydn, Mozart and Schubert are all Austrian. Beethoven is a German who lives in Vienna. In fact, Schubert and Beethoven never even *visit* England, so what am I doing suggesting that this might be the zenith of music in England?

If this is indeed what you are thinking, you are not alone. In December 1826, Prince Hermann Pückler-Muskau sees Mozart's opera, *The Marriage of Figaro*, advertised at Drury Lane. He is delighted – and buys a ticket. But his delight turns to astonishment when he realises that the soloists only sing their *arias*; their main parts are played by other people, actors. And Mozart's music is rearranged to suit English popular taste. It causes him to write to his beloved Lucie in the following words:

> The English national music, the coarse heavy melodies of which can never be mistaken for an instant, has, to me at least, something singularly offensive; an expression of brutal feeling both in pain and pleasure, which smacks of roast beef, plum pudding and porter… Poor Mozart appeared to me like a martyr on the cross and I suffered no less by sympathy.

In truth, there is a great deal more good music to be discovered than Prince Hermann realises. But it is hidden away in the private salons and drawing rooms of wealthy families. They have their collections of scores – sometimes thousands of them – and the best music libraries include a large number of foreign compositions. But this is not why I have chosen classical music as the zenith of Regency England. It is rather because of the awareness of what is happening musically in Europe and the contribution of the English to one of the greatest pieces of music ever written.

In 1791 the German violinist Johan Peter Salomon invites Haydn to come to London. For the last five years, Salomon has been playing the role of an impresario, bringing Mozart and Haydn's symphonies to his adopted city. This alerts people to the musical wonders being composed and played on the Continent. Salomon has no doubt that both composers would be very welcome here. Unfortunately in 1791 Mozart is not in good health: he dies later that year. Hence Salomon asks Haydn. Although Haydn is almost seventy, he agrees to leave Vienna and come to England to compose and perform the first six of his London symphonies. The trip is a great success from everyone's point of view. Three years later, Haydn revisits England and the other six London symphonies are composed and performed.

Salomon's next target is Beethoven. In 1801 he advertises in *The Times* a forthcoming performance of Beethoven's septet, drawing attention to this new composer, *Luigi* van Beethoven. The performance is again very positively received. But Beethoven does not come to England in person. This is a shame because, after Haydn's death in 1809, Beethoven is the one person everyone wants to hear.

In 1813 a number of musical gentlemen decide that they must do something to inspire and invigorate English classical music. On 6 February, the Philharmonic Society meets for the first time in London. They agree to hold a season of concerts every year in the Argyll Rooms in Regent Street, where they will perform a piece by Mozart, another by Beethoven and two or three others by Haydn or another recent composer. These concerts prove very popular, so in 1817 they try to tempt Beethoven to come in person with the offer of £300 for two symphonies. He declines. The Society tries again a few years later. Again he refuses. But in 1822 they offer him £50 simply to dedicate a symphony to the society – and he says yes.

That is probably the best £50 ever spent. Because what Beethoven delivers into the hands of their agent on 27 April 1824 is not just a symphony. It is the score of the great work about the human spirit he has been thinking about for more than thirty years – since the French Revolution. It is his setting of Schiller's 'Ode to Joy'. The Philharmonic Society has commissioned Beethoven's Ninth Symphony.

As it happens, the first performance takes place in Vienna on 7 May 1824. And what a performance it turns out to be! Everyone who is anyone on the Viennese musical scene is there. Beethoven is nominally conducting – despite being deaf – accompanied by the actual conductor, Michael Umlauf. The reaction at the end is ecstatic. The audience does not stop applauding. But Beethoven hears nothing. So the young soloist Caroline Unger, seeing him still staring ahead, goes over to him and gently turns him around to face the audience.

When the reviews are published a few days later, they surpass anything any artist has ever received. 'Beethoven is the musical Shakespeare' declares one. 'He has revealed the divinity in humanity,' states another.

Now, I have to confess that the first English performance of Beethoven's Ninth Symphony on 21 March 1825 in the Argyll Rooms is not such a success. For a start, the English musical bigwigs think music should be sung in Italian, so they translate the 'Ode to Joy' into that language from the original German. The conductor, Sir George Smart, has difficulty understanding the musical structure of the symphony. And the reviewers are very snooty. They think the piece too long. Five years pass before it is played again in London – and that performance is also not a success. But in the 1830s people start to think again and, after that, and they continue to reappraise Beethoven's achievement.

Nowadays, as I am sure you are well aware, Beethoven's great work is ubiquitous. It is the most requested piece of music on Desert Island Discs in the seventy-plus years the programme has been running on BBC Radio 4. It is the national anthem of Europe. It is played everywhere that people reach for hope. In Chile in the 1970s, women protesting against the detention and torture of their menfolk by the regime of Augusto Pinochet sang Beethoven's 'Ode to Joy' outside the prison walls. In Tiananmen Square in 1989 it was played repeatedly during the students' campaign against the Chinese government. In Berlin in 1989 it was played as the Berlin Wall came down.

All this is impressive but it is not why I have chosen classical music as the zenith of the period. My reason comes from Beethoven himself and his reworking of the 'Ode to Joy'. Because in one line, 'you millions, I embrace you', there is a sense that, in this piece of music, he is embracing *everyone* – not just the millions who are alive now but everyone who will ever hear his music. Not just Germans, Austrians and English people but men and women everywhere. And in recognising the timelessness of his work and that of his greatest contemporaries, especially Mozart, Schubert and Haydn, I realise that all humanity's greatest achievements have a quality of escaping time and yet still being intimately *of* their time. Individualistic yet all-embracing. The cathedrals are timeless medieval wonders that join the mind and the soul. Shakespeare too transcends Elizabethan England, being not only a man of his time but also for *all* time – as Ben Jonson remarked – and for people of all nations. Newton and the natural philosophers embrace both the natural and the divine, and establish the mathematical principles that, in their eyes, link the two, thereby shifting our entire understanding of the world. And then, after all that, Haydn, Mozart, Beethoven and Schubert set everything to music – the spirit of humanity – and unite us in that feeling of being one people, in all our infinite variety, in an everlasting embrace.

Most of our history is about ordinary daily life in the great shadow of our own mortality. The darker shades and struggles account for the greater part of our existence; glimpses of ecstasy are few and far between. But every so often, someone touched by genius opens our eyes and our ears – and makes us realise what a glorious thing it is to be alive.

PART FIVE

A TO Z

OF
HISTORICAL REFLECTIONS

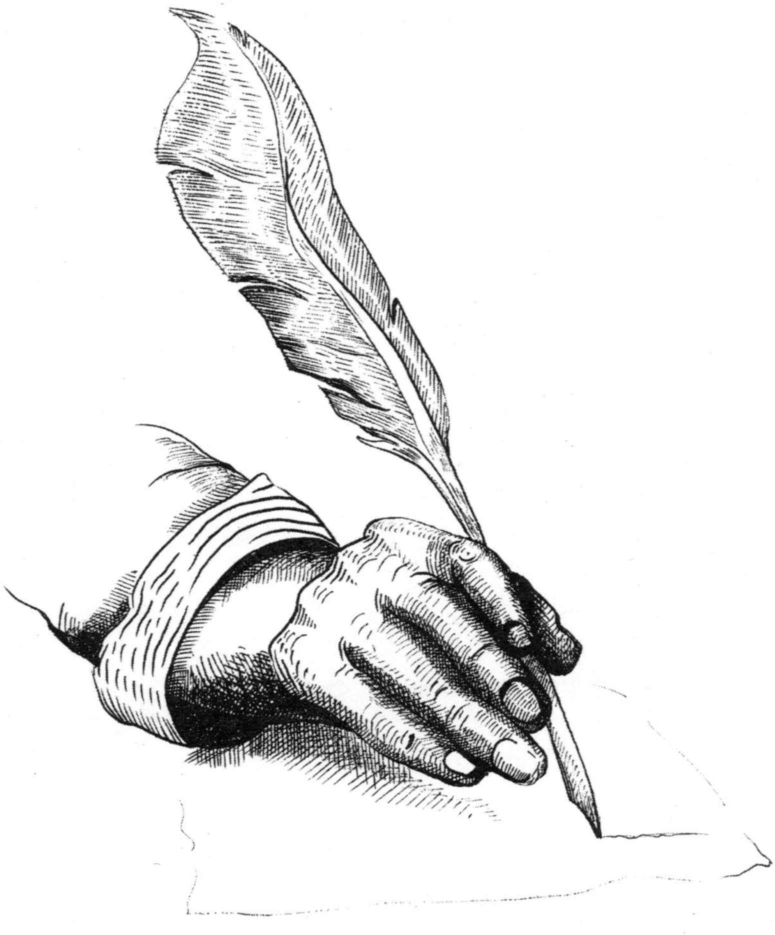

ENVOI

That concludes the four A–Zs that I originally devised to promote my *Time Traveller's Guides* and which I have continued to develop in the years since starting to perform them. But things do not end there. What a historian writes about the past should only be the start. Now it's over to you. You need to do some thinking. Were people really crueller in Elizabethan times than now? Is justice a relative concept in all ages? What are the vices and virtues of the English and have they changed over time? I hope such questions make you mindful of the prime purpose of addressing the past so directly, which is to put different ways of living – including our modern way of life – into some sort of context. What does all this history mean for you? Could you have borne living in any of these past ages? Would you have *preferred* to live in any of them? Just as beauty lies in the eye of the beholder, so the meaning of these historical reflections lies in the mind of the reader and listener.

The thing is, in preparing these A–Zs for publication, I myself have become one of my readers. I find myself noticing new meanings in what I have said and suggested. So this envoi consists of my thoughts about the whole process – from boiling poisoners to death to Beethoven's Ninth Symphony and everything in between. And as I've now developed a bit of an A–Z habit, that is how this envoi will pan out. However, as these last twenty-six points are my thoughts on history as a matter of the past (as opposed to a different time we might metaphorically visit), I will revert to the past tense.

A IS FOR APPROACHES TO HISTORY

A fellow writer once told me that he thought I was probably the only qualified historian who regularly used the second person in his books, as if I was having a chat with my readers. It's true that most historians who have spent a long time studying at a university have had the chattiness trained out of them. You may therefore be wondering, where does it come from, this idea of describing the past, as if *you* could go there? To answer, I have to tell you something about my childhood.

It would be an understatement to say I was keen on history as a boy. My school report for the end of the academic year 1975–76, when I was eight, says 'here surely is a future historian in the making'. I learnt a lot of dates at a very tender age. I cannot now be sure how old I was when I knew the regnal dates of all the post-Conquest English monarchs but I see that gaining such knowledge very early in life benefitted me in the way that it benefits musicians to learn their scales when they are very young. Once you have that framework in place, you can spend a lifetime building on it. What other people struggle to remember, you just *know*.

When I was about twelve years old, I was taken by my parents to see three castles in the Welsh Marches: Skenfrith, White Castle and Grosmont. I was particularly eager to see the last of these because it was the birthplace of Henry, duke of Lancaster, one of the greatest military leaders of the fourteenth century. As we drove there, I imagined being inside the castle hall, with its whitewashed walls and the stones delineated in red paint, as was the custom of the day. I pictured the fire on the hearth in the centre of the room, with the smoke rising into the rafters. I could see straw on the floor, the benches along the sides of the hall, and the principal table beneath a baldequin or canopy on the dais. I could see Lady Lancaster, heavily pregnant, making her way down the steps of the spiral staircase from the solar to eat a late-morning dinner, with her ladies around her and her priest at one side. Standing beside the table, she washed her hands, one servant pouring water from a ewer as another held a basin underneath. The more I thought about the scene, the more things I saw: the servants feeling the cold when they went outside to fetch more firewood; the long tables covered with linen cloths; the silver-gilt salt cellar in the shape of a ship; the serving boys taking care not to trip as they brought in the food from the kitchens; a minstrel tuning his gittern; dogs looking for scraps beneath the table.

When we finally arrived at the castle, I was shocked. It was a ruin. The bare stone shell of the hall gaped open to the sky. I had just seen Lady Lancaster a moment ago, looking very pregnant, and now she was gone. The only noise was the sound of the leaves in a nearby copse rustling in the breeze.

I walked up to one end of the hall and read a page of the guidebook. It had the date of the duke of Lancaster's death after his name: 'd. 1361'. That suddenly seemed most peculiar. People don't go through life with their deaths in brackets after their surnames. It made 'Henry of Grosmont, duke of Lancaster (d. 1361)' sound like it was the corpse of a butterfly pinned out in a museum case. As it happened, I had been on a school trip to the Horniman Museum in South London a week or two before and had seen hundreds of butterflies displayed just like that, in glass-fronted cases. I could remember thinking at the time that butterflies are best seen alive and fluttering about. Now I realised the same was true of Henry of Grosmont and his mother. They *were* alive once, and almost everything interesting about them dates from their lifetimes, so we should think of them as being alive, before that crushing end date and the pinning out of their bodies in the display case of history.

This philosophy was never going to go down well at Bickley Park School. Sitting in Mr Turner's classroom, I realised that even if I could go to the past and come back to tell him what it was really like, he'd never believe me. He'd want to see some evidence. That was when I realised that history is not the study of the past itself, it is the study of evidence. Documents. Buildings. Objects. Quite simply, without evidence there is no history. But most people want to know about the past itself, not the ways in which we find out about it. And that included me at the age of twelve. It also included me at the age of twenty, when I was reading for my first degree. It was only later, when working in archives in my mid-twenties, that I came fully to realise that *how* we know something is just as important as *what* we know.

My experience at Grosmont taught me that there are different ways of approaching the past. Yes, you can do history in the traditional, objective way – and there's nothing wrong with that – but why not imagine *being* in the past, like our subjects? After all, historians have to use their historical imaginations – their creativity, logic and understanding of human behaviour – to translate a mass of evidence into a historical narrative. Why not translate that evidence into a present-tense description rather than a past-tense one? That way you can create an up-close, intimate view of another time. You can 'show, not tell' people about the past. You can raise questions that traditional, educational history does not normally ask, being led by an analysis of the evidence, not the past *per se*. We think of medieval people as dirtier than us. But were they actually? And if they were, did they realise they were dirty? Did they care, even?

This was how the *Time Traveller's Guides* came into being. If we really know our stuff as historians, we should be able to describe how the past would appear to us if we could actually go there. W. H. Auden once suggested that if people wanted to understand their own country, they should have lived in at least two others. I realised that, by referring to other periods as different countries, I could do something similar for time. In short, if you want to understand your own *time*, you need to understand what life was like in at least two others. My books, I decided, would present readers with the opportunities to 'live' in other ages. On behalf of my readers, I would ask questions of the past that normal history books ignored, such as where did breakfast come from, how did people brush their teeth, and why did Regency gentlemen drink so much port. And, as they say, the rest is history. In this case, literally so.

So when I say 'A is for Approaches to history', I hope you can see that taking an alternative look at the past can be stimulating, revealing and entertaining. History is not just a classroom exercise. When you go to an opera or a rock concert, you don't treat that as a lesson in how to sing or how to play an electric guitar. History too has its operatic side and its rock 'n' roll. We should feel free to play around with our perspectives, improvising and innovating with regard to literary form, moving up close to inspect our subjects, or drawing back to see the bigger picture. After all, the way in which a historian chooses to write doesn't in itself lessen the accuracy of his or her historical analysis.

The bottom line is that we, the readers, matter in any piece of historical writing. By taking ourselves into consideration – in this case, working out what *we* need to know to get by in, say, Elizabethan England – we can see not only Elizabethan people's values in relation to our own but also our values in relation to theirs. The past gives context to the present – and vice versa. Or, to put it another way, the great value in studying history is not that it teaches us about the past but that it teaches us about ourselves.

B IS FOR BUILDING

One day in the 1990s, while walking along a street in north London, I noticed a block of new houses being erected. Outside the front was a sale board, which informed me that this development was 'architect-designed'. My first thought was, 'why do they need to say that? Every house in England except for the occasional self-built one is designed by an architect.' My second thought was that the houses in question looked ugly. They were utilitarian blocks with no sense of proportion, no style and no decoration. I can remember thinking that the little design features you see in almost every nineteenth-century residential and commercial building in London – the carved keystones above a window, the mouldings around a door, the finials on the roof above a bay window – were entirely lacking from the structures in front of me. The architect's prime concern had been to squeeze the maximum number of residential units on to the plot. It suddenly occurred to me how attractive our traditional houses are – even though very few of them were designed by architects. And I say that as the son of an architect who designed many hundreds of flats and houses for Lambeth Council in the

1960s and 1970s. Some of them won awards. But with all due respect to my father, they look like concrete boxes compared to a humble thatched cottage.

When writing my medieval A–Z, I found myself waxing lyrical about the medieval cathedrals. When writing my Elizabethan A–Z, Hardwick Hall reminded me how far domestic architecture had come in the previous 200 years. In discussing the grand designs of the Restoration period, I noted, with regard to Chatsworth, that it is difficult to think of any other house that so many people find aesthetically satisfying. I said very positive things about Regency architecture too. If I were to write an A–Z for the twentieth century, there would be few architectural references and most of them would be negative. The cathedrals and great churches built in this country since 1900 are not a patch on those built in the Middle Ages; no modern terraced houses are as desirable as those built during the Regency period. The London skyline of today is an unplanned hotchpotch of competing icons rising haphazardly above a welter of utilitarian buildings. And at ground level, although the Industrial Revolution might have given us terraces that became slums, we have replaced those slums with urban wastelands, polluted highways and concrete jungles.

You will be thinking from this that I am no fan of twentieth-century architecture. That is not the case: there are many important exceptions to that simplistic 'old is good and modern is bad' impression. The garden cities built north of London in the early twentieth century are one. There are thousands of outstanding examples of stunning contemporary homes around the country, curated by their owners to be as aesthetically pleasing as they are functional. Having sat on a planning authority myself for twelve years, I know there are good examples of modern architecture as well as mundane, uninspiring ones. But a consideration of English domestic building and urban planning over the last 700 years has left me thinking we lost sight of the historical principles of architecture in developing our towns in the twentieth century, especially after World War II. We prioritised mass-produced housing, the absence of ornamentation, and the right of way of road transport.

It meant we abandoned traditions that had stood us in good stead for centuries. Those traditions had taught hundreds of thousands of master masons and builders to produce homes that were both functional and aesthetically pleasing to their communities. When modernism came along, the drive was to create something new and bold. The emphasis shifted away from pleasing the community to presenting designs that architects and planning committees found new and interesting. It reinforced the myth of progress – that continual change would result in everlasting improvements in our standards of living.

What did we lose! Already by 1500 people could build cottages that are as desirable now as they were when first constructed. More so, in fact. They have matured, like fine wines. We might think them quaint; we might bash our heads on the low doors; we might curse when rats get into the cob walls or thatched roofs; but they are lovely and characterful. They all have stories to tell, in a manner of speaking. They have proved remarkably adaptable over the centuries. And they have been extremely efficient in terms of sustainability: they have lasted twenty times as long as the ordinary builder's guarantee on a modern building.

That is the serious point arising from this – and why it is not just a matter of personal preference. As observed with regard to the medieval cathedrals, aesthetic appeal provides an impetus for a community to cherish its old buildings and to continue to use them. Modern tower blocks have the opposite effect – as do long lines of cheap, characterless housing and featureless concrete offices – not to mention buildings blighted by major roads and airports. While we might hope that ugly and unsatisfactory structures will be swept away in due course and replaced by something better, that is not going to happen. We cannot afford to demolish millions of houses and offices just because they look ugly or are poorly located, or are filled with asbestos or collapsing concrete. The environmental and financial costs would be too great. Besides, walking through the less-attractive parts of a city centre reminds you that these are people's homes, shops and workplaces; they need these places, now, however ugly they look.

So we are stuck with them – in many cases until they become derelict or start to collapse. With such a backdrop, it is hardly surprising that modern developers prioritise generating short-term profits over leaving an uplifting architectural legacy. What is the point of spending extra on an architectural legacy, they might say, when other buildings in the area looks cheap, utilitarian and run down?

Here, I think, is a lesson we could learn from our engagement with the past. We love our old houses and cottages. If modern homes were as aesthetically pleasing and as well-built as those that survive from past centuries, more people would look after them and invest in them. There is no reason why a comfortable modern building should not have the proportions of a Tudor cottage, a Regency townhouse or a Victorian villa. It could even use the same materials, albeit at an additional cost. But there would be a saving too. It would last. It is difficult otherwise to imagine 'architect-designed' mass-produced newbuilds still being here in another 500 years.

C IS FOR THE CLASS SYSTEM

These days you will find a lot of references to the class system in social-media and the mainstream press. These regularly refer to the fact that the upper classes still dominate property ownership. For example, an article in the *Independent*, dated 1 November 2013, stated that 'the British upper class have been masterful in maintaining their privileges'. This view was strongly supported by responses to Guy Shrubsole's book, *Who Owns England?* published in 2019. One review in the *Guardian* (10 May 2019) stated,

> What's astonishing about his research is how little has changed in the last 1,000 years. His figures reveal that the aristocracy and landed gentry – many the descendants of those Norman barons – still own at

least 30 per cent of England and probably far more, as 17 per cent is not registered by the Land Registry and is probably inherited land that has never been bought or sold.

It is, of course, undeniable that the aristocracy and landed gentry still own a large proportion of the land. But are these the same people? Is it true to say that 'little has changed' when it comes to land ownership in the last thousand years?

When you consider the vast sweep of time, the individual families dissolve into a bigger picture. And that picture is one of constant change. Everyone with English ancestry is descended from 'those Norman barons' mentioned in the *Guardian* review, not just the aristocracy. As remarked in the medieval A–Z, everyone is descended from Edward III and the kings of England before him – as well as Philippe IV and the kings of France before him, and Ferdinand III and the kings of Castile before him – and many other noble and ruling European houses besides. On top of that, consider the *thousands* of Elizabethan people from whom you are descended: do you think they were all equally poor or rich? People today who own no land or who own just their house and garden are the descendants of the younger sons and daughters and the illegitimate progeny of the wealthy, as well as the poor and the not-quite-so-poor. It's not that things haven't changed, it's that rich men and women today are descended from a higher proportion of eldest sons who, due to primogeniture, have inherited more of the assets of 'those Norman barons'.

That is just one side of the coin. The other is that you, me and everyone else of English ancestry is also descended from all the eleventh-century peasants and slaves in the country who have living descendants. After this much time, you cannot *not* be descended from them. That includes the landowners who form 'the upper class' of today. They too have to be descended from peasants – due to the way that DNA permeates through the whole of a surviving population after thirty generations or so. That even includes the present royal family, who have many commoners among their ancestry. They too must be descended from tenth- and eleventh-century slaves, as well as kings, like the rest of us.

So the question is not whether the upper class is still rich but how open it is to social mobility. To what extent does it allow in new blood? Both now and in the past?

The twelfth-century aristocracy was not very flexible at all. The very wealthy were indeed the children, grandchildren and great-grandchildren of Norman barons; they intermarried with other descendants of Norman barons as a matter of course. But the next social rank down and the next were not so exclusive. They were prepared to marry Anglo-Saxon women almost as readily as women of Norman parentage. The Church too acted as an engine of social mobility, so that many relatively poor boys who were lucky enough to gain an education ended up attaining the rank, wealth and power of archdeacons and bishops. Consequently they were able to raise their relations to similar positions of wealth and authority. By 1340, when the law of Englishry was repealed, it was no longer possible to discern who was of Norman descent and who of English ancestry.

Social mobility increased further after the Black Death, as capital was increasingly freed up for ambitious descendants of peasants to make themselves wealthy. Lords sometimes had to sell off their manors to their tenants because they could not raise a workforce to manage their land. Social mobility accelerated even further thereafter. In the late sixteenth century the richest merchants and lawyers were as wealthy as barons. In the Regency period industrialists could make enormous fortunes and become millionaires in the money of the day. They might marry the daughters of aristocrats and join the upper classes within a generation or two. Their own daughters might marry noblemen. Thus the constituent elements of the class system were (and are) constantly shifting. The classes remain – the family names often remain too – but the DNA of the families who make up those classes is constantly being mixed with that of families from lower down in the social hierarchy, like the boiling water in a kettle.

You might point out that aristocratic people normally marry other aristocratic people. This is true, both now and in the past. It is also true that the nineteenth-century upper classes looked down on those who made their money in trade. But these exceptions do not give us the full picture. Aristocrats don't always marry other aristocrats. Elizabeth II's maternal grandfather, the fourteenth earl of Strathmore and Kinghorne, married a commoner, as did his father (the thirteenth earl) and all four heads of the family before him (back to the eighth earl). Thus many of Charles III's ancestors were *not* of noble blood. Furthermore, the snobbery against someone being in 'trade' was soon overcome if the 'tradesman' in question made a large enough fortune. James Morrison began life as a publican's son but, when he died in 1857, he owned property in England worth more than £3 million and had a similar level of investments in the USA. His granddaughter married a viscount. Aristocratic prejudice against a fortune made in trade did not last that long. Not if the fortune was big enough.

It is meaningless therefore to say that 'the British upper class have been masterful in maintaining their privileges'. That's like saying 'the premier division has been masterful in maintaining its dominance of football'. It is those teams that dominate the game that make up the premier division. Just as the premier division sheds declining teams and takes on up-and-coming ones from the tier below, so upper-class families relegate younger sons and daughters into a middle-class periphery and embrace new bloodlines from that periphery. And the same goes for the middle classes. In fact, I rather suspect that this flexibility is the real reason for the resilience of the class system in the UK today.

D IS FOR DREAMS

One day in 2017, when I was writing a book called *Why Running Matters*, the question popped into my head, 'how far can you dream?' If you could put that question to a cross-section of medieval society, I think you would be startled at how close to home their wildest dreams were. Yes, some fourteenth-century people did traipse off across Europe to Asia but not many. Long-distance seafarers and explorers were far more common in Elizabethan times. And that expansion of horizons mirrors people's hopes for self-betterment. You can't really dream of becoming super wealthy in a world in which you have to seek permission from your lord to leave your manor. In that situation, you can't even dream of sending your sons to school.

The furthest-flung medieval dreams were religious ones: dreams about the life to come. Some held it as their greatest ambition to visit one or more of the three great international pilgrimage destinations: Santiago de Compostela, Rome and Jerusalem. Others dreamt of taking part in a crusade. Others still of seeing a particular shrine when suffering from a degenerative illness, or receiving the blessing of the king's touch when suffering from scrofula. Medieval people dreamt of what they might *do*, not what they might be; what they might *be* had already been decided for them, by God. Many lords and religious leaders were inspired to perform acts of charity as a result of literal dreams. The rebuilding of the abbey of Cluny in the eleventh century came about because of a paralysed monk being told in a dream by St Peter that he would be cured if he told the abbot that St Peter was disappointed with the existing church. The abbot could dream of building a great new church. The paralysed monk could dream of being able to walk.

These ambitions stand in marked contrast to our modern hopes for self-betterment. Ask children today what they would like to be when they grow up and they will often say a pilot, firefighter, popstar, film star, professional footballer, racing driver, social media influencer or some other glamorous occupation. We can dream of being the prime minister or president; we can dream of travelling around the world or even going into space. We can dream of being rich. We can dream of being famous. We can dream of our books becoming bestsellers.

People often ask me how I think we would get on in the past if we were actually to travel there. One of the most unpredictable hurdles we would face, I think, is how we would deal psychologically with having our dreams taken away from us. Can you imagine being a medieval peasant doing nothing with your life except working the land? Or a machine operative working the same mechanised loom six days a week in the dust and heat of a five-storey factory? Our ancestors had to put up with some of the most mind-numbing jobs. They had no choice: it was that or starve. They dreamt of fine food, no doubt. We, with our dreams of reaching distant horizons and fulfilling great ambitions, would struggle to find meaning in such hard, unchanging lives.

E IS FOR EXPECTATION OF LIFE AT BIRTH

Just after I completed *The Time Traveller's Guide to Regency Britain*, I read a report in a newspaper that claimed the poorest people today can only expect to live 90 per cent as long as the well-off. That made me think. Was that true of past ages too? I looked at the figures for the Middle Ages and it seemed to be so – discounting the early deaths of monks, whose monasteries were hives of communal infection. Looking at Elizabethan England, the difference was similar: the poor lived approximately 90 per cent as long as the rich. The same was true for the Restoration period. But then I reflected that the figures I had just included in my Regency book told a very different story. Working-class Londoners in the early nineteenth century had a life expectancy roughly half that of the wealthy: twenty-two years compared to forty-four. And as you have heard, in the industrial regions of the north, it was even less than that – less than a third in some places.

That contrast made me pause and think about the industrial progress of the Regency period. I started to incorporate it into my A–Z talks. One day, a man in the audience told me that life expectancy was only so low then due to the high level of infant mortality and that, if I ignored young children, things weren't that bad. I was dumbfounded. But I gathered my wits. 'Do you have children?' I asked him. He did. Three. So I asked him the obvious question, 'Would it not bother you and your wife if they all died before the age of five?'

It disturbs me that some people think young children don't count. To the argument that counting infant deaths is 'skewing the data' I have to respond, no, it *is* the data. Life expectation at the age of twenty is quite a different thing from life expectation at birth. Besides, infant deaths are indicators of dire misery throughout the whole family. In Liverpool in the 1830s, 55 per cent of children did not survive to the age of five. In London, a third did not make it to the age of two. That is why many working-class families insured their young children in burial clubs so that the cost of their funeral would be covered. But insured children had a 30 per cent higher chance of dying. You can guess why. Sometimes a family was so wretchedly poor that they allowed their sick children to die so they could claim the burial money to pay the rent. Low life expectancy reflected the suffering that affected everyone in a poor community, not just the very young.

We live today in an age when politicians talk about 'trickle-down economics' – the idea that the wealth generated by rich entrepreneurs will benefit the whole of society – but that was certainly not the case in the industrial towns of the early nineteenth century. There the wealthy became phenomenally rich and the poor were ground down into abject poverty. Reading about inspectors stepping on piles of bricks placed like stepping stones in pools of excrement to reach slum dwellings, and the contents of graveyards oozing out through cemetery walls into the street, made me realise just how bad things were by the 1830s. We may think of the Regency in terms of opulence and taste but these qualities are like the beautiful, iridescent shells that are left on the shore after the animal inside has died and decayed. We don't see the suffering and the hard work that went into creating the fortunes which allowed rich men and women to commission so many beautiful things.

F IS FOR FANTASY

When I was writing about fourteenth-century England, I was struck by the fact that a medieval thinker was not constrained by modern scientific knowledge. As I commented in that A–Z, their intellectual boundaries were limitless; their belief in miracles meant that they could conceive of all sorts of phenomena and were 'more open-minded about the natural world'. I should add that they were hugely imaginative too. Who on earth originally dreamt up the idea of the *sciopods* (men with one giant foot) or the *cynocephales* (the dog-headed men) or the *blemmyae* (men with faces in their chests)? Who came up with the idea that crocodiles shed tears for their victims? That last detail is mentioned by the thirteenth-century writer Bartholomew the Englishman but I doubt he was the original source. I am sure you remember the 100ft-long dragon on the Isle of Lango, which John Mandeville tells us was once a beautiful woman who now awaits some knight errant to come along and kiss her on the lips. As for the fantasy in Marco Polo's writing, or, rather, that of his amanuensis, Rustichello da Pisa, who recollected what Marco Polo had told him in gaol – well, his imagination knew no bounds.

In today's world we have a habit of assuming that we do everything so much better than our forebears, especially our medieval ancestors, whom we tend to look down on as violent and ignorant. But in terms of fantasy, medieval people are easily our equals. At the very least, I feel confident in saying that although the imagination has altered in *content* over the centuries, it has remained consistent in its range, brilliance and vibrancy. Indeed, perhaps it fulfilled a vital function for the medieval peasant ploughing his strips of land. The ability to imagine all sorts of threats and rewards – in heaven as well as on Earth – was perhaps what kept him and his ilk sane.

G IS FOR GLASS

We tend to overlook glass. We overlook it because we look through it. When we look in a mirror, we see ourselves; we don't see the glass. When we look at a clock face, we see the hands telling the time, not the glass. But just looking around my study, I notice there are at least a dozen pictures behind glass in here. I can also see a glass-covered clock face; a glass face on my watch; a glass of water beside me; a whisky glass; two Belgian beer glasses; window glass; a glass paperweight; three glass-fronted bookcases; an hourglass; an old magnetic compass with a glass front; several old wine bottles; and an antique pair of binoculars with glass lenses. What else? The woodburner has a glass front. I almost missed the lightbulbs: five of those. And this is just in a single room – and one in which there are no mirrors, perfume bottles, china cabinets, lanterns, spectacles, measuring jugs or oven dishes or jars of any sort, as there are elsewhere in the house.

It seems this obliviousness to glass was just as common in the past as now. The Elizabethan clergyman William Harrison, in his description of England, remarked that three great changes had recently taken place in people's houses: chimneys instead of central hearths; metal spoons instead of wooden ones and pillows instead of logs on which to rest the head. He doesn't mention glass, which was then allowing many yeomen's houses to be flooded with light for the first time. Francis Bacon's famous assertion in 1620 that three inventions had changed the world – printing, gunpowder and the compass – similarly omits glass. Yet a thousand years ago, you'd have come across very little glass in England. No secular buildings had glass windows and few churches, if any. I suspect Francis Bacon did not know that. Nevertheless, how different our standards of living would be today if we had no glass. Hardwick Hall would be very draughty. So would my study.

The point I draw from this is that we see the importance of things unevenly. Even when objects are right in front of noses – even when they are all around us – we don't notice them. The same can be said for people in the past, who created our historical records. We can trace the ownership of an eighteenth-century farmhouse but rarely do we know anything about its garden. We can often tell who owned which fields in past centuries but only occasionally can we identify what they cultivated there. We might know which books someone owned but not which ones they read. That's true of so many things. Often when we write 'the history' of something all we are really doing is tracing its ownership.

People have always seen things unevenly and failed to notice the significance of the most mundane objects and substances. Glass is among them. Just looking out of my window, as the light fades and I turn on a table lamp, makes me realise how much it underpins the ways we live today.

H IS FOR HEROES AND HEROINES

It was while writing about Edward Bushell – the man who took action in 1670 to stop judges locking up juries if they came to a verdict with which the judge did not agree – that I realised there are quite a few social heroes and heroines in our history. By 'social hero' I mean ordinary people whose selfless actions benefitted the rest of the nation. Think of Henry Winstanley, who decided to build a lighthouse on the Eddystone Rock in the English Channel, and then manned it himself until both he and it were destroyed in a storm in 1703. He was not looking for profit, only to save lives. When a French privateer captured him and destroyed the foundations of his lighthouse, Louis XIV ordered the captain to return Winstanley to Plymouth and make good the damage. 'We are at war with the English, not with humanity,' the king declared.

When I came to write about the Regency period, it seemed these social heroes and heroines were everywhere. There were the prison reformers John Howard and Elizabeth Fry. There was the campaigner against the death penalty, Sir Samuel Romilly. And those who led the crusade against the slave trade, particularly Granville Sharp, Thomas Clarkson and William Wilberforce. To these names we could add that of Hannah More, who fought for women's education and the relief of poverty, as well as the end of slavery. There was James Braidwood, who pioneered modern firefighting in Edinburgh and himself died fighting a fire when chief of the London Fire Brigade. There was Thomas Braidwood, who opened the country's first school for deaf children. Two clergymen stand out for drawing attention to the plight of the poor – David Davies and Thomas

Robert Malthus. Sir William Hilary founded the National Institution for the Preservation of Life from Shipwreck (which became the RNLI). You've heard about Charles Thackrah, the pioneer of occupational health, and Edward Harrison, the medical reformer. And the list could be extended to include educationalists, missionaries, people trying to prevent cruelty to women and children or to animals, men and women who founded hospitals for the blind, and many more virtuous causes besides these.

Only at the end did I stop and think, why were there so many social heroes and heroines in the Regency period? Why is it harder for me to think of their ilk in Elizabethan times? The name of William Tyndale jumped out for early Tudor England: he wanted the Bible to be translated into straightforward English so that even a ploughboy could understand it. But the further back I looked, the fewer names seemed to fit the pattern of a social hero. There were philanthropists in all ages but they sought to improve other people's lives through donations of large amounts of money. The social heroes were different: they all took action themselves, directly. Why was this so noticeable in the eighteenth and nineteenth centuries and yet difficult to perceive in an earlier age?

In the Middle Ages, you needed independence and wealth to make a difference. You might establish a monastery, a bridge, a school, a hospital or even a monastic order – but these things required large sums of money and the cooperation of other donors. The options were there for charitable giving but medieval charity was normally as much for the benefit of the soul of the donor as the improvement to the beneficiaries' lives. Elizabethan and seventeenth-century charitable donors often left bequests for the poor of their parish or provided Bibles to teach poor boys to read; but these were almost always on a local basis. And they were primarily pious benefactions.

Many social heroes were, no doubt, motivated by their Christian values. There was also an increased awareness that things *could* be better – that it was not just a matter of praying to God to make them so. However, the underlying impulse seems to have been a growing sense of fairness. Or, to put it another way, people were spurred into action by the fundamental idea that one man or woman is worth the same as any other, regardless of social rank. And where did this come from? You have to consider the Last Judgement and the idea that we are all equal in the eyes of God. You can see that same sense of fairness underlying William Tyndale's declaration that even a ploughboy should be able to read the Bible. You can see its consequences in Puritanism and in the urban reforms of the Elizabethan period whereby towns and cities started to look after their poor – not as a matter of charity but one of social duty.

This explains why it is hard to find social heroes in the Middle Ages. Medieval people did not believe that 'one man or woman is worth the same as any other'. The medieval understanding was that the social hierarchy was ordained by God and was in itself divine. Earls had been born to be earls, kings to be kings and peasants to be peasants. But the sixteenth, seventeenth and eighteenth centuries saw a rise in those who believed in fairness. Or to be specific, more and more people were able to separate the concept of fairness from that of the social hierarchy. The idea developed that all men and women should be equal in the eyes of the law even if they were not equal in social status. Boys and girls equally deserved an education, whether they were the offspring of an earl or one of the earl's tenant farmers. And people who were blind deserved the support of society, so that they could learn to help themselves and not be a burden on their loved ones.

The other noticeable thing about the social heroes was that they were altruistic in their pursuit of fairness. John Howard had nothing to gain personally from seeing prison conditions improved. Nor did Samuel Romilly from preventing pickpockets and shoplifters from being hanged. Granville Sharp, Thomas Clarkson and William Wilberforce likewise did not profit from the abolition of slavery. And although their causes are now in the past, they have left a legacy in the character of the English people. Today that sense of fairness – separate from social rank, and altruistic in intention – may be regarded as one of the cardinal virtues of the English. At the very least, it signifies why saying you are 'proud to be English' is not just a patriotic statement.

I IS FOR INFLATION

I often tell people that they cannot say what medieval and early modern amounts of money would be worth today. According to the Office for National Statistics, the median household income in 2022 in the UK (before taxes and benefits) was £35,000. The Bank of England inflation calculator declares that that sum was the equivalent of £60 5s in 1322. That is hugely misleading. If half the population had had an income that high then, every other person would have been lord of two or three manors, and eligible to be knighted (as the benchmark for knighthood was set at £40 of income). The actual median household income was less than a tenth of that, under £5. As I explained in the medieval A–Z, the main reason for the distortion was the relative value of food. Hence I introduced the idea of evaluating wealth in terms of chickens.

As you might recall, in the late fourteenth century, a chicken was the equivalent of a whole day's wages for a skilled worker such as a carpenter or a mason, 4d or 4½d per day. How did things change in later centuries? A skilled labourer in Elizabethan times would have earned about 10d per day and had to pay 6d for his chicken – so 1.67 chickens per day's work. That's a slight improvement but don't turn on the oven just yet. A Restoration craftsman would have earned about 2s per day: at 1s per chicken, he could have afforded two of them. And his successor in the same skilled role in Regency times, earning 8s per day, could have bought 2½–3 chickens. Today, in marked contrast, when a skilled worker earns more than £110 per eight-hour day, he or she can buy at least ten free-range chickens. More than ten times as many as a skilled worker in the fourteenth century.

We think primarily of illness and violence when we consider the trials and tribulations of our ancestors. But every day they faced a struggle to find sufficient food. Conversely, when we ask ourselves what sets our age apart from the past, we automatically think of technology. But in so doing we have already missed the most important difference. Most of us don't have to worry where our next meal is coming from. To return to the point about life expectancy, if you're wondering why so many children died in infancy, there's your answer. Not enough chickens.

J IS FOR JOY

If you tell a traditional historian that 'historians don't include enough jokes in their books', he or she may well take offence, presuming you're accusing him or her of lacking a sense of humour. Obviously, that is not what you mean. Nevertheless, it is generally taken that the seriousness of a piece of scholarship is reduced if it includes any levity. Sobriety and a severe humourlessness contribute to the myth of objectivity on which traditional historians pride themselves.

This seems more than a little odd to me, if not plain tedious and unnecessary. It's all very well for *research* to be limited to the facts and processes – and thus somewhat humourless – but that is just a professional matter. Research is not history. Rather, undertaking research is like preparing the ingredients for a lavish feast: the ingredients alone don't make the meal. You need to cook them or prepare them in some way, to make them desirable, uplifting and memorable, not just edible. Likewise, history is as much about the presentation of knowledge as it is the acquisition of information. It should be engaging and interesting, multifaceted and entertaining. If it eliminates the humour, it is not only cutting out a bit of reality but the very part that most people find most attractive. History books without any joy in them are thus rather like a gallery of portraits in which the curators have cut out the eyes and mouth of every subject who is smiling. Such unmitigated seriousness is not true to life.

K IS FOR KINGSHIP

In May 1993, the rock musician Frank Zappa gave one of his final interviews to Alex Kershaw. In the version printed in the *Guardian*, he declared that Britain is a 'third-world country' because:

> As long as you adhere to the idea that the monarchy is a necessity and everything is going to spring from some sort of regal perspective, you get to be subjects instead of citizens. Until you change yourself from subjects to citizens you are going to be eating shit, aren't you?

I normally have a lot of time for Mr Zappa – always unconventional – but an examination of the monarchy since 1300 raises a very different question. Who are the real subjects: kings or their people?

On the face of it, the people are, by definition. In fact, citizens of the United Kingdom are officially known as His Majesty's subjects. However, history shows us that kings can only rule over their people whereas the people can both overrule and dethrone their kings.

Let's start with Edward I. Even before 1300, he had had to acknowledge that he could not raise extraordinary taxation without parliamentary approval. This effectively meant that the king could not go to war without Parliament's backing. Then came the disastrous reign of **Edward II**. From early on, the king was required to obey a set of ordinances and to have his rule supervised by a committee of noblemen. In 1327 Parliament agreed to depose him unless he abdicated in favour of his son and heir, Edward III, which he did. In 1399 Parliament forced **Richard II** to abdicate and then dethroned him for good measure, electing his cousin, Henry IV, king in his place. Henry IV himself was threatened with deposition several times in the course of his short reign, as well as being the target of several assassination attempts. At one point he was forced to allow his son to become head of the royal council and effectively prince regent. In 1461 **Henry VI** was dethroned and locked up. In 1469 **Edward IV** was ousted from the throne. In 1471 he returned and had Henry VI murdered in prison. In 1483 Parliament declared that Edward IV's marriage to Elizabeth Woodville had been unlawful and that therefore **Edward V** was a bastard. That ended his brief reign. Two years later, opposition to **Richard III** resulted in his death at the Battle of Bosworth. In 1554 **Jane Grey** was proclaimed queen after the death of Edward VI but her Catholic cousin Mary I had her arrested and beheaded, and took the throne herself. Elizabeth I had to deal with multiple attempts on her life. In 1646 **Charles I** was defeated by a parliamentary army; three years later he was beheaded as a traitor. Charles II was stopped from passing legislation in favour of religious toleration in 1662 and 1672. The Glorious Revolution of 1688 saw **James II** ousted and William III and Mary II crowned on condition that they and their successors had no power to countermand the statute laws of the realm. In 1811 Parliament replaced the mentally unstable **George III** with his son and heir, the Prince Regent. Note: it was not the prince himself who made that decision, still less was it the king. In 1937 **Edward VIII** was forced to abdicate purely on the basis that the government deemed his intended bride inappropriate. Just looking at the names in bold, that amounts to eleven instances of reigns being cut short due either to the monarch's failure to live up to public expectations or to the stronger power of a rival. That's 35 per cent of the thirty-one monarchs who ruled between 1272 and 1937 (including Jane Grey). The royal family would have had considerably better odds playing Russian Roulette with a loaded revolver.

L IS FOR LITERACY

This is another of those developments which, like glass, is easily overlooked. Yet its importance cannot be overstated. In fact, I would give it priority over the three things that Francis Bacon said had changed the world – printing, guns and the nautical compass. Printing is useless unless people can read. Given that 'the pen is mightier than the sword', I reckon literacy has got a good chance against guns too. As for the compass, all the furthest-flung inhabitable regions of the world were settled by human beings without any navigational aid except the sun and the stars. Besides, what was the first thing that Columbus did when he returned from the New World? He had a letter printed announcing the fact – for everyone of consequence to *read*.

Think about how many needs literacy fulfils. Without it you can only have local laws. You cannot have standardised national law because it is impossible for it to be applied in all parts of the kingdom equally without it being written down. Nor can there be international law. You can have no jurisprudence. You can have no accounting or banking. You can have no records of tax liability and thus no taxation. You can have no development of scientific thinking. Important health messages like Dr William Buchan's exhortations to the working class to keep themselves clean for their own good would go unheard. Nothing can be remembered except by way of oral tradition and that, as we all know, is unreliable. The lack of banking means everyone has to survive on a relatively limited local economy, leaving them dependent on local production and vulnerable to fluctuations in the weather. In short, without the ability to read, society is reduced to a primitive state in which might is right; rulers have to exact tribute from their subjects; there are no public services other than defence; superstition flourishes; and all that matters otherwise is the struggle to stay alive.

As you have heard in the Elizabethan A–Z, the biggest boost to reading came in the sixteenth century, when the male literacy rate improved from 10 to 25 per cent and the female one from almost zero to 10 per cent or more. The key to those changes was the English Bible. Not only were William Tyndale and his fellow translators some of the earliest 'social heroes', as mentioned before, their English Bible and the literacy they prompted contributed to the basis of modern civilisation.

Perhaps the best way to show how much the Bible translations contributed to English literacy is to look at those countries that did not produce a Bible in their own language at an early date. Portugal, for instance, did not have a vernacular Bible until 1753; in 1900, only 36 per cent of its men and 18 per cent of its women could read and write. The first Bulgarian Bible did not appear until 1871: in 1900, only 55 per cent of Bulgarian men and just 13 per cent of women could read and write. The English, on the other hand, having benefitted from a complete vernacular Bible since 1535, had literacy rates in 1900 in excess of 97 per cent for both sexes. It is true that those high levels were partly due to compulsory education from 1870, but even in 1800, male and female literacy rates in the UK had been more than 60 per cent and 40 per cent respectively. Countries that had no interest in reading the Bible had even lower rates of literacy in 1900. In Egypt, the rates were 13 per cent of men and 1 per cent of women – more or less the same as England in 1500. China and Japan had similarly low levels of literacy. If you want to understand why the West had such a commanding lead over other parts of the world in 1900, particularly with regard to science, technology, engineering, civic administration, finance and medicine – a major part of the answer lies right there, in the high levels of literacy resulting from the availability of cheap Bibles in the vernacular.

The spread of literacy, then, from very low levels in the Middle Ages to nearly 100 per cent by 1900, is one of the most important social trends in English history. It is up there with shifting our faith in our well-being from prayer to professional help. Indeed, the two are not unrelated. Literacy underpins both civilisation and healthcare, so we owe our very survival to the fact that most of us can read and write. Those parts of the world with the lowest life expectancy at birth have low literacy rates; the highest rates are to be found in countries with high levels of literacy. Correlation does not imply causation, of course: it does not necessarily follow that life expectancy depends on literacy. However, when civilisation demonstrably *does* depend on literacy, and just writing a prescription can mean the difference between life and death, you'd be a fool to think that if we were all suddenly to become illiterate, our life expectancy would not plummet.

M IS FOR MEMORY

Following on from literacy, we might ask what is the value of knowing our past? Why is our collective memory important?

One answer to this question has already been mentioned – that written records are essential for the smooth running of a legal system. For example, written evidence is needed to demonstrate ownership of land. A second answer is contained in the famous line by the philosopher George Santayana, that 'those who cannot remember the past are condemned to repeat it'. A third is the message with which I started this envoi: that history does not just teach us about the past but also about ourselves. It allows us to see our present age in context.

Allow me to elaborate on the second and third points – particularly with regard to what these mean for strategic thinking.

History shows us that people have always lied as they do today and, in all probability, they always will. It also shows us that people have always fought as they are wont to fight today, both on a small scale and a large one. In war, men will destroy and kill with incredible cruelty and, when the safety of their homeland is at stake, women will support them in doing so. Those things hardly need pointing out. History shows us that even if people were to lie less in the future, and be less prone to fighting, this would be a temporary situation. Imagine that the most perfect form of society were to be reached at 12 midday on the clock. After the hands of the clock had briefly pointed to perfection, they would start moving further and further away from that ideal world.

What is important is not the dream that one day people will not lie or fight: it is knowing how to deal with the fact that they always will. We need to learn from the past how to manage, inspire, defend, protect, nurture and educate the next generation. We need to know that, as a result of our collective experience, we can cope with all the difficulties that the world and other human beings can throw at us. You may agree with Benjamin Franklin's view in his 1816 letter to John Adams – 'I like the dreams of the future better than the history of the past' – but dreams are not practical solutions. In that sense, the value of history is like that of swimming. When you are in deep water, the important thing is not the dream of standing on dry land but knowing how to swim.

N IS FOR NATURE VS NURTURE

I am sure you have frequently heard people discussing whether nature or nurture is of greater importance in conditioning our behaviour. Frequently the lives of identical twins who have grown up independently are compared. Sometimes their experiences reveal remarkable similarities, confirming what people often suspect: that it is nature that has the upper hand. But as any psychologist will tell you, the question is not one of whether nature or nurture is more important but rather how they work together – how our genetic makeup and our environment complement one another, or clash.

When we widen this consideration from individuals to the whole of society, the genetics even themselves out. In terms of our DNA, the human race is genetically homogenous: any two human beings are 99.9 per cent identical. DNA changes very slowly so we are genetically almost identical to our medieval ancestors. But our environments most certainly are not.

Take any one of the four periods we've been looking at and you can see how people who were genetically almost identical lived very different lives from us. We would have difficulty accepting in daily life today our ancestors' cruelty, propensity to fight, sexism, racism, hostility to strangers, superstition, class-related elitism, lack of care for the homeless, and harsh treatment of children. The different conceptual frameworks they employed are also startlingly unlike our own, especially in the earlier periods. Nevertheless, however nasty they might appear, they were all just as human as we are. Their weaknesses were like our weaknesses; their instincts were like our own. If you were to take a baby boy from the 1320s and raise him now, the chances are that he would thrive in the modern world, just as if he had been born recently. He would speak and behave as we do. Conversely, if we took a baby girl from her modern hospital incubator and raised her in the 1320s, she would grow up to be like any other girl from that time. Or die young, like about half of her fourteenth-century contemporaries.

How do we really differ from our pre-1830s ancestors? In respect of our nurture – enormously, as I have tried to show. In respect of our nature, however, we only differ very slightly – we have greater height, bigger feet and possibly less muscle development. Even the landscape of disease probably doesn't make a huge difference. It is possible that our hypothetical baby girl born in the twenty-first century but raised in the 1320s would have some genetic resistance to medieval diseases – being descended from those who'd survived them – but it is equally likely that she would have less resistance to those diseases that were around 700 years ago but which have vanished in the interim. Much the same is true for the fourteenth-century baby boy raised in the twenty-first century: he might suffer terribly from diseases that only affect us mildly, because they did not exist in the fourteenth century.

We take it for granted that the way we live today is a standard below which we should not slip. But remove the civilising factors that benefit us – education, literacy, the law, healthcare, midwifery and the availability of affordable food – and, as a society, we could easily revert to a state comparable to that of our ancestors. Social change is not a one-way street. We were taught that lesson in the harshest way possible in the early fifth century. After the withdrawal of the Roman army and administrators from Britain, there was a complete collapse of taxation, defence, the legal system, education, healthcare, urban markets and people's standards of living. The result was bloodshed and mayhem. I am not predicting that that will ever happen again. But I do think that the point William Golding makes in his novel *Lord of the Flies* is a good one. If you remove the civilising factors that have conditioned us to be different from our cruel, violent, sexist, racist, superstitious, foreigner-hating, hierarchical, child-beating ancestors, the chances are that we will quickly come to resemble them.

O IS FOR 'ONCE UPON A TIME'

When did people become aware that life in the past was different? Not in the Middle Ages. When medieval people painted scenes from the Bible or the ancient world in their churches and manor houses, they showed them in medieval costume sitting in medieval buildings and sailing medieval ships. Even in the early sixteenth century, you had to be highly educated to know that men and women in Ancient Rome wore togas and ate lying down on couches. You had to be able to read the Bible to know that the ancient Jewish kings practised polygamy. To the medieval mind, battles and famines might come and go but the substance of daily life did not alter.

This started to change in England in the late sixteenth century. People looked at the castles that were falling into disrepair and realised that the introduction of cannon had rendered them practically obsolete as defensive structures. Ruined abbeys similarly told them that times had changed. In the 1570s writers started to use the term 'the Middle Ages' to describe the period between the Roman occupation and their own time. Despite this, Shakespeare still presented his medieval kings as having all the technology available in Elizabethan England. In *King John* he refers at least six times to cannon being used in sieges in the early thirteenth century. Likewise the characters in *Julius Caesar* tell the time by the chimes of a public clock.

The phrase 'once upon a time' is another way to approach this question of when people became aware of society's development. The earliest reference in the *OED* is from Chaucer's *The Knight's Tale*, 'Although thee ones on a tyme mysfille'. However, in modern English this means 'although for you, things once fell ill': it simply equates to 'at some time in the past' or 'once' – with no reference to *society* being different. The same can be said for all the medieval instances of 'once on a time'. Not until the late sixteenth century do we have the earliest uses of the phrase meaning a cultural difference. In 1591 the countess of Pembroke wrote in her poem 'Yvychurch', 'Once on a time when Nymphs and Pastors chanc'd to be sporting'. George Peele in his *Old Wives Tales*, published in 1595, has his character Madge start a story with the words, 'Once upon a time, there was a king or a lord or a duke, that had a fair daughter, the fairest that ever was...' But still these uses refer only to the worlds of imagination and fairytales. They do not refer to the real past. The phrase 'once on a time' only starts to be used to refer to a different epoch around 1700. Jonathan Swift employed it in his humorous poems. His 'Ballad to the Tune of the Cut-Purse', written in 1702, begins with the lines, 'Once on a time, as old stories rehearse, / A friar would need show his talent in Latin'.

Another phrase that may be taken to indicate awareness of the past being different is the 'old days' or the 'olden days'. Anglo-Saxon uses of this phrase are mostly biblical or about the political past. The first reference in the *OED* to things being done differently in the 'old days' comes from about 1500 with a reference to how 'In old time enchanters would put quick-burning coals in the four parts of the house.' The phrase became more common around 1700. In William Congreve's first play, *The Old Batchelour*, published in 1693, the main character Heartwell says 'Ay, ay, in old days people married where they lov'd; but that fashion is chang'd.' Daniel Defoe in his *Complete English Tradesman*, published in 1727, says that 'In the good old days of trade there were no Bubbles, no Stock-jobbing.' It seems that popular awareness of social change has its roots in the sixteenth century but was not ubiquitous until the late seventeenth.

'Once upon a time', then, is a way in which Jonathan Swift – writing in the age of Queen Anne – might have described the reign of Queen Elizabeth. And although the term 'social history' was not employed for another hundred years after that, people generally understood by 1700 that daily life had altered dramatically between the two queens' reigns.

P IS FOR PROGRESS

The awareness that our way of life is continually changing gave rise in the eighteenth century to the concept of progress. The marquis de Condorcet's *Outlines of an Historical View of the Progress of the Human Mind* was published in 1794, with its English translation appearing the following year. This broke history into ten epochs, all of which were described as periods of progress. The first was when people 'united into hordes'; the second when people started farming: 'the pastoral state of mankind'. After dealing with Ancient Greece and Rome and the Middle Ages in the third to seventh epochs, it went on to look at the development of the sciences between the invention of printing in the eighth epoch; the period from Galileo to the French Revolution in the ninth; and the 'future progress of mankind' in the tenth.

The marquis de Condorcet's legacy in this regard was that many people across Europe came to believe that things had got better, were getting better, and would always continue to get better. His last chapter told them one day there would be equality and prosperity everywhere. You can see why people wanted to believe this: it's an attractive idea. Not everyone was convinced. Thomas Robert Malthus responded in *An Essay on the Principle of Population*, first published in 1798, that Condorcet was deluding himself and his readers. As Malthus pointed out, the poor were starving in ever greater numbers. However, it was Condorcet's vision that became popular. There was so much more to like about it than Malthus's dire realism. Progress thus became entrenched in popular thinking. Even today we hear people say 'you can't stand in the way of progress' when they want to stamp on all opposition to something they want to see happen.

As most historians from the 1920s and later have noted, it is difficult to argue that there is such a thing as 'progress' in the positive sense of the word, when 'progress' results in the killing of more people in war than ever before. Herbert Butterfield dealt another blow to the whole idea of 'progress' in his book *The Whig Interpretation of History*, first published in 1931. In this he argued it was simply distorting our view of the past to present it as one long glorious march of progress to the present day. Ever since then, generations of historians have been taught to judge people according to the standards of their own time, not those of the present. And to decry those who talk of the inevitability of progress.

Does this mean that there is no such thing as progress?

In these A–Zs you have comes across many reasons to conclude that there isn't. I don't suppose you think it a mark of progress that the English started to torture Catholics in the reign of Elizabeth, having previously been proud that they didn't torture anyone for state purposes. Nor do I imagine you consider it a mark of progress that we started trading in slaves in the sixteenth century and did not stop until the early nineteenth. Nor that we started hanging people – mostly women – for witchcraft in the sixteenth century and carried on until the 1680s. Nor do I expect you'll consider it progress that life expectancy at birth in the industrial towns was allowed to fall below the age of twenty. If your only benchmarks of 'progress' are technological achievement and economic growth, then perhaps you *do* equate nineteenth-century industrialisation with progress. But I doubt the workers who made it happen would see it the same way.

Having said these things, these A–Zs have also shown that there are areas of life in which progress has undeniably taken place. Food production is the most obvious one. From the fourteenth century to the present, we have not just seen a growing number of proverbial chickens pile up on our dinner tables but a much greater variety of foodstuffs too. We might also point to undeniable progress in literacy. The medical sciences can hardly be disregarded in this respect, especially if we consider that life expectancy at birth today is more than three times what it was in the Middle Ages. These things are all measurable and obviously beneficial to the people involved. Thus real 'progress' is possible – in terms of more people living longer lives without there being a detrimental impact on anyone else's life anywhere in the world.

Where things get difficult is in those aspects that have negative consequences as well as positive. We might say that the Industrial Revolution saw tremendous progress in levels of manufacturing output and the amassing of enormous profit – but also resulted in greater inequality, the destruction of large swathes of the countryside and the start of a cycle of factory pollution that has yet to end. The railways brought huge benefits but they also destroyed the prosperity of the smaller market towns, many of whose inhabitants emigrated to the larger centres rather than remain in their shrinking provincial backwaters. Steam engines also caused significant damage to the atmosphere. Motor vehicles have similarly had both negative and positive consequences: accidents and pollution on the one hand; rapid mobility and the transportation of goods on the other. Aeroplanes continue to destroy the atmosphere and harm the landscape, while providing the invaluable service of swiftly transporting things and people around the world. As these examples show, the damage is normally done to the environment whereas the benefits are personal. Can we really refer to something as progress when it might benefit us individually but contributes to making parts of the planet uninhabitable for others, possibly forever?

In no other area of life are the negative consequences of 'progress' more apparent than in war. In 2013 I debated the question 'Is humankind naturally violent' with the novelist Martin Amis at an event in Brighton. He adopted the point of view advanced by Stephen Pinker in *The Better Angels of our Nature*, that we are 'progressively' becoming less violent. My response, first outlined in my book *Centuries of Change*, was (and is) that this is naïve. Our tendency to violence is ever-present; it is just that it is suppressed by social forces and threats. But suppressed violence is still a potentially destructive force. You can only equate such potential forces with greater peace – as Pinker does – if they are *never* used. But you have no way of knowing if they ever will be. Pinker might be able to point to fewer wars and steadily declining proportions of populations being killed, but that is only due to the military threats not being implemented to their fullest extent. Is it 'progress' that America and Russia each have more than 4,000 nuclear weapons rather than none? Is it 'progress' that now seven other countries have nuclear weapons too? A nuclear war that annihilated most or all of humanity would clearly demonstrate that the Pinker thesis is wrong but, in the meantime, the idea that we are all becoming ever more peaceful encourages complacency. Neither outcome to my mind is a sign of progress.

To sum up, a review of the last seven centuries leaves me thinking that the academic dismissal of progress is unhelpful and saddening because it denies the positive things we have achieved. But I think we should focus on true progress as relating only to those aspects of life that are wholly positive – discounting developments that also damage the environment or have negative consequences for other people.

Q IS FOR QUALITY OF LIFE

The question I am most frequently asked at public events is 'when would you most like to have lived?' I always say that I am very happy to have been born when I was, in 1967, because it means I had a good education, have lived during a long period of domestic peace and freedom, and was able to raise a family without much difficulty despite having relatively little money. But it's not these positives that persuade me of this so much as the absence of the negatives of living in past centuries. Everyone who says they would have rather lived in a past age is deluding themselves as to the difficulties people faced. Even if you were rich, your life was likely to be blighted by tragedy. Just remember the statistic mentioned in the Restoration A–Z: 90 per cent of the legitimate babies born to members of the royal family between 1660 and 1700 did not live to adulthood.

Of course, the twenty-first century is by no means perfect. We're a long way off the high point of 12-noon perfection. It could be said the hour hand is no longer moving in that direction. But even if things never get better than they are today, we have come a long way from where we were in the early nineteenth century – let alone the fourteenth.

R IS FOR RESPECT

When I stand in a medieval cathedral, I always think about the men who built the walls and the arches around me. I think of the high-ranking clergy who had the will and vision to take on the enterprise. I think of the labourers who had to clear and level the site; the craftsmen who had to identify and buy the best stone; the carters who transported that stone; and the ordinary masons who shaped it and made each piece fit according to the design. I think of the carpenters who built the scaffolding and the lifting mechanisms and the frames for the arches to be constructed. I think of the artists, glaziers and lead workers who designed and made the stained glass. I think of the smiths, plasterers, painters and sculptors and all their apprentices and helpers. Then I reflect that the whole edifice was constructed by illiterate people without a standardised language, let alone the means of calculating the colossal forces exerted by the weight of the structure. And yet it has stood for 700 or 800 years.

I am left with the most profound respect for their achievement.

When I find myself walking along a country lane between fields, I often think of all the men and women who cleared the land around me in the twelfth and thirteenth centuries. Unnamed labourers one and all – but they each contributed in their way to making the land useful and productive, which in turn led to the surpluses necessary to build the cathedrals and churches. And I reflect on how they worked without modern tools, shifting rocks and trees, ploughing in the cold of January and sowing seed as the hungry birds came down and tried to help themselves. They took in the crops without any machinery too. All the manorial tenants worked together to maximise the efficiency of the harvest: the women with their babies swaddled close to them, the children also doing their part.

Again, I have the greatest respect.

You can think your way around every aspect of the pre-industrial past like this. You develop a respect for the visionaries and the builders of the seventeenth and eighteenth centuries, the workers and the traders, the mothers and the teachers, the playwrights and the poets, the explorers and the inventors – almost everyone you can envisage playing their part. But then you snap out of your reverie and look around and realise there are many people in the modern world for whom you have much less respect. Did they have their counterparts in earlier eras too? Yes, of course – in their millions. The court records of past centuries are full of ne'er-do-wells, underworld characters, criminals, bullies, thugs and misers. The testimonies of vagrants in the eighteenth century often attest to their living rootless, irresponsible lives. It forces us to acknowledge that there has always been a range of people, from the worthy to the unworthy – those deserving of respect and those less so.

The thing is, though, that historical respectability is not related to contemporary respectability. Many people in 1830 had great respect for the king, George IV. As a historian, I do not – except in his role as a patron of the arts. In marked contrast, few people in 1330 had any respect for Sir Roger Mortimer, the first earl of March. This is understandable: he invaded England with a mercenary army, started a revolution against Edward II, arranged for Parliament to depose him and then faked the old king's death and governed the country in the name of Edward III for the next three years, executing the young king's uncle in the process. Yet I do have respect for him: he was the subject of my first book, *The*

Greatest Traitor. I respect him because he made so many things *happen*. And although I just dismissed underworld characters as among the 'unworthy' in that last paragraph, it is noticeable that many common criminals became folk heroes soon after they were no longer an imminent threat to society. Just think of the highwayman Dick Turpin, or any number of pirates, smugglers and Robin Hood-like characters.

There is a sense in which every historical character may earn our respect. We don't even need to remember their names to respect them, as my comments about the cathedral builders and clearers of medieval fields show. We sit in judgement on everyone whose deeds are known to us: we praise some and condemn others. But even those we condemn we respect in a manner of speaking – by remembering what they did. The only historical damnation lies in becoming unknown.

S IS FOR SPEED

When looking at a broad sweep of seven centuries, certain things become apparent which are not obvious if you are just looking at a short period of time. One is the importance of speed. Anyone considering an aspect of English history before 1830 in isolation is unlikely to discern any significant changes in the speeds at which people travelled. Even the Regency does not show a marked alteration, despite the advent of trains. People could sometimes travel at 10 mph when riding with the post in the Elizabethan period. The fastest Regency stagecoaches could maintain a steady 12 mph. The steam locomotive *Rocket* demonstrated its superiority at the Rainhill Trials in 1829 by hauling a train with more than twenty passengers up an incline at 15 mph. Presumably it went down the other side much faster but even if it achieved 30 mph that would have been a world record. These modest speeds seem all singularly unimpressive when compared to what became possible in the twentieth century.

The development of speed in the long term, however, tells a very different story. It is impressive not so much for the rapidity of travel itself but for its implications.

The easiest way to appreciate this is to consider the impact of the telegraph over long-distance communications in the nineteenth century. In governing Australia in 1800, the British government needed to put in place a trusted man. It was simply not possible to govern directly. If there was a problem in Australia requiring a political decision to be made, it necessitated a letter to be sent to England by ship, which could take up to three months to arrive. After due deliberation, it would take the same period of time for the reply to be delivered. A six-month delay between a problem arising and action being taken was obviously impractical. The government in London had to delegate absolute authority to their man on the ground. After a telegraph cable was laid to Australia in 1872, however, it became feasible to think of direct government. Serious issues could be relayed from the Australian administration to London and an answer given almost immediately. In this way, the British government could be held directly accountable for decisions affecting Australia. This is how increased speed results in a shift from devolved trust to centralised control and responsibility.

The same principle applies across much shorter distances. In the early fourteenth century it was rare for messages to travel at more than 20 miles per day. Eighty per cent of royal writs travelled at less than half this speed. Very occasionally urgent communications travelled much faster – such as the announcement of the king's death in July 1307, which took between 3½ and 4½ days to reach London from Burgh by Sands in Cumberland (330 miles, via York), which equates to a speed in excess of 73 miles per day. But less than 1 per cent of royal messages travelled more than 40 miles per day in the Middle Ages. What changed in the late fifteenth and sixteenth centuries was the regularity of rapid communications. By 1600 the post routinely carried letters at 80 miles per day and sometimes more than 100 miles per day. News of Queen Elizabeth's death in March 1603 was taken to Edinburgh in three days, with the messenger averaging 149 miles per day for the first two days (he fell off his horse and injured himself on the third). By 1805 messengers could travel even faster: Lieutenant Lapenotière took just thirty-eight hours to cover the 271 miles from Falmouth to the Admiralty in London with news of the Battle of Trafalgar, which equates to 171 miles per 24 hours or 7.13 mph all the way.

Speed mattered. You can guess as much if you think about the need for intelligence concerning threats to national security to be reported to the government as quickly as possible. An eighteenth-century prime minister whose information routinely travelled in excess of 100 miles per day was in a far more commanding position than a thirteenth-century king whose information usually travelled at less than a tenth of that speed. But speed also mattered at a local level – in reporting crime and calling out magistrates and constables. It mattered in maintaining links between central government and the localities. Most important of all, it mattered in terms of accountability. Lords of remotes areas who had once been unassailable in their domains and practically above the law became aware they could be swiftly brought to heel by government officers. The abolition of private armies in 1504 was very much a part of this slow development. Speed of information and bureaucratic efficiency led to new responsibilities and greater authority in centralised government and altogether a more united and peaceful kingdom. That, it should be noted, was long before *Rocket* achieved 30 mph at the Rainhill Trials.

T IS FOR TIME TRAVEL

Is it reasonable to talk about travelling in time? Yes, for the simple reason that we are all doing it now. We are all moving forward through a succession of present moments, second by second, hour by hour. Moreover, as Einstein informed us, time is relative. The faster we physically move, the slower we move in time. If you were to travel in a spacecraft for ten years at 90 per cent of the speed of light (603.554 million mph), you would return to Earth to find that twenty-three years had elapsed here. Travelling forwards in time is simply a fact of life.

Whether we will ever travel backwards in time is a very different question. We can answer it in two ways. First, there is the theoretical response. As a physicist once informed me, you would need more energy than exists in the entire universe to do it. The second answer is simple logic. If ever travelling backwards in time were to become possible, we would have met the said travellers from the future by now.

U IS FOR UNIVERSALITY

When I wrote that 'K is for Kissing' entry for the Elizabethan A–Z, I found myself thinking that it was ironic that we pay the least historical attention to the most common elements of human behaviour. The fact we don't discuss how people looked after their hair before 1777, when William Kent started manufacturing the first hairbrushes, clashes with the fact that almost everyone who has hair does this on a daily basis. We pay extra attention to things we deem important but we pay almost no attention to universal aspects of life. Thus we have perhaps fifty books on the Battle of Agincourt in 1415, which directly involved less than half of 1 per cent of the population at the time, and only one or two on personal cleanliness in the early fifteenth century, which directly mattered to everyone.

The problem lies not in the plentiful attention given to major events and battles; it lies in the lack of it paid to the minutiae of everyday life. Why is there no history of defecation? Because it's a dirty subject. Yet we all do it on a daily basis. And it most certainly has an important history. There is the architecture of the various garderobes – from those in aristocratic dwellings set at the end of long passages and over high drops to lessen smells, to plain ones built over water courses. There is the advent of contraptions from Sir John Harrington's flushing loo in the sixteenth century to Joseph Bramah's eighteenth-century water closets and then later ones. There is the history of close stools, chamber pots, bed pans and commodes. There is the history of the various urinals and pissoirs – for medical inspection as well as the removal of waste. Then there is the range of material employed to 'wipe the nether end'. There is the matter of the economics of removing the waste from a latrine pit and the disposal or use of the matter taken out. That too has a social history. Urine was used for centuries for fulling and cleaning cloth. There is the social aspect of propriety, of when and where it was appropriate to defecate and urinate in company and in public. Pepys reports having to defecate in a fireplace when feeling the urge late one night in someone else's house. Most important of all is the matter of disease. At the siege of Harfleur in 1415, just before the Battle of Agincourt, approximately 2,000 English soldiers contracted dysentery and either died or had to be sent home. Excrement thus even plays a part in a battle. In ignoring such things, we are ignoring the fundamental bedrock of social history.

V IS FOR VIRTUES

What are the virtues of the English? You might respond that that is such a subjective question that no one can say. But the nature of 'Englishness' is so frequently discussed in our newspapers that it is worth considering, especially when bearing in mind large chunks of the last 700 years. In addition, you have already heard me expound on what I believe to be one of the cardinal virtues – that we believe in fairness, regardless of social rank. What other ones come to mind?

Sifting the thoughts that arise from writing about these four periods of time, I find several aspects of English culture in my mental sieve. There is the ocean-crossing courage of our mariners in the sixteenth century as they sailed off to discover new lands. There is also the boundless curiosity of our natural philosophers as they tried to determine the truth of Creation. There is the boldness of our writers and architects, and the entrepreneurial spirit of our businessmen and manufacturing pioneers. All these qualities could be matched with comparable ones in other nations but, when taken together, they suggest an innate spirit of adventure in the English people. That spirit also underpins our scientific achievements – the drive to investigate and innovate – which correlates with our geographical discoveries, our engineering achievements and many of our economic success stories, from the start of the Industrial Revolution to the present day.

To my mind, there are two virtues at work here: intense curiosity and considerable enterprise. They are clearly connected. English curiosity combined with English enterprise is what led to steam engines changing the world and Darwin writing *The Origin of Species*. It led to Robert Falcon Scott and his team perishing in the cold of Antarctica and Tim Berners-Lee designing the Enquire system, which later became the World Wide Web. In suggesting curiosity and enterprise as cardinal virtues, I am not saying that the English possess more of these things than other nations but merely that they underpin many of our achievements, including several of the points raised in the foregoing A–Zs.

My fourth suggestion for a cardinal virtue of the English is simply good fellowship. In the sixteenth century, 'good fellowship' was the term used to describe what people sought in company, especially when they were in the alehouse. However much foreigners might label the English as cold, reserved and aloof, the fact is that together we are social creatures. We like nothing more than the companionship of kindred souls. It is no coincidence that it was the English who developed the concept of the public house or pub – which is much more than a bar or a hotel. Again, this is not to say that the English are closer to each other than people of other nations but merely that good fellowship is one of our cardinal virtues.

My fifth suggestion is our love of freedom. I think this led to the development of the English Parliament and the bold challenges to the king's power from the Middle Ages onwards. It led to two revolutions against monarchical tyranny in the seventeenth century.

Those are my five suggestions: (1) a sense of fairness; (2) intense curiosity; (3) boundless enterprise; (4) good fellowship; and (5) the love of freedom. Of course, there are many other attributes of the English – and some of them I would *not* call virtues. Some are definitely vices. The most obvious one is our hostility to foreigners – which is attested in every period we have looked at and reflected in many unpleasant exchanges in our own time. It also has to be said that the five virtues I have chosen are not shared by every English person. But they do, I think, characterise the English as a whole. We have a spirit that has sailed around the world with Francis Drake and William Dampier, climbed on board the train pulled by Stephenson's *Rocket*, and dared to ask the most challenging questions of nature – such as why an apple accelerates as it falls from a tree, and whether it is better 'to be or not to be?' We might not have the finest traditional cuisine but these five virtues have proved enduring and are, I think, things of which we should be mindful and even proud.

W IS FOR WOMEN

When was the best time to be born female in the last 700 years? I cannot see how anyone could argue any time other than now, in the twenty-first century. Although modern society might still be sexist, unequal and exploitative of women, at least there is legislation to limit that sexism, inequality and exploitation. Practically the only law protecting women before 1830 was the common law concerning rape. In all the periods we have looked at, no laws were passed with the intention of empowering women in relation to men. The first Act of Parliament intended to protect women – the Mines and Collieries Act of 1842 – actually disempowered them by making it illegal for women to be employed underground. The first of the Matrimonial Causes Acts, which collectively enabled women to get divorced from abusive and violent husbands, was not passed until 1857. The law allowing married women to keep their own inherited property and income (rather than it legally belonging to their husbands) was not passed until 1870. No Englishwomen had the vote before 1918 and most didn't until 1928. Equal pay was not a legal matter until 1970. The Sex Discrimination Act was not passed until 1975.

All this suggests that twenty-first-century Englishwomen are less sexually disadvantaged than their female ancestors. But I would add that in writing my Regency A–Z I was left with the strong impression that the world Jane Austen conjures up – in which women are the centre of their society and the focal points of its interactions, despite their legal and economic disadvantages – probably existed in previous ages too. It is just that those ages did not have the writers to make it apparent. We may read the comments of foreign visitors to Elizabethan England who noted the freedoms Elizabethan Englishwomen enjoyed, specifically talking about them going out together without any menfolk to enjoy a night on the town. We may read John Skelton's poem, 'The Tunning of Eleanour Rummyng', about groups of working-class women in the early sixteenth century turning up at an alehouse run by Eleanor and drinking ale as they sat side by side on the benches. We can imagine the Elizabethan forebears of Jane Austen's women gossiping and laughing just as much as their nineteenth-century descendants. I suspect, therefore, that in stressing the challenges women faced, I have paid too much attention to their legal disadvantages – which are well documented – and too little to the many occasions they found joy in each other's company, which are hardly evidenced at all.

X IS FOR XENOPHOBIA

When were the English least xenophobic? I have to say, the points made about our hostility to foreigners in every period make for wearisome reading. They leave me with the inevitable conclusion that English people have never been that welcoming – only the most privileged, highly educated and most widely travelled individuals excepted.

Why were we so unfriendly? My first thought is that perhaps

this is not just an English thing and that it is natural for ordinary people everywhere to be suspicious of those they don't know. It is not difficult to find reasons why this might have been the case. First, there was the fear of invasion. In the early Middle Ages, the dangers of being killed or raped by marauders and seeing your children abducted and sold into slavery were real. In later centuries it was dangerous to live on the south coast on account of the French, with whom we were often at war. Large towns were thought to be safer but even then, some south-coast ports were vulnerable to sea-borne assault. The French destroyed Southampton in 1338, Rye in 1377, Brighton in 1514 and Teignmouth in 1340 and 1690. In addition, they attacked Sandwich, Rye, Hastings and Winchelsea in 1360, then Winchelsea again in 1366, 1377, 1388 and 1418. They attacked Dartmouth in 1404 and Fishguard in 1797. In this context, you can understand the reluctance to welcome the French with open arms. Especially in Winchelsea.

Invasion fears were not the only reason why foreigners were regarded with suspicion. There was also the fear that peaceful incomers would take advantage of local resources. There was hostility to those immigrants who stuck together in groups and did not give up their own culture, especially when they practised a different religion with an alternative moral code. The antisemitism of the Middle Ages was characterised by suspicion of a group that not only did not mix with the English but also maintained a strong grip on the money-lending business. Anti-Irish feeling during the Regency period was exacerbated by Irish workers offering to undercut already hard-pressed English ones. Racism from the sixteenth century to the nineteenth was amplified by the social stigma of slavery, together with the denigration of the poor in general.

Having said all these things, it is important to provide the antithesis to the general premise that the English were generally unfriendly towards strangers. Hundreds of Continental merchants lived peacefully in London and the south-coast ports in the later Middle Ages. London and the home counties took in thousands of Dutch Protestants after the massacres perpetrated in the Low

Countries by the Spanish in 1567–71. Thousands of French Huguenot refugees came here after the St Bartholomew's Day Massacre in 1572. Thousands more came after the revocation of the Edict of Nantes in 1685. The industrial towns were melting pots of national difference as English, Welsh, Scots and Irish all lived alongside each other, most of the time in a tolerant way. Black people chose to live in England in the late eighteenth century because they would not be presumed to be runaway slaves and could not be sold back into slavery. The ex-slave and merchant Olaudah Equiano was baptised in England, married an Englishwoman, raised a family, bought property, had the vote and contributed to the abolitionist movement. He published a memoir in 1789 which went through multiple editions, showing English people were genuinely interested in his life and misfortunes, as well as in the story of how he overcame adversity. All these things are reassuring of the fact that, while the poorly educated and unadventurous may well have harboured a natural suspicion of foreigners, there were many who were able to rise above it.

Y IS FOR YOUR ANCESTORS

Family history is addictive. With every new generation you discover, you double the number of people who are relevant to your research. I love the fact that even the basic shape of an ancestral chart is uplifting – forming the Y-shape of a 'Yes'!

Father   Mother

Y

You

That Y-shape is like two arms reaching back into the past and touching the previous generation. And when you add the generations before that, you have an even bigger affirmation containing more Yeses, over and over again. A chart reaching back seven generations to your great-great-great-great-grandparents includes 127 names and is one great expanded embrace reaching back 200 years. And 'embrace' is the right word because without all that physical contact, you would not be here. All the DNA from every single one of your ancestors has, in some small way, contributed not only to your personality but also to your very existence.

Having said that, an ancestral chart or family tree is often just so many names and dates. Family history is a marvellous way to discover the past but many people miss out on the meaning of it all. Too often genealogists are predominantly concerned with adding another name to lines of names so they can claim they are descended from this king or that lord. Family history is much more meaningful when you find out more than just the names and dates of your ancestors. To me, the completeness of a family history does not depend on identifying more and more forebears but knowing how they lived. Understanding what life meant to them. Were they religious, law-abiding, hard-working, inventive, enterprising, conscientious, faithful to their spouses, caring, adventurous and responsible – or were they none of these things?

A family tree without the personalities and achievements of the people involved is like a tree in winter, barren of leaves, and stark and lifeless against a grey sky. Add the leaves of the ways in which they all lived and the tree comes alive. Now add the details of exactly *how* they lived their lives – from brushing their teeth with cuttlefish powder to baking their daily bread in a fireside oven heated with hot ashes – and all the buds on the tree come out into blossom.

Z IS FOR ZENITH

Finally, what was the zenith of the last seven centuries? Is it one of the four 'zeniths' we have already encountered – the medieval cathedrals, Shakespeare, the shift from natural philosophy to science, or classical music? No. These were all selected for the way they represented the greatest cultural achievements of their time, so it doesn't seem appropriate to pick one out to stand for the last 700 years as a whole. What then of widening them out, to encompass all architecture, all literature, all science and all music? Again, no. How can any one of these be given precedence over the others? A re-thinking is necessary.

I took as my starting point for this re-thinking the most basic requirement for survival, namely food. The chronic shortages that killed people on a regular basis prior to the Black Death no longer afflict us, so we rarely have to deal with the lack of necessities. People haven't starved to death in large numbers in England since the terrible famines of 1597 and (in the north) 1623. Perhaps, then, I should point to the food supply – the combination of agricultural production, the market system and the Old Poor Law – as the zenith of the last 700 years? That would not be unreasonable because we have transformed society from frequent hunger to abundance. However, food is food and, although it can be an end in itself, it is uninspiring as a cultural achievement. What is a loaf of bread compared to the achievements of Shakespeare, Newton, Mozart and Beethoven? Bread only means more to you than poetry and music if you are starving.

With these things in mind, I went for a long walk – walking being as important to historical thinking as documentary research. And I found myself pondering the condition of labourers on this manor at the start of the fourteenth century, who had so little to eat, so few rights and, on the face of things, so few prospects. I thought of the peasant woman who was denied the right to marry the man of her choice because he was a free man and she was an unfree serf. How had people allowed themselves to be trapped like that? They had had no choice. They were born to it – as their ancestors had been for centuries. The very development of the manor as a unit of administration had been a matter of survival.

Imagine you were living in England in the tenth century, tending to a few acres. Then the harvest failed and your land was ravaged by intruders, with the destruction of your house and your reserve food supplies. And the next year the harvest failed again. If you had four children and your community could spare enough food for only one besides you, what should you have done? Give them all a quarter of what they need, knowing that doing so will mean they will probably all die? Or should you have tried to feed one and sold the other three into slavery, in which state they would at least have had a chance of living? Or should you go for a third option, which was to give up your freedom to a lord and work hand-in-hand with your neighbours using heavy ploughs to obtain a richer food supply for the benefit of your community, your family and your lord?

This third option became the popular choice across Northern Europe, including southern England and the Midlands. It required people to live together, pray together and defend themselves and their land as a community. It required them to give up their individuality and behave as a group. They had to accept the manor as their family and the manorial lord as the head of their family, with rights over them and their children. Given the other options of death and slavery, losing their individuality was a price worth paying if it meant they and their children had a better chance of staying alive.

As I thought about these things on my walk it seemed to me that one of the greatest social-history stories of the last 900 years – if not *the* greatest – is England's recovery from that nadir. It is marked by the end of slavery in the twelfth century; the decline of serfdom in the fourteenth century; the rise in the independence of enterprising men as merchants; the rise of the yeomen class; the spread of education; the rise of individualism; the broadening of our geographic horizons; the growth of towns and trades; the growing equality of men and women; and the growth in the number and range of opportunities for self-betterment. All this amounted to a story of people satisfying their collective yearning for freedom – individual liberty.

That settled my mind. For me, the zenith of the last 700 years is the freedom of the individual. In 1300 few people were free to come and go as they pleased. Even fewer were able to obtain an education that allowed them to acquire new knowledge from outside their own community. Very few were free to choose their course in life.

Do I think individual freedom counts as 'progress'? Yes, I do. Today, more people are able to fulfil their personal ambitions and derive satisfaction from their lives than in the past without there being a detrimental impact on anyone else's wellbeing. Do I think this change was inevitable? No. I think it has been achieved through a colossal collaborative effort against the forces of nature, the limitations of the nation's resources and people's instinctive competitiveness. Is it irreversible? No, both overpopulation in relation to land and radical changes in weather patterns could see things slipping back into a situation where people do not have the wherewithal to maintain their independence or their freedom. Hence I believe this epoch is experiencing the zenith of individual liberty.

Finally, has this zenith benefitted everyone? In a manner of speaking, yes. Without it, Shakespeare would not have learnt to write, Newton would not have learned to calculate. Nor would people have been free to buy tickets to hear the music of Mozart and Beethoven. Nor, for that matter, would I myself be able to think and write about the past. I would be forced to labour for the lord of the manor and my community in the fields. But as a result of the growth of individual liberty, I can go for a walk when I want. I can wander more or less where I want. And at the end of the day, I can come back home to write down my thoughts. I feel fortunate indeed – not just in the sense that I am not at risk of being killed in a cruel and inhumane way like a cook in Henry VIII's kitchens but for lots of positive reasons, most of which are rooted in our precious, fragile English freedom.

FURTHER READING

Needless to say, a lifetime's reading has gone into the making of these A–Zs. Also a lifetime of visiting houses, abbeys, castles, museums, art galleries, archives and public buildings. On top of that, there is the experience of simply being in the street, looking around me. One of the most inspirational moments that went into writing *The Time Traveller's Guide to Medieval England* was in Holborn, London, in the 1990s, looking at workmen putting up scaffolding outside a four-storey building and trying to imagine the equivalent scene in the fourteenth century. History is not just what we make of the relics of the past but also what we make of the world around us.

Those who are familiar with my other books will know that I normally include extensive sections of endnotes. Indeed, I hold it to be one of the principles of history that writers should always cite their sources in full. That way, other people can not only check their work to make sure it is truly rooted in past reality but also can extend it, building on a particular line of enquiry. It is fair for readers to wonder, therefore, why there are no notes in this book. The answer is simply that most of the themes are based on the four *Time Traveller's Guides*, so if you want to check the references for what I say in one of these A–Zs, I suggest you first refer to the relevant guide on which the A–Z was originally based. The four are:

- *The Time Traveller's Guide to Medieval England: a Handbook for Visitors to the Fourteenth Century* (2008)

- *The Time Traveller's Guide to Elizabethan England* (2012)
- *The Time Traveller's Guide to Restoration Britain* (2017)
- *The Time Traveller's Guide to Regency Britain* (2020)

In addition, some themes highlighted in these A–Zs are based on chapters in other books of mine. The section on speed in the last A–Z, for example, is based on the detailed research presented in my book, *Medieval Horizons* (2023). Other aspects of social change touched on in various parts of the last A–Z, such as the significance of the mirror and individualism, are based on research incorporated in *Centuries of Change* (published in paperback in the UK as *Human Race* and in the USA as *Millennium*). Elements of the discussions on kings are drawn from my biographies of Edward III and Henry IV, entitled *The Perfect King* and *The Fears of Henry IV* respectively.

Beyond my own books, there are many wonderful descriptions of life in past centuries by other historians. It was an electrifying moment for me, in about 1993, in the grand setting of the Round Room of the old British Library (now part of the British Museum), when I opened *Standards of Living in the Later Middle Ages* by Professor Christopher Dyer. Here was a book that I had never imagined finding: it did not talk about medieval life in terms of stories but in measurable quantities – dimensions of houses, calorific values of peasants' diets, comparative wealth of monastic houses. It made everything I had ever read on medieval social history up to that point appear amateurish. So the lists that follow are four eclectic selections of fifteen books that I found particularly engaging, revealing or thought-provoking when writing about each of the periods covered in this book.

The Fourteenth Century

There is no better starting point for making a foray into fourteenth-century England than the *Canterbury Tales* by Geoffrey Chaucer. In addition, I do recommend reading William Langland's poem, *The Vision of Piers Plowman* and the anonymous poems *Pearl* and

Gawain and the Green Knight which are also vivid descriptions of life at that time.

Otherwise, in writing about the past with an eye for saying what *did* happen (as opposed to what life *might* have been like), I was most energised by precise studies that promised certainty rather than romantic vagueness. The following books are the ones that I found particularly inspirational. Some have been updated with later editions but these are the ones I used.

1. Jonathan Alexander & Paul Binski (eds), *Age of Chivalry: Art in Plantagenet England 1200–1400*. Exhibition at the Royal Academy of Arts (1987)
2. Tanya Bayard (ed.), *A Medieval Home Companion: Housekeeping in the Fourteenth Century* (1991)
3. Ole J. Benedictow, *The Black Death 1346–1353: the Complete History* (2004)
4. Georges Duby (ed.), Arthur Goldhammer (trans.), *A History of Private Life: Revelations of the Medieval World* (1988)
5. Christopher Dyer, *Standards of living in the Later Middle Ages: Social Change in England c. 1200–1520* (1989; revised edn., 1998)
6. Christopher Dyer, *Everyday Life in Medieval England* (1994; revised edn., 2000)
7. Christopher Dyer, *Making a Living in the Middle Ages: the People of Britain. 850–1520* (2002)
8. Jean Gimpel, *The Medieval Machine: the Industrial Revolution of the Middle Ages* (1976; 2nd edn., 1988; Pimlico edn. 1992)
9. Barbara Harvey, *Living and Dying in England 1100–1540: the Monastic Experience* (1993)
10. Colin Platt, *The English Medieval Town* (1976)
11. Colin Platt, *Medieval England: a Social History and Archaeology from the Conquest to 1600 AD* (1978)
12. Henry Thomas Riley (ed.), *Memorials of London and London Life in the XIIIth, XIVth and XVth Centuries* (1868)
13. L. F. Salzman, *Building in England Down to 1540* (1952)
14. C. M. Woolgar, *The Great Household in Late Medieval England* (1999)
15. C. M. Woolgar, *The Senses in Late Medieval England* (2006)

Elizabeth I

Elizabethan England is rich in documents and I was familiar with many from my PhD and from spending the early part of my career in archives. Volumes of inventories and wills, my own transcriptions of probate accounts and masses of other routinely created records were helpful. Obviously I do recommend reading the plays of William Shakespeare and Christopher Marlowe as a starting point. Otherwise, books that were particularly useful to me in learning about the sixteenth century include the following.

1. Tom Arkell, Nesta Evans & Nigel Goose, *When Death Do Us Part: Understanding and Interpreting the Probate Records of Early Modern England* (2000)
2. Janet Arnold, *Queen Elizabeth's Wardrobe Unlock'd* (1988)
3. Jonathan Bate & Dora Thornton (eds), *Shakespeare. Staging the World*. British Museum Exhibition (2012)
4. David Cressy, *Birth, Marriage & Death: Ritual, Religion and the Life-cycle in Tudor and Stuart England* (1997)
5. Mark Dawson, *Plenti and Grase: Food and Drink in a Sixteenth-Century Household* (2009)
6. F. G. Emmison, *Elizabethan Life: Disorder*. Essex Record Office Publications no. 56 (1970)
7. F. G. Emmison, *Elizabethan Life: Morals & the Church Courts*. Essex Record Office Publications no. 63 (1973)
8. F. G. Emmison, *Elizabethan Life: Home, Work & Land*. Essex Record Office Publications no. 69 (1976)
9. Julie Gardiner and Michael J. Allen (eds), *Before the Mast: Life and Death aboard the Mary Rose*. The Archaeology of the Mary Rose, 4 (2005)
10. Mark Girouard, *Elizabethan Architecture* (2009)
11. Ralph A. Houlbrooke, *The English Family 1450–1700* (1984)
12. A. V. Judges (ed.), *The Elizabethan Underworld: A Collection of Tudor and Early Stuart Tracts and Ballads* (1930; rep. 1965)
13. Alan Macfarlane, *Witchcraft in Tudor and Stuart England: a Regional and Comparative Study* (1970)

14. Barbara Howard Traister, *The Notorious Astrological Physician of London: Works and Days of Simon Forman* (2001)
15. Clare Williams, *Thomas Platter's Travels in England 1599* (1937)

The Restoration

Restoration England is even richer in documents than earlier centuries. But this was also the period when foreign visitors started to come to England and describe their journeys, and the diary as a form developed properly, so there are a number of published accounts of tours in England. As for a good literary starting point, the Restoration comedies would be my recommendation, especially the works of William Congreve, William Wycherley and Aphra Behn.

1. Guy de la Bédoyère, *The Diary of John Evelyn* (1995)
2. D. J. H. Clifford, *The Diaries of Anne Clifford* (1990)
3. Maurice Exwood, H. L. Lehmann (eds), *The Journal of William Schellinks' Travels in England 1661–1663*, Camden Fifth Series, 1 (1993)
4. Kenneth Fenwick (ed.), *The London Spy by New Ward* (Folio Society edn., 1955)
5. Peter Laslett, *The World We Have Lost* (1965, rep. 1979)
6. Robert Latham and William Matthews (eds), *The Diary of Samuel Pepys* (11 vols, 1970–83)
7. Lorenzo Magalotti, *Travels of Cosmo the Third* (1821)
8. M. Misson's *Memoirs and Observations in his Travels over England. With Some Account of Scotland and Ireland* (1719)
9. Christopher Morris (ed.), *The Illustrated Journeys of Celia Fiennes* (1982)
10. David Ogg, *England in the Reign of Charles II* (2 vols, Oxford, 1934; 2nd edn., 1956)
11. David Ogg, *England in the Reigns of James II and William III* (Oxford, 1963)
12. Geoffrey Parker, *The Global Crisis: War, Climate Change and Catastrophe in the Seventeenth Century* (2013)

13. Stephen Porter, *Pepys's London* (2011)
14. Paul Slack, *The Impact of Plague on Tudor and Stuart England* (1985)
15. Gladys Scott Thomson, *Life in a Noble Household, 1641–1700* (1937)

The Regency

In conducting the research for Regency England, I took advantage of a number of government reports compiled slightly later, in the 1830s. I haven't included such routine publications here but the volumes on the state of the industrial towns were compelling. I should add that my literary starting point was the poetry and biographies of Byron, Keats and Shelley – Byron having been a boyhood hero of mine. The following lists include several of the diaries I used, as well as some secondary sources that contained particularly interesting and arresting information.

1. William Daniel, Richard Ayton, *A Voyage Around the Coast of Britain* (8 vols 1814–25; Folio Society edn., 2008)
2. Rose Collis, *The New Encyclopaedia of Brighton* (2010)
3. Caroline Davidson, *A Woman's Work Is Never Done: a History of Housework in the British Isles, 1650–1950* (1982)
4. Janet Ing Freeman (ed.), *The Epicure's Almanack* (2013)
5. Mark Girouard, *Life in the English Country House* (1978)
6. W. O. Henderson (ed.) *Industrial Britain under the Regency: the Diaries of Escher, Bodmer, May and de Gallois 1814–18* (1968, rep. 2006)
7. Prince Hermann Pückler-Muskau (trans. Sarah Austin, ed. E. M. Butler), *A Regency Visitor: the English Tour of Prince Pückler-Muskau Described in his Letters 1826–1828* (1957)
8. Carl Philip Moritz, *Journeys of a German in England* (paperback edn., 1983)
9. Nicola Phillips, *The Profligate Son or a True Story of Family Conflict, Fashionable Vice, and Financial Ruin in Regency England* (2013; paperback edn., 2015)

10. Louis Simond, *Journal of a Tour and Residence in Great Britain During the Years 1810 and 1811 by a French Traveller with Remarks on the Country, its Arts, Literature, and Politics, and on the Manners and Customs of its Inhabitants* (2 vols, 1815)
11. E. P. Thompson, *Customs in Common* (1991; paperback edn., 1993)
12. Nathaniel S. Wheaton, *A Journal of a Residence for Some Months in London; Including Excursions through Various Parts of England; and a Short Tour in France and Scotland* (1830)
13. Helena Whitbread (ed.), *The Secret Diaries of Anne Lister, 1791–1840* (paperback edn., 2010)
14. Jerry White, *London in the Eighteenth Century: a Great and Monstrous Thing* (2012)
15. Alun Withey, *Technology, Self-fashioning and Politeness in Eighteenth-Century Britain: Refined Bodies* (2016)

Acknowledgements

These talks have grown with me since the first one, the A–Z of Elizabethan England, was presented at Waterstones in Cirencester in April 2012. On that occasion I was sharing the stage with Dr Marc Morris, who had to interrupt me because I was going on so long he wasn't going to have enough time to do his own presentation on *The Norman Conquest*. Sorry, Marc, my apologies.

Since then I have incurred a number of debts – not least to the organisers who invited me to speak; I am grateful to them all for thinking of me. The editor of the four *Time Traveller's Guides*, Jörg Hensgen, is a man to whom I owe many sage words and wise re-evaluations since we started working together in 2002. I would also like to thank two men who have constantly inspired me over the course of my career, namely Euan Clarke, my history master at Eastbourne College, and Professor Jonathan Barry, who supervised my PhD more than twenty years ago and has been a fount of wisdom ever since. My thanks also go to my agent, Georgina Capel, and her hard-working team, especially Irene Baldoni and Rachel Conway. I am grateful too to Ben Yarde-Buller and Kieron Connolly of Old Street Publishing for having faith in this book and helping me bring it to its finished form.

Finally, my deepest debt of gratitude is to my family – my brothers, Robert and David; my inspirational children, Alexander, Elizabeth and Oliver; and my conscientious wife, Sophie. One lesson that history teaches us is how lucky we are to be alive in the first place; I am even luckier to have their love and support.

NEW AND FORTHCOMING HISTORY FROM OLD STREET

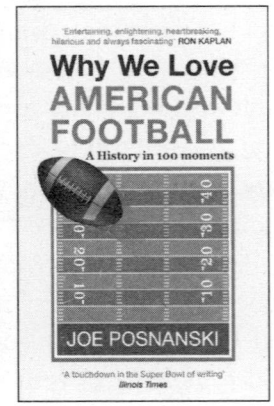

THE SHORTEST HISTORY of FRANCE
Colin Jones

'Vital, incisive, revelatory'
HILARY MANTEL ON THE FALL OF ROBESPIERRE

THE SHORTEST HISTORY of AUSTRIA
Nicholas T. Parsons

'Incisive but comprehensive, entertaining and well-illustrated... the perfect introduction'
TIM BLANNING

THE SHORTEST HISTORY of ANCIENT ROME
Ross King

'King's supreme ability is to imagine himself into the past. The scope of his knowledge is staggering'
JOHN CAREY, SUNDAY TIMES

The Death of Stalin
Sheila Fitzpatrick

'Wise, comprehensive and brilliantly succinct'
Owen Matthews

Bombard the Headquarters!
The Cultural Revolution in China
GREAT EVENTS
Linda Jaivin

'Brilliant... a tour de force'
Jumping Pen

Why We Love AMERICAN FOOTBALL
A History in 100 moments
JOE POSNANSKI

'Entertaining, enlightening, heartbreaking, hilarious and always fascinating' RON KAPLAN

'A touchdown in the Super Bowl of writing'
Illinois Times

Old St

A   C
   D
H B
 M I
   N
R S
   T
V W